NOT
for Sale

NOT
for Sale

*The Return of
the Global Slave Trade—
and How We Can Fight It*

David Batstone

HarperSanFrancisco
A Division of HarperCollinsPublishers

In order to protect the identity and ensure the safety of former slaves, and to prevent disruption of current legal proceedings, pseudonyms are used throughout this book, and locations are sometimes obscured.

FIRST EDITION
Designed by Joseph Rutt

Library of Congress Cataloging-in-Publication Data is available.

isbn: 978–0–06–120671–9

07 08 09 10 11 RRD (H) 10 9 8 7 6 5 4

To Wendy, Rusty, Ruth, Jade, Linda, and Loie
Your love surrounds me and your actions inspire me

"A little more matriarchy is what the world needs,
and I know it. Period. Paragraph."
—Dorothy Thompson

Contents

NOT
for Sale

Introduction

Finding Slavery in My Own Backyard

Defeating human trafficking is a
great moral calling of our time.

Condoleezza Rice,
U.S. Secretary of State

Twenty-seven million slaves exist in our world today.[1] Girls and boys, women and men of all ages are forced to toil in the rug loom sheds of Nepal, sell their bodies in the brothels of Rome, break rocks in the quarries of Pakistan, and fight wars in the jungles of Africa.

Go behind the facade in any major town or city in the world today and you are likely to find a thriving commerce in human beings. You may even find slavery in your own backyard.

For several years, my wife and I dined regularly at an Indian restaurant near our home in the San Francisco Bay Area. Unbeknownst to us, the staff at Pasand Madras Indian Cuisine who cooked our curries, delivered them to our table, and washed our dishes were slaves.

It took a tragic accident to expose the slave-trafficking ring. A young woman found her roommates, seventeen-year-old Chanti

Prattipati and her fifteen-year-old sister Lalitha, unconscious in a Berkeley apartment. Carbon monoxide emitted from a blocked heating vent had poisoned them. The roommate called their landlord, Lakireddy Reddy, the owner of the Pasand restaurant where the girls worked. Reddy owned several restaurants and more than a thousand apartment units in northern California.

When Reddy arrived at the girls' apartment, he declined to take them to a hospital. Instead, he and a few friends carried the girls out of the apartment in a rolled up carpet and put them into a waiting van. When Reddy and his cronies tried to force the roommate into the van as well, she put up a fierce fight.

A local resident, Marcia Poole, happened to be passing by in her car at that moment and witnessed a bizarre scene: several men toting a sagging roll of carpet, with a human leg hanging out the side. She slowed down her car to take a closer look and was horrified to watch the men attempt to force a young girl into their van. Poole jumped out of her car and did everything in her power to stop the men. Unable to do so, she stopped another passing motorist and implored him to dial 911 and report a kidnapping in progress. The police arrived in time to arrest the abductors.

Chanti Prattipata never regained consciousness; she was pronounced dead at a local hospital. A subsequent investigation revealed that Reddy and several members of his family had used fake visas and false identities to traffic perhaps hundreds of adults and children into the United States from India. In many cases Reddy secured visas under the guise that the applicants were highly skilled technology professionals who would be placed in a software company. In fact, they ended up working as waiters, cooks, and dishwashers at the Pasand restaurant or at other businesses that Reddy owned. He forced the laborers to work long hours for minimal wages, money that they returned to him as rent to live in one of his apartments. Reddy threatened to turn them in to the authorities as illegal aliens if they tried to escape.

The Reddy case is not an anomaly. Well over one hundred thousand people live enslaved at this moment in the United States, and an additional 17,500 new victims are trafficked across our borders each year. Over thirty thousand more slaves are transported through the United States on their way to other international destinations. Attorneys from the U.S. Department of Justice have prosecuted slave-trade activity in ninety-one cities across the United States and in nearly every state of the nation.[2]

Like the slaves who came to America's shores two hundred years ago, today's slaves are not free to pursue their own destinies. They are coerced to perform work for the personal gain of those who subjugate them. If they try to escape the clutches of their masters, modern slaves risk personal violence or reprisals to their families.

Just how prominent a global crisis the slave trade has become was apparent when President George W. Bush took the podium before the United Nations General Assembly in September 2003. As expected, the president first addressed international concerns over the U.S. intervention in Iraq. As he neared the end of his speech, Bush shifted his attention to "another humanitarian crisis" of global proportions. "Each year 800,000 to 900,000 human beings are bought, sold, or forced across the world's borders," he said. "The trade in human beings for any purpose must not be allowed to thrive in our time." Bush went on to underscore how the slave trade targets vulnerable women and children and fuels a thriving organized crime syndicate that threatens global security.[3]

President Bush did not exaggerate the crisis. The commerce in human beings today rivals drug trafficking and the illegal arms trade for the top criminal activity on the planet. The slave trade sits at number three on the list but is closing the gap. The Federal Bureau of Investigation (FBI) projects that the slave trade generates $9.5 billion in revenue each year.[4] The International Labour Office (ILO) estimates that figure to be closer to a whopping $32 billion annually.[5] Whichever figure is closer to the mark, no one doubts that slave commerce is booming. "In terms of profits, it's on a path to overtake drugs and arms trafficking," says Barry Tang, an Immigration and Enforcement attaché with the U.S. Department of Homeland Security.[6]

In recognition of the fact that human trafficking was spinning out of control, the U.S. Congress created a high-level position at the State Department specifically to combat the slave industry. President Bush appointed former congressman John Miller to the post in March 2003 and promptly lifted his position to the ambassador level.

The primary mission of the Office to Monitor and Combat Trafficking in Persons is to motivate and support governments to address their own participation in the global slave trade. To that end, one of its most potent tools is a report card called the Trafficking in Persons (TIP) Report, published annually since 2001 as mandated by the U.S. Congress.

No nation wants to be known as a haven for slaveholders and traffickers. Nonetheless, the 2006 TIP Report documents that over 150 countries around the globe function as a source, a destination, or a transit country for the slave trade; some countries serve as a base for all three activities.[7] The exhaustive research that the State Department conducts makes it clear that modern-day slavery plagues every country, including the United States. "This is one of the great moral struggles of our day," says Ambassador Miller. "We need to bring the same passion and commitment to this struggle that the abolitionists of this country brought to the struggle against slavery based upon color 160 years ago."[8]

Many people bristle to hear the word *slave* used to describe the modern practice of exploitation. Deeply engrained in the collective psyche of western culture is the notion that slavery ended in the nineteenth century. It is not unusual to read a newspaper account of "slavelike conditions" in a copper mine in, say, Bolivia. The laborers were kidnapped, coerced to work without pay, and prohibited from leaving the mine. So why would the writer refer to the laborers' condition as "slavelike"? Because the writer buys into the cultural myth that "real slavery" was vanquished long ago.

It certainly was a momentous day in 1833 when the British Parliament passed the Slavery Abolition Act, which gave freedom to all slaves held captive in the British Empire. Likewise, the Thirteenth Amendment to the U.S. Constitution, passed in 1865 at the conclusion of the Civil War, left no ambiguity about the legal standing of slavery in America: "Neither slavery nor involuntary servitude … shall exist within the United States, or any place subject to their jurisdiction."

The establishment of laws that criminalized the slave trade meant a major advancement in the cause for human freedom. Though slavery persisted for decades thereafter, legislation gave abolitionists an effective tool to hold slaveholders accountable for their inhumane activity. Abolition laws eventually spread to nearly every nation in the world.

In our own day, however, a thriving black market in human beings has emerged once again. It is a criminal enterprise involving both local scoundrels and sophisticated international syndicates. Corruption among law enforcement agents and government officials plays a key role in its success. And it's not limited to one specific region of the world—it respects no borders. Hence, modern slavery cannot be eliminated with a single stroke of the pen like Abraham Lincoln achieved when he signed the Emancipation Proclamation.

The European Union (EU), for example, cannot figure out how to stop the flood of 120,000 women and children trafficked each year into its member states. Most of these slaves are abducted in Africa or the beleaguered former republics of the Soviet Union and transported through porous borders. Ninety percent end up coerced into Europe's proliferating sex industry.[9]

As late as 2002, the UN human rights chief (and former president of Ireland) Mary Robinson admitted to "a tendency in Europe to consider trafficking as illegal immigration and penalize the women involved." Robinson lamented that the destination countries "tend to get off lightly on the matter of [sex] trafficking because it has been a sort of subterranean, invisible, criminal dominated ... form of modern slavery."[10]

The European Ministers got serious about the slave trade in 2002 when they required all member states to implement the Palermo Protocol, a strong UN initiative that aims to nurture effective antitrafficking measures across borders. Most western European countries subsequently created ambitious community-education campaigns and poured resources into law enforcement aimed at traffickers. All the same, traffickers somehow managed to maintain a steady flow of new sex slaves into the region. As Benita Ferrero-Waldner, the "secretary of state" for the EU, admitted in March 2006, "Despite efforts to tackle this trade, the uncomfortable truth is that trafficking people is sometimes an even more profitable business than trafficking weapons."[11]

Indeed, more slaves are in bondage today than were bartered in four centuries of the transatlantic slave trade. Nowhere has its impact been felt more brutally than on children in the underdeveloped nations. Slaveholders prey on the defenseless, and children so easily become vulnerable.

Ten Million Children Exploited for Domestic Labor—this title for a 2004 UN study on the exploitation of children internationally hardly needs explaining. The UN's surveys found 700,000 children forced into domestic labor in Indonesia alone, with staggering numbers as well in Brazil (559,000), Pakistan

(264,000), Haiti (250,000), and Kenya (200,000). The UN report indicates that children remain in servitude for long stretches of time because no one identifies their enslavement: "These youngsters are usually 'invisible' to their communities, toiling for long hours with little or no pay and regularly deprived of the chance to play or go to school."[12]

That "invisible" tag often gets attached to descriptions of modern slavery. Just as I never suspected that my favorite restaurant had become a hub for a trafficking ring, slavery likely crosses our path on a regular basis without our awareness. We may pass a construction site and never think twice whether the laborers work of their own volition. Or we might drive along city streets at night, see young girls on a street corner peddling their bodies, and wonder how they could ever "choose" such a life.

That's the paradox: slavery is in reality not invisible. Except in rare circumstances, slaves toil in the public eye. The truth is we do not expect to find it in "respectable" settings. To learn that slaveholders press children into forced labor in the cacao plantations of the Ivory Coast may not surprise us. But we regard it as unthinkable that an otherwise upstanding citizen might be a slaveholder.

Kim Meston wishes that she had not been so invisible to her New England community. In a rural town near Worcester, Massachusetts, the minister of the local church used her as his domestic sex slave for five years without raising the slightest suspicion in the community.

Kim's parents were Tibetan exiles living in a refugee camp in southern India. When Kim was in her teens, her sister's husband introduced the family to a church minister visiting from the United States. The reverend offered to bring Kim to America where he would provide a formal education and opportunities for a better life. "He told my parents that he would treat me as his own daughter," Kim recounts.[13]

Her brother-in-law lobbied the family persuasively to let Kim go. He even offered to accompany her to Delhi, where he could help her secure a visa to travel to the United States. In the ultimate betrayal, the brother-in-law made his own financial arrangement with the minister to traffic Kim.

At the age of sixteen, Kim began a double life in America. Everything would have appeared normal to the casual observer—she attended the local high school, ran on the track team, and attended church on Sundays. The minister even had a wife and a stepdaughter living in his home. But behind closed doors, she became the household servant, doing nearly all the cooking, housecleaning, ironing, and even tending the church grounds. Moreover, the minister sexually abused Kim frequently over a five-year period.

The minister threatened to have Kim's Tibetan family back in India thrown into jail if Kim told her school friends a word about her treatment. So she suffered in silence, and no one in the community thought to ask how she might be faring. They simply assumed the best intentions of the minister and his family. "His deception was well constructed," notes Kim. "The minister was a pillar in the community, and I was viewed as the poor child from the third world who was the lucky beneficiary of his generosity."

Finally, at the age of twenty-one, Kim escaped her tormentor. She initially planned to run away and never turn back. Yet she received news from her family in India that the minister had trafficked two of her cousins into the United States to take her place inside his home. Kim mustered the courage to take her case to the local police. The minister was arrested, convicted, and sent to jail. Today Kim owns a retail store in the Boston area and volunteers her time to prevent more vulnerable women from falling into sexual exploitation and enslavement.

Elements of Kim's experience are disturbingly common in the modern slave trade. She was a young girl in a transient environment (a refugee camp). A trafficker (the minister) conspired with someone close to the family (her sister's husband) to extract her from the community and take control of her life. She was trafficked to another country where she did not understand the culture or the laws, and her family would be harmed if she did not fully cooperate. The slaveholder used her sexually and exploited her labor. Once she escaped, the slaveholder went out and quickly found two more girls to replace her.

To write this book, I conducted hundreds of interviews with young girls from Cambodia, Thailand, Peru, India, Uganda, South Africa, and eastern Europe. I encountered this essential story line time and time again. Of those individuals extracted out of impoverished countries and trafficked across international borders, 80 percent are female and 50 percent are children.[14] They are taken to unfamiliar destinations where, in the absence of legal protections and family networks, they can be kept in slavery. The consistency of the story line in fact suggests overarching mechanisms of a global industry.

Like any other commercial market, the slave trade is driven by the dynamics of supply and demand. Criminal agents make handsome profits off unpaid labor: it is cheaper to produce goods or, in the case of sex slavery or domestic servitude, to offer valued human services. Due to these financial advantages, slaveholders can compete successfully in almost any market. The profit margins will rise as high as the demand will bear.

We may not even realize how each one of us drives the demand during the course of a normal day. Kevin Bales, a pioneer in the fight against modern slavery, expresses well those commercial connections: "Slaves in Pakistan may have made the shoes you are wearing and the carpet you stand on. Slaves in the Caribbean may have put sugar in your kitchen and toys in the hands of your children. In India they may have sewn the shirt on your back and polished the ring on your finger."[15]

To ensure a steady stream of recruits, slaveholders will rely on slave traders to fulfill their supply. The slave trader may be a recruiter or a trafficker; often individuals will play both roles. Their capacity to meet the demand for slaves only becomes a problem if one of two conditions comes into effect: there is a scarcity of new recruits, or engaging in illicit activity becomes a real risk. In most of the world today, neither condition presents itself as an obstacle. To the contrary, there exists a glut of potential recruits and a negligible threat of prosecution. Hence the slave trade grows at a rapid pace.

Widespread poverty and social inequality ensure a pool of recruits as deep as the ocean. Parents in desperate straits may sell their children or at least be susceptible to scams that will allow the slave trader to take control over the lives of their sons and daughters. Young women in vulnerable communities are more likely to take a risk on a job offer in a faraway location. The poor are apt to accept a loan that the slave trader can later manipulate to steal their freedom. All of these paths carry unsuspecting recruits into the supply chains of slavery.

"The supply side of the equation is particularly bleak," says Senator Sam Brownback of Kansas. "While there are one hundred thousand places in the developed world for refugee resettlement per year, 50 million refugees and displaced persons exist worldwide today. This ready reservoir of the stateless presents an opportunity rife for exploitation by human traffickers."[16]

During the era of the American plantation economy, the slaveholder considered slave ownership an investment. The supply of new recruits was limited. The cost of extracting and transporting slaves and ensuring that they would be serviceable by the time they reached their destination was considerable. Though the slave owner usually treated the slave like a beast, it would be equal to the treatment of a prized bull. The slave owner aimed to extract the value of his investment over the course of the slave's lifetime. Proof of legal ownership therefore served an important purpose.

In the modern slave trade, the glut of slaves and the capacity to move them great distances in a relatively short period of time drastically alters the economics of slave ownership. As relative costs plummet, slaves cease to be a long-term investment. The fact that slave ownership is almost universally illegal today is of little consequence. The owner need not be too concerned about maintaining the health of the slave. Kevin Bales's description of modern slaves as "disposable people" profoundly fits: just like used batteries, once the slave exhausts his or her usefulness, another can be procured at no great expense.[17]

Notwithstanding these emerging trends in global markets, traditional modes of slavery also persist. Bonded labor has existed for centuries and continues to be the most common form of slavery in the world today. In a typical scenario, an individual falls under the control of a wealthy patron after taking a small loan. The patron adds egregious rates of interest and inflated expenses to the original principle so that the laborer finds it impossible to repay. Debt slaves may spend their entire life in service to a single slaveholder, and their "obligation" may be passed on to their children. Of the 27 million people worldwide held captive and exploited for profit today, the Free the Slaves organization estimates that at least 15 million are bonded slaves in India, Pakistan, Bangladesh, and Nepal.[18]

The tale of Bonda, a slave I met during my travels in South Asia, graphically illustrates the plight of a bonded laborer. The owner of a rice mill used small loans to enslave Bonda's entire village. The villagers labored eighteen hours daily and were banned from passing beyond the walls of the rice mill without supervision. After years of relentless oppression, Bonda's wife broke down one day and killed herself. Disconsolate over his loss, Bonda threw caution to the wind. He found a gate in the rice mill left open one day, and he bolted.

The owner did not treat insubordination lightly. He sent bounty hunters after Bonda and they captured him without much trouble. Once they brought Bonda back to the rice mill, the owner gathered all the slaves into an assembly in the center of the compound. For their edification, he used a cane to beat Bonda within an inch of his life. The owner then chained the unconscious man to a wall in the slaves' living quarters. And that became his bed for the rest of his days at the rice mill. He did his daily chores and then was ushered back to his chains.

Bonda's tale, I am pleased to report, ends on a happy note. An abolitionist agency called International Justice Mission (IJM) instigated a raid on the rice mill and emancipated Bonda along with his entire village. Local police arrested the owner and put him on trial for his crimes. In this book I detail how IJM's fearless team of criminal investigators and lawyers works with local law enforcement agencies to rescue slaves from dire situations around the world. Their relentless pursuit of justice on behalf of the innocent, despite considerable personal risk and sacrifice, inspired me beyond words.

That, in fact, was the unexpected surprise of my journey to monitor the rise of modern global slavery. I had steeled myself emotionally to end up in the depths of depression and despair. To be honest, I made some unpleasant stops in my journey. The day I went undercover to investigate a brothel in Phnom Pehn, for instance, broke my heart. A brothel owner invited me to take my pick of any one of the thirteen-year-old girls that crowded the sofas in front of me. A few extra bucks and I could have two of them for the night, he offered. I could not bear to think of these little girls passing through this ritual a dozen times each night.

But my journey did not end at the station of despair. The prime reason: I met a heroic ensemble of abolitionists who simply refuse to relent. I felt like I had gone back in time and had the great privilege of sharing a meal with a Harriet Tubman or a William Wilberforce or a Frederick Douglass. Like the abolitionists of old, these modern heroes do not expend their energy handicapping the odds stacked against the antislavery movement. They simply refuse to accept a world where one individual can be held as the property of another.

Kru Nam is one of those abolitionists who operates on the front lines in the fight against sex slavery. A painter with a university degree in art, she decided to use her natural gifts to bring healing. She launched a project to reach street kids in Chiang Mai, the second largest town in northern Thailand. Once she turned the kids loose with paintbrushes, they created a series of disturbing images that added up to a horror story.

Kru Nam soon realized that most of the kids did not come from Thailand. Most came from Burma, with a sprinkling of Laotians, Vietnamese, and Cambodians tossed in the mix. Through their painting they could tell her how they had arrived on the streets of Chiang Mai.

The Burmese boys spoke of a well-dressed Thai gentleman who had visited their village in the south of Burma. Accompanying him was a fourteen-year-old Burmese boy who wore fine-tailored clothes and spoke Thai fluently. The man explained to parents that he was offering scholarships for young boys to attend school back in Thailand. He would pay their school fees and cover their living expenses. "Look how well this child from your region is doing," he said, pointing to his young companion. "If you let me take your son back to Chiang Mai, I will do the same for him."

Though the tribal people of Burma are reluctant to part with young girls, they give more license for sons to travel afar in search of a livelihood. Many families therefore agreed to let their sons go with the Thai man. Once they reached Chiang Mai, the

Thai man immediately sold them to owners of sex bars and brothels.

The boys living on the streets were the lucky ones; they had escaped. They told Kru Nam that many more boys remained captive in the sex bars. Her blood boiled. She could not stand by and do nothing.

Kru Nam did not exactly have a plan when she marched into the sex bar for her first raid. Only her mission was clear: rescue as many of the young boys as she could find. The street kids had informed her that the owner held captive a dozen boys between the ages of ten and thirteen. He forced the boys to have sex with paying clients.

Kru Nam did not even attempt to negotiate with the owner; she knew better than to waste her time. But to her disappointment, only six boys sat at tables entertaining the male customers. The other boys were out on "dates" with the johns.

She had no need for histrionics. One by one she approached a table where a boy sat and calmly said, "Let's go. I'm taking you out of here." Several moments later, she was leading six little boys out the door and to her safe house in Chiang Mai.

Though Kru Nam made several more impromptu raids on sex bars, she eventually had to tread with more caution. Owners put the word out that they would kill her if she walked into their bars.

Deploying a fresh strategy, she organized street teams to scourge the night market of Chiang Mai and connect with young children who just got off the bus from the northern Thai-Burmese border. Recruiters for the sex bars also trolled the streets on the hunt for vulnerable kids. It became a life-and-death contest to find them first.

One day it struck Kru Nam that if she moved upstream before the kids hit Chiang Mai she would have an edge over the recruiters. So she moved about forty miles north to the border town of

Mae Sai, a major thoroughfare for foot traffic between Burma and Thailand.

In Mae Sai she set up a shelter to take in kids on the run. Nearly sixty boys and girls today find safe refuge each night in Kru Nam's shelter. She has had to move her safe house several times. Neighbors on each occasion have forced her out; they do not want "these dirty kids" living on their block. So Kru Nam purchased a block of land some fifteen miles outside of Mae Sai in the region of the Golden Triangle where the borders of Laos, Burma, and Thailand intersect. She does not have the money she needs to build a proper residence, so for the time being Kru Nam and the children will live on the land in temporary shelters.

Kru Nam is irrepressible. She does not have a large organization standing behind her; a skeletal staff of three assists her, and she receives modest funding from a tiny nongovernmental agency based in Thailand. What she does have is a burning passion to rescue young boys and girls so that they do not fall into the treacherous control of slaveholders.

Kru Nam does not know Lucy Borja, who rescues girls and boys forced into the brothels of Lima, Peru, nor has she met Padre Cesare Lo Deserto, who steals trafficked girls away from the mafiosi of eastern Europe. But she shares a special calling with these characters whose stories are featured in this book. Not one of them went out looking for slavery. Each simply reached out a compassionate hand to a refugee in need or a homeless street child, and it exposed him or her to the ugly undercurrent of human trafficking. Their passage from a single act of kindness to fighting for justice on a grander scale is the quintessential story of the abolitionist.

This book aims to be a handbook for the modern-day abolitionist. As such, it does not pretend to be an exhaustive study of global slavery in the twenty-first century. Rather, it follows the trail of a select group of extraordinary abolitionists into their respective settings. We get a feel for the people around them who have fallen into captivity. We delve into the historical antecedents and social forces that frame their time and place. We learn how the slave traders they resist use power and violence to exploit the weak. And we gain an insight into the specific strategies these abolitionists deploy to bring about emancipation for the captives.

These stories make it clear that modern-day abolitionists are not cut from the same mold. The women who embrace the child soldiers of Uganda move in a different universe from those abolitionists in Los Angeles who confront forced labor in garment factories. A Swiss-born entrepreneur launches business enterprises for ex-sex slaves in Cambodia, while an American-born lawyer uses the public justice system to free entire villages in South Asia. Some abolitionists rely on their faith in God, while a dedication to love and justice inspires others.

Despite their unique bearings, these abolitionists do share a common sense of their moment in history. They recognize that human freedom stands poised at a crucial crossroads in our time. Powerful forces aim to turn human beings into commodities that can be bought and sold like any other piece of property. To declare "not for sale" affirms that every individual has the inalienable right to be free, to pursue a God-given destiny.

To inspire others to join their movement is my overriding purpose for writing this book. The abolitionists featured herein are truly extraordinary, but they cannot win the fight alone. They are overwhelmed and beleaguered. Although Kru Nam is brave and resourceful, she cannot single-handedly stop sex trafficking in Thailand. The size and scope of her project is about the norm for abolitionist organizations. They sorely need reinforcements, a new wave of abolitionists, to join them in the struggle.

My students at the University of San Francisco often remark that they feel as if they were born in the wrong era, after all the important issues of history have been decided. It's as if they were born in 1975 in Liverpool with a burning desire for pop music. They have a real passion for a craft, but it's already been done.

They could not be more wrong. We have arrived at a momentous stage in the struggle for human freedom. The curtain has gone up, and the future waits for what unfolds.

All of us wonder how we would have acted in the epic struggles of human history. Would we have stood up and been counted among the courageous and the just?

How would we have responded in 1942 when Nazi soldiers came to our door in pursuit of our Jewish neighbors? Would we have been the collaborator who reveals to the soldiers where the Jews on our block might be found? Or would we have played the role of the spectator who pleads ignorance, minding our own business and watching the drama unfold from our front room window? Or might we have dared to act as an advocate, giving our neighbors shelter in our attic or helping them escape across the border? Would we have stood up and been counted among the just?

Imagine we lived in rural Tennessee in 1855 and Harriet Tubman came to our door. "We are smuggling fugitive slaves across an underground railroad, and we need safe houses where they can receive shelter, food, and rest," she might have said, bringing us to our moment of truth. "Contacts in the network say that you might be willing to open your home as a way station. Will you help us?" If Harriet Tubman had come calling, would we have stood up and been counted among the just?

Or what if we were in the company of Jesuits who established a mission in the New World in 1624? The Spanish slave traders warn us to dismantle our mission where the natives work and keep their tribal structure intact. "We control this territory," they would have said, "and you are undermining our lucrative trade in natives. End the missions now, or we will shut them down our own way." Would we have stood up and been counted among the just?

There are times to read history, and there are times to make history. We live right now at one of those epic moments in the fight for human freedom. We no longer have to wonder how we might respond to our moment of truth. It is we who are on the stage, and we can change the winds of history with our actions. Future generations will look back and judge our choices and be inspired or disappointed.

A bit overdramatic, you might think. I do not know any other way to express the urgency of rescuing 1 million children whom UNICEF estimates are forced today to sell their bodies to sexual exploiters. In a single country, Uganda, nearly forty thousand children have been kidnapped and violently turned into child soldiers or sex slaves. In South Asia each day, millions of children are forced to crush rocks in a quarry or roll cigarettes in a factory. The destinies of children around the globe hang in the balance, and they are powerless to break free.

As Edmund Burke presented the challenge so eloquently two centuries ago, "All that is necessary for the triumph of evil is that good men [and women] do nothing."

Shining Light into the Sexual Darkness: Cambodia and Thailand

I paid good money for you!"

How Srey Neang loathed those words. They made a claim on her, excusing any abuse, justifying every chore.

The old woman bought her not long after she turned seven. Srey Neang's parents were struggling to care for five children in a camp for internally displaced Cambodians. The camp was situated near the border with Thailand where food was scarce and jobs nonexistent. The old woman and her son came to the camp seeking a young girl to be a house servant. Her parents sacrificed one child for the survival of her siblings.

Memories of her family now lurk in shadows. She recalls playing in a dusty field with other children. Are those kids rolling on the ground her brothers and sisters? Rumors that her parents were Khmer Rouge militants follow Srey Neang. Of course, pinning that history on a child could be a form of manipulation. A daughter of the Khmer Rouge merited a tragic karma.

The old woman lived in a small structure; a single space served as bedroom, kitchen, and living room. At night, Srey Neang pulled out a mat to sleep on a knotty wood floor in the corner of the house.

She cooked the woman's meals, bathed her, washed clothes, scrubbed the floors, and performed any other chore demanded of her. Her master demonstrated neither affection nor malice; she expected only obedience. Srey Neang was never once addressed by name. "Hey you, get me some water," the woman would say, or "Girl, go sweep the floor." Did the old woman know her name? Some days Srey Neang whispered her own name softly to herself simply so that she would not forget.

Three years passed, and then her master turned very ill. Some days the woman did not even rise from the bed. During that period Srey Neang rarely left the house; morning and evening she tended to the dying woman's needs. The loneliness felt heavy at times.

Once the woman died, her son acted decisively to consolidate his mother's property. "Pack your stuff," he ordered Srey Neang no more than an hour after burying his mother. "You now will serve my family."

Srey Neang grabbed the few clothes she owned, rolled them up in the sleeping mat, and departed the old women's home for the final time. The son lived on the other side of the village, perhaps a walk of fifteen minutes. Though short in distance, the journey transported her to a new and dangerous universe.

Srey Neang sensed the rotten air as soon as she arrived. The wife of her new master treated her gruffly, as if to blame Srey Neang for an unwanted intrusion into her home.

She now had four people to serve—the married couple and their two young children. Srey Neang worked steadily from the break of day until the final member of the family fell asleep at night. Yet no effort proved good enough for her owners. Both husband and wife beat her with a reedy switch for the slightest offense: the porridge was too salty, or the front door of the house had been left open. Often they beat Srey Neang for things she did not even do.

No matter, it was their right. After all, they would declare, "We paid good money for you!"

A RECIPE FOR MASS VULNERABILITY

In June 2006, Cambodia was ranked as one of the worst countries in the world for human trafficking. The report card, published annually by the U.S. State Department, pulled no punches: "Cambodia is a source, destination, and transit country for men, women, and children trafficked for the purposes of sexual exploitation and forced labor."[1] The report further declares that "corruption, lack of training and funding for law enforcement, and a weak judiciary" stand in the way of Cambodia "making significant efforts" to eliminate its slave trade.

Unfortunately, Cambodia does not stand out as an exception in Southeast Asia. Sex traffickers in Thailand, Vietnam, Laos, and Burma also move women and children across borders with brazen disregard for law enforcement—and oftentimes with their help! The majority of their victims end up staying in Southeast Asia to service a robust sex industry. The sex bars and massage parlors in Phnom Penh, for instance, are highly populated with young girls from Laos and Vietnam. Southeast Asia is one of the world's largest exporters of sex slaves as well to brothels in Japan, China, Australia, Europe, and the United States.

So why does sex slavery thrive so in Southeast Asia? Four powerful forces collude to rip apart stable communities in the region: 1) devastating poverty; 2) armed conflicts; 3) rapid industrialization; 4) an exploding population growth. Though political scientists and economists may reach no definitive consensus about which of these social forces is paramount, they all would concur that Southeast Asia is passing through a period of radical transition. Whenever a society faces seismic changes, the powerless suffer most.

The impoverished masses of Cambodia represent the economic challenge. At least one in three of Cambodia's 15 million people live below the poverty line today. Cambodian women, above all, do not get the chance to study formally or learn vocational skills; 41 percent of the country's adult women are illiterate.[2] While finding a job in Cambodia can be difficult under any circumstances, an uneducated and impoverished woman does not fit the profile that most legal employers seek to hire. Desperate to secure the well-being of their parents or perhaps their own children, a poor woman can become easy prey for a trafficker.

The present situation in Burma—or Myanmar under the current regime—demonstrates the far-reaching impact of armed conflict. A military dictatorship maintains a fragile hold over a plethora of tribal groups and warlords, each of whom fight for their autonomy. Violent conflict can erupt at any given moment. As a result, Burmese families fleeing the violence or looking for a more sustainable livelihood pour into neighboring countries.

Refugees all over the world walk a perilous path. They become a minority in a new society, often without legal standing, that more powerful individuals will seek to exploit. So traffickers today view the Burmese population as a deep recruitment pool. According to one reputable organization that monitors sex trafficking in Thailand, nearly two-thirds of the girls brought into Thai brothels during the past five years came from Burma.[3]

The Southeast Asian region at large has experienced more than its share of armed conflicts over the past fifty years. The Vietnam War obviously left a dramatic mark on the Vietnamese people. It's easier to overlook the long-term impact of that war on the people of Laos, Cambodia, and Thailand. Combatants are not the only casualties of war; communities take years to heal from the wounds. Many hill tribes in Laos, for instance, have yet to regain their mooring. Cambodia, meanwhile, went on to experience the Khmer Rouge and its "killing fields," then sunk deep into its own civil war. The Cambodian conflict only ended after Vietnam invaded the country and propped up a regime to its own liking.

Added to the chaos of civil conflicts, Southeast Asia has made a dramatic leap toward industrialization. Its base of production has been shifting from subsistence farming to cash-crop agriculture and manufacturing (though certainly not at the same pace in each country within the region). Peasant families find it increasingly difficult to make a livelihood off the land. In many cases, they head to urban areas in hopes of finding a job in a factory. In Thailand, for example, nearly 10 percent of the population migrated from the rural areas to industrialized centers over a three-year period from 1993 to 1995.[4]

Although industrialization may stimulate growth to the overall economy, the distribution of wealth is not being evenly distributed. An elite sector benefits from the concentration of land and capital and makes financial arrangements that do not take into account the needs of the poor masses. Students of history recall the social crises that accompanied the process of industrialization in the Western world. While it is hoped that modernization in Southeast Asia eventually will bring economic progress to the many, in the short term the poor get tossed to and fro like flotsam on a raging sea.

As if the foregoing trends do not bring enough of a challenge, a population boom puts added strain on the region. In many countries of Southeast Asia, over half the population alive today falls under the age of fifteen. Confronted with a scarcity of jobs and food, local communities do not have sufficient resources for their young people. As harsh as it sounds, the young are the first to become expendable.

Amid all these disruptions to social stability, slavery emerges as a tempting financial solution. Extreme poverty contributes to family breakdowns and deserted children. Human traffickers are most successful in finding young girls among destitute rural villages. Best estimates indicate that thirty thousand Cambodian children are exploited in the sex trade and as many as one-third of these are under eighteen years old.[5]

The owner of a brothel in Southeast Asia can buy a women or child for as little as $50. Virgins fetch anywhere from $500 to as much as a $1000. To put those figures in perspective, $1000 corresponds to three and a half times the annual average income in Cambodia.

Annie Dieselberg—A Light in the Darkness

Annie Dieselberg embraces abolition as her vocation. She calls her Bangkok-based project NightLight Design, playing off the image of a light that brings to safety individuals who are lost in darkness. The creativity that fuels her project matches the compassion that brought it into existence.

When Annie launched NightLight Design in 2005, she aimed to offer an alternative for young girls who work in commercial sex bars. Annie and her husband had worked in various Christian ministries in Thailand for more than a decade. Witnessing so many women in Bangkok engaged in demeaning sexual exploitation drove Annie to dream in full color. She could continue to help broken individuals after predators had disposed of them, or she could confront the problem head on. She chose the steep path.

Annie is accustomed to taking the road less traveled. She grew up for most of her childhood in Zaire, the daughter of parents involved in international church ministry. In her teens, her parents relocated to Thailand. Annie spent one year living with them in Thailand, and then attended boarding school in India. After high school graduation, she showed up at the University of West Virginia wrapped in a salwar and sporting bangles on her wrist. "The other students did not know what to make of this strange white girl with blonde hair who dressed and acted like a total foreigner," Annie says with a laugh as she reminiscences. "I may have looked like any other American, but I sure brought some unusual ideas to the classroom."

Even today, her appearance can be deceiving. Frankly, she does not cut an imposing figure—in her early forties, a mother of four children and of slight build and stature. She could be a "soccer mom" at any suburban park.

Fire in the belly—no better description fits Annie's persona. Only time will tell if she is constructing a castle in the air, but there is no doubting her commitment to the cause. She speaks and acts with the intensity of a Hebrew prophet.

"Women on the streets may look like they are free when you tour Bangkok, but they are not!" Annie begins her orientation to the sex trade. "Trafficked women are often moved around, and many of them do not know the language or the money currency. They feel alone, isolated from friends or family who might give them a helping hand."

So Annie decided to step in and be that helping hand. In early 2005, she took a visiting American church group to a sex bar. While the men in the delegation remained outside praying, Annie led a small team of women inside.

"We sat down with a young woman—only twenty-two years old with two children of her own," Annie says, recounting the episode. "She told us how much she hated working at the bar. When I asked her where she would like to be, she told me that she would like to be home with her kids."

So Annie and her spiritual sisters paid the bar owner 600 baht (roughly $15) to "rent" the woman for the night—the standard price a customer pays for a full evening of "entertainment." The payment unexpectedly turned into a redemption fee.

Over the previous year Annie had taught herself how to make jewelry. So she spontaneously offered the bar girl a job to work alongside her producing jewelry for commercial sale. The young woman accepted and became employee #1 in NightLight Design.

Annie did not even have an office or work studio for her company at that moment. So she told the (now retired) bar girl to meet her at a McDonalds restaurant in central Bangkok. With the waft of burgers and fries deep in their nostrils, Annie delivered to the young woman her first training session in jewelry production. She then sent her new employee off with a suitcase of beads and stones under her arm.

Srey Neang—A False Rescue

Srey Neang, at twelve years old, learned to anticipate when her masters would beat her. Not that she could do anything to prevent it. She paid for every failure or misfortune with blows from the reedy switch. She endured the abuse in silence. Yet whenever the opportunity arose, she would run from the house and, at a safe distance, release the pain screaming inside her.

That was precisely her condition when Sovanna found her. He lived in Phnom Penh but often came to her small village to visit relatives. Though he looked sixteen, Sovanna was actually in his early twenties and had a wife in the Cambodian capital.

"So what did those ogres do to you this time?" he would ask sympathetically.

Sharing the story with Sovanna did not take away the sting, but it made her feel better to talk about it.

One afternoon, after a particularly bad beating, Sovanna planted a subversive idea: "Hey, these people treat you like a dog! Why don't you come to Phnom Penh and live with my family?"

Srey Neang looked long and hard at Sovanna; could he be

kidding? His next comment erased her doubt: "My mother could use your help in her shop. You could attend school and work for her on weekends."

Her heart made a leap. Though she could not imagine what life in a busy city might be like, it had to be better than this living hell. Together they devised an escape plan.

One week later, Srey Neang was living in Phnom Penh. Sovanna's mother immediately put her to work, dispatching Srey Neang out to the city center with a tray of fresh-baked cakes to sell. In the evenings Srey Neang would tend the shop that the family ran out of its home. Neighbors came to buy cigarettes, alcohol, and an assortment of sweets.

School, however, dropped off the agenda. Only once did Srey Neang ask when she might take classes with other kids in the neighborhood. Sovanna responded that the family needed her to work full-time to cover her expenses.

Sovanna otherwise continued to show her kindness. He often would take her with him to run errands around Phnom Penh. She especially liked visiting the riverfront, where they would watch a parade of small vessels move in and out of the city.

Sovanna's wife, Ly, quickly became jealous of the tight bond that Srey Neang had developed with her husband. Though Srey Neang still had not reached fourteen, Ly convinced herself that the two were involved romantically. Ly would become cross whenever they returned from an outing. Her anger eventually turned abusive. She began calling Srey Neang "that little Khmer Rouge bitch." After a nasty fight with Sovanna, she would scream at her husband, "Get out of this house, and take your little prostitute with you!"

Neither Sovanna nor Srey Neang could persuade Ly of the innocence of their relationship. Srey Neang sensed danger. A child walking alone, bereft of family and community, always has cause to fear.

Pierre Tami—If Heaven Could Cry

In 1994, Pierre Tami established Hagar Shelter in Phnom Penh, Cambodia, as a haven for women who had fallen victim to violence and sexual exploitation. Since its establishment, Hagar has provided assistance to over one hundred thousand women and children through its social programs and economic projects.

Despite this resounding success, Pierre does not feel totally satisfied: "I get discouraged at times because there are so many tragedies, so many people dying, so much poverty and helplessness, and there is only so much I can do."

This humble confession speaks volumes about Pierre's character. He stays focused on the needs and rarely brings a conversation around to his accomplishments. But truth be told, Hagar represents a remarkable achievement. The U.S. State Department in 2004 selected Pierre and the Hagar project as one of its six international heroes in the struggle against the global slave trade. The story of how Pierre created one of the most innovative programs for freed slaves will inspire even the most entrenched cynic.

Sometimes you know your destination before it is clear why you should go there. For Pierre, Cambodia was that destination. He already had devoted twelve years to helping people in crisis—including a long stint in Japan aiding the homeless in the parks of downtown Osaka and several years more building up a youth drop-in center in Singapore. He could not explain why, but he understood these ventures as a training ground for some greater project. When he received the invitation to visit Cambodia in June 1990, it was destiny calling.

At the time, a communist regime had taken over Cambodia and a civil war threatened to throw the country into chaos. Though the ruling regime were paranoid about the presence of foreigners, it asked the Swiss-born Pierre to evaluate the potential of providing aid to its impoverished masses. Only twenty-five nongovernmental aid agencies were operating in Cambodia at the time.

Government agents kept Pierre's delegation under close watch during the course of its stay. They strictly forbade movement beyond the official agenda. Under military escort, the delegation visited the starkly underdeveloped northeast region of the country. The roads were filled with soldiers and studded with land mines.

Though no stranger to poverty, Pierre felt a bit overwhelmed. The absence of health facilities and the oppression of minority groups had led to some of the most devastating social conditions he had ever witnessed.

The intensity magnified on a visit to one particular village. When Pierre first arrived, silence blanketed the town. Actually, not complete silence—for a single, terrible wail disturbed the calm. A mother had just lost her six-month-old baby, a casualty of malaria. She spilled out her agony and protest.

A traditional Cambodian (Khmer) proverb muses, "If Heaven could cry, then Cambodia would never know drought." For Pierre, the mother's wail became the cry of a people, and it continued to haunt him long after he had left the country.

Two weeks after he had left Cambodia, Pierre personally experienced the ravage of a potentially fatal disease—on his travels he had contracted a rare strain of malaria peculiar to northeast Cambodia that travels directly to the brain. Doctors gave him only a 50 percent chance of survival. He spent several weeks in the hospital and barely survived.

While recuperating, Pierre regularly read his Bible—his faith in God served as an anchor in his life. The near-death experience now gave him a greater sense of urgency about the future. This became his daily prayer: "I was born for a purpose. Show me what that purpose might be."

One morning he came across a passage in Paul's second letter to the church in Corinthians that seemed to be speaking directly to him: God helps us in all our troubles, so that we are able to help others who have all kinds of troubles, using the same help that we ourselves have received from God.

Upon reading the passage, images of the Cambodian people whom he had just visited crystallized in Pierre's mind. He had received a dramatic healing. Now it was his turn to bring comfort to Cambodian women and children who suffered from poverty and violence.

Srey Neang—The Conspiracy

Srey Neang did not go on excursions beyond the occasional outing with Sovanna. She had no friends—she "celebrated" her fifteenth birthday alone tending the shop. Work was her life.

So when Tevy asked Srey Neang to accompany her on a trip to the ancient Buddhist temple of Angkor Wat, she practically fell speechless. Tevy lived down the street and was a close friend to Sovanna's wife, Ly, which made the invitation all the more unexpected. Because Ly had soiled her reputation in the neighborhood, Srey Neang had resigned herself to being a social leper. Miraculously, both Sovanna's mother and Ly gave her leave to go on the trip. During the three years she had lived at their home, Srey Neang had never had even a single day off.

Tevy borrowed a car for the journey. As soon as they had left Phnom Penh, Srey Neang lost her bearings. She had heard the name Angkor Wat on the lips of tourists to whom she sold cakes in the city plaza. But it could be located on the moon for all she knew.

After a long morning on the highway, a sign welcomed them to the town of Siem Reap. Tevy suddenly announced, "My cousin lives here, and I promised him that I would drop in and say hello." A few minutes later, she pulled over to park in front of a karaoke club.

They jumped out of the car and walked to a set of stairs attached to the side of the club. Tevy's "cousin" awaited them on the top landing. He introduced himself as Chuan and offered both his visitors a cold drink. After a few minutes of small talk, he ushered Tevy into an adjoining room and shut the door. Srey Neang awkwardly sat alone in the living room.

Nearly half an hour passed before the two reemerged. Tevy did not hesitate to drop a bombshell: "I've run out of cash. Before we go on to Angkor Wat, I need to pick up some money. You stay here with my cousin, and I'll come back and pick you up later."

The words packed a punch to Srey Neang's stomach. She could not identify the precise story line, but she sensed danger. "Oh, please let me go with you," she begged Tevy. "I won't be any trouble."

"No," Tevy snapped, "you'll just get in the way."

Tevy then walked swiftly to the door and down the stairs to her car. Srey Neang stood motionless for a few seconds before breaking into a convulsion of sobs.

"Oh, come on now, what are you worried about?" she heard Chuan's voice behind her. Srey Neang turned and saw his outstretched hand holding a tissue. "You'll have lots of fun here," he said.

Srey Neang did not respond, but cried quietly into the now-drenched tissue.

"Hey, why don't we go out to a nice restaurant and celebrate your arrival in Siem Reap?" Chuan suggested. "I guarantee that you'll love the food."

Chuan raised his hand as if to say, "Wait here for a moment," and scurried off to the adjoining room. A few moments later he returned holding a beautiful black dress and matching shoes.

"These should cheer you up," he said enthusiastically. "We are going to a very nice restaurant, the best in town, and you have to look like you belong there."

Srey Neang never imagined herself in such an elegant dress. Her wardrobe consisted of a skirt, two shirts, and a single pair of pants, all of which had turned threadbare from regular use. Perhaps, she thought, it was a stroke of luck that Tevy had left her with Chuan.

Nor had Srey Neang dined at a restaurant where servers wait on customers. During the meal, Chuan asked her lots of questions about herself. Yes, she was fifteen years old. No, she did not live with her parents. She did not allow the small talk to interfere with the enjoyment of her meal.

The dinner over, they strolled back to the karaoke bar. "Let's go inside the club," Chuan said upon their arrival. "I want you to meet a couple of my friends."

Srey Neang followed him through the entrance. At first her eyes had trouble adjusting to the darkness of the room. Slowly, she could make out the scene. At nearly every table a middle-aged man enjoyed the company of two or more young women who casually draped their bodies around him.

Chuan led her through the club, occasionally pausing to give a brief greeting to a male patron. Once they reached a staircase at the back of the club, he pointed upward with his index finger. Srey Neang went first. At the top of the stairs they reached a small hallway with three doors, all shut. She turned around to get further instructions. Chuan jerked his head deliberately to the right, indicating which door she was to open.

Srey Neang turned the knob and tentatively pushed forward. It startled her to see a man standing in the middle of the room as if he were anticipating her arrival. She heard the sound of the door click shut behind her. She did not need to turn her head to know that Chuan had not entered the room with her.

The room did not hold much furniture, save a bed and a small nightstand. The man, in his mid–thirties, appeared to be a Cambodian. He uttered a simple, shocking command in the local dialect: "Take off your clothes."

Srey Neang reeled backward toward the door. "I'm sorry," she said, trying her best to keep a steady voice. "You must be confusing me with someone else."

"No, I'm not mistaken," he replied. "I paid good money for you." He then held out the palms of his hands, whispering, "Now be a good girl, and show me what you've got under that dress."

Srey Neang spun around and flew out the door in retreat. Chuan, however, was waiting for her on the other side of the door. He wrapped his arms around her torso and squeezed her in a strong bear hug. Srey Neang struggled with all her might but could not break free.

"Let go of me, you brute!" she screamed.

"You aren't going anywhere until you pay back what you owe me!" Chuan yelled as he dragged her toward the room.

"What do you mean 'what I owe you'?" she asked incredulously. "You never gave me any money!"

"Oh yeah, how about your dinner tonight?" he said. "You also owe me for those clothes you're wearing. And I gave $150 to that woman who brought you here this afternoon."

Once he finished listing her debts, Chuan shoved her toward the man, saying, "Now unless you have some other way of paying me, get to work!"

"Tevy had no right to sell me!" Srey Neang protested in red rage. "I've never had anything to do with that witch until she tricked me into coming on this trip."

Chuan could not have shown any less interest in fairness. Ignoring her plea, he changed tactics: "You aren't fooling me with your fake innocence. I know you're already used goods."

"What do you take me for?" asked Srey Neang. "I'm still a virgin!"

"That's not the story I got," Chuan said as he chuckled. "Young girls should not be screwing around with other women's husbands."

In a flash the veil fell from Srey Neang's eyes. So here was her punishment for being a close friend to Sovanna. She had fallen for an intricate conspiracy. The air went out of her rebellion.

Chuan, sensing his victory, offered encouragement: "Hey, don't worry. After a few times it's not hard. You'll get used to it."

By night's end, four adult men had raped Srey Neang. The nights to follow never got better.

SHAME AS A WEAPON

Shame is a club that beats enslaved women at practically every turn. It starts when young girls from impoverished families are blamed for the destitution of their parents. "Good" daughters manage the health and welfare of their mother and father. Their suffering translates into her shame, so she is willing to make any sacrifice to change their condition.

The community's perception of sexual purity also plays a major role in a young girl's shame. Once an unmarried girl has lost her virginity, she is considered despoiled. It does not matter if a family member sexually abused her or a stranger raped her. Purity is all or nothing—either you have it or you don't. Her family will treat her as blight to its honor, and no 'respectable' man will want to marry her. The girl might as well be sold into a life of prostitution, for she has lost her innocence. So strikes the club of shame.

Traffickers and brothel owners alike also use this cultural value to manipulate girls. If a new recruit resists the idea of having sex with a paying customer, the slaveholder might rape her himself and say, "Now you are used goods; you might as well give it up for other men." Tragically, the girl is apt to understand the logic of this brutal indoctrination and resign herself to life in the brothel. She has lost everything—her family will reject her and her neighbors will treat her as a pariah. And each day she stays, the possibility of rejoining respectable community life diminishes. She lives in exile.

Annie Dieselberg—Designing a Future

Like a prism, NightLight Design can be viewed from a number of angles. For starters, it is a for-profit business that trains women in how to make and sell jewelry. The products are made in NightLight's humble factory in central Bangkok and sold primarily through religious networks in Thailand and the United States. The jewelry is high quality, and the design ranges from classic to trendy.

Programs that encourage girls to escape the sex trade but leave them poor and jobless do not yield long-term success stories. The girls remain vulnerable to being trafficked once again. Annie therefore created her project to equip young women for life beyond the sex trade.

"Everyone makes money off these women: the recruiter, the trafficker, the owner of the bar, you name it," says Annie. "But the woman herself stays mired in poverty." Just naming the injustice has gotten Annie fired up, and she cuts loose with one of her prophetic statements: "Society won't pay a poor woman a decent wage, but men will shell out big bucks just so they can abuse her body for a few minutes!"

Despite a limited budget, NightLight pays twice the minimum wage established by Thai law. Obviously, the workers will not become wealthy off this pay, but the compensation does offer a sustainable livelihood. In order to be considered for employment, the women must agree to leave the sex industry completely. They also must commit to a forty-hour week, working Monday to Friday from nine to five.

The policy of paying a salary rather than on a fee per produced item facilitates NightLight's other mission, to develop healthy women. During the course of a normal workday, women engage in workshops on health care, HIV/AIDS prevention, personal financial management, spiritual formation, and how to speak English. The workers also are invited to daily worship services and a weekly spiritual formation class. (Participation in religious activities is not a requirement for employment.)

NightLight now employs nearly fifty women in its jewelry business. Financial resources present the biggest hurdle for expansion. Frankly, Annie never intended NightLight to grow as fast as it has. The project took on a life of its own as word spread throughout the sex bars that escape was possible. And Annie, understandably, finds it hard to put on the brakes.

"At one point early on, I felt like we had to halt our progress," she said. "But then one young woman for whom I had been praying for six years called and asked if I would help her leave the sex trade. I took it as a sign from God to move forward."

Srey Neang—The Police Raid

From the moment she arrived at the karaoke club, Srey Neang looked for a chance to escape. But Chuan operated the club like a prison. Whenever they were not seeing johns, the girls were kept captive in the apartment atop the club. Each door had a deadbolt that locked from the outside. Steel wires covered the windows.

He forced the women to have sex with ten men each day on average. Most of the johns hailed from Cambodia, though a decent portion came from Thailand, China, and India. The customers began trickling into the karaoke club in the late afternoon, and the final engagement might not end until two in the morning. On rare occasions, a john would pay to keep a girl for the entire night. More typically, johns put out $2.50 for a visit that might last twenty minutes.

Chuan aimed to keep a steady stable of young women working in the club at any given time. Few showed up as young as Srey Neang; most had turned seventeen or eighteen years old, and none were older than twenty-four. Regardless, once at the karaoke club, they aged at an accelerated pace. A woman seemed to add two days for every one day she spent there.

To prevent rebellion, Chuan regularly sold individual women to other brothel owners. A network of recruiters had little trouble replenishing his supply. Due to the constant turnover, the women rarely formed relationships where trust and solidarity might take root. They shared a nightmare, yet faced their suffering alone.

In a departure from his pattern, Chuan did not sell off Srey Neang. He had his reasons. A good number of the johns specifically requested a young girl, and that made Srey Neang a valuable commodity. Chuan's second reason made Srey Neang even more ill. He confessed that he had fallen in love with her.

As far as she was concerned, love had nothing to do with their relationship. Chuan raped Srey Neang at least three times a week. He treated her no better or no worse than the other johns she met each day. Occasionally Chuan brought her small gifts such as perfume or new earrings. He never failed to mention—usually the next day—that he had added the cost of the gift to her debt.

Only on one occasion did Srey Neang feel hopeful about getting away from the karaoke club. Late one morning, while nearly all of the girls still lay asleep in their beds, she awoke to the sound of pounding at the front door. She stumbled out of the bedroom and heard a clear voice bark: "It's the police! Open up the door immediately!"

"I can't," she yelled back through the door. "The door locks only from the outside. You'll have to get the key from Chuan."

"Stand back then," the voice advised. "We're going to break down the door."

"Be my guest!" Srey Neang squealed with delight.

Within seconds a band of uniformed police officers came bursting through the entrance. By now, all of the girls had spilled out of their bedrooms and stood pensively in the front hallway. The officer in charge paced slowly in a circle around them. He used exaggerated gestures to show that he was counting the number of girls present. He then announced, "You are all under arrest for the illegal solicitation of sex."

"Boy, I never thought I would be so glad to be arrested," quipped an older girl. She then added to the policeman who grabbed her arm, "But you got the wrong criminal. Find that bastard Chuan, and throw him behind bars."

Ignoring her comment, the commanding officer ordered his team to escort the girls down the stairs to the cars parked below. Once at the police station, they placed all the girls in a single holding cell.

Nothing much happened over the next twenty-four hours. Srey Neang kept waiting for the opportunity to tell the police her story. Surely Ly and Chuan committed a crime when they bartered her like a prized cow. And can someone be forced to perform unmentionable acts with men? She thought not.

The following afternoon a guard opened the door of the jail cell and invited only Srey Neang to accompany him. She assumed that she would get first crack at testifying against Chuan. To her surprise, the guard led her straight out of the police station. There, waiting for her on the sidewalk, stood Chuan.

"I bet you missed me," he crowed.

She turned to run back into the police station, but Chuan grabbed her by the arm. "You're wasting your time," he said. "How do you think I got you released? The police are more than happy at the moment with their cash bonus."

Chuan drove her back to the karaoke club. Once they arrived, he walked with her up the stairs to the apartment and then raped her. Before departing the bedroom, he whispered into her ear, "So glad you're back." Lying still in her bed, Srey Neang heard the key lock the door.

In the weeks to follow, Srey Neang sank into a deep depression. Sleep once had been her refuge, but the events of the day seeped into her dreams. She now tossed and turned her way through the night. Food lost its appeal. She lost nearly twenty-five pounds. Though she had always been somewhat slight, at sixty-six pounds she now looked all skin and bones.

Perhaps death would be her only escape. She counted it among her options.

Sean Litton—Busting a Trafficking Ring

"Imagine yourself in a dark room. You stick out your hand to grab what you believe to be a snake, but you realize that you are actually holding the tail of an elephant."

That's how Sean Litton, the International Justice Mission's vice president of interventions, describes the serendipity involved in the investigation of sex trafficking. A routine lead may result at any moment in a major bust.

International Justice Mission (IJM) deploys a corps of seasoned public justice professionals—criminal investigators, prosecutors, political analysts, and diplomats—to confront slavery wherever it exists in the world. Its staff gathers detailed evidence of illegal bondage and encourages local police authorities to free the slaves. The agency then collaborates with local prosecutors to build against slaveholders or traffickers a case that might stick in a court of law.

Litton points to the relatively innocuous alert that he received from a Thai-based nongovernmental organization (NGO) in late 2004. A Thai man had approached the NGO after he had been forced to pay $1,500 to buy his niece out of bondage. Pressed for details, the man explained that Siri, his niece, had called him on the phone from a country in Southeast Asia, pleading for help. A heavily armed group of men had held her captive in a brothel and were demanding a ransom for her release. Siri's captors had released her upon receiving the money, and she was now safely back home. But Siri's uncle wanted justice for the men who had forced his niece into prostitution.

The NGO committed to assisting the family, but sensed that it was out of its depth dealing with heavily armed sex traffickers, so it called IJM for assistance. IJM strongly discourages the practice of paying traffickers a redemption fee to release slaves. Siri, however, was able to provide IJM with a few financial and personal details concerning the traffickers, and this created an opportunity to pursue an investigative trail.

An IJM investigator met with Siri to recover everything she knew about this trafficker. She identified a man called Johnny as the leader of the syndicate that had trafficked her into the brothel. Johnny was a citizen in Southeast Asia and of Chinese decent.

Siri described how one of Johnny's recruiters had deceived her into the sex trade. She had been working as a tailor in the city of Mae Sai in the north of Thailand. Her income of $75 a month was fairly decent by Thai standards, especially for a woman in her early twenties. But the recruiter had promised her a job in a restaurant in Malaysia with a starting salary of $250 a month. "Besides, you are only twenty-one years old and single," said the recruiter, herself a woman, in a crafty ploy to persuade

Siri. "You're likely to meet a wealthy Chinese man who will marry you."

Once the young tailor had agreed to the proposal, the recruiter helped her apply for a passport and made travel arrangements. On the appointed day of departure, she put Siri in a minibus along with several other young women "lucky" to have landed a restaurant job. As soon as they had crossed the southern border of Thailand and passed into the destination city, Johnny met them.

To their dismay, he informed the women that his "investment" to bring them to this destination bound them to a "six-month contract to work in his entertainment business." To reinforce his control, Johnny demanded that they turn over their passports for "safekeeping." The minibus then continued on to another, smaller city known for retail shopping and gambling.

Siri provided the IJM investigator with enough clues to indicate that Johnny was not operating alone, but as part of an organized crime syndicate. During the few weeks she stayed in the city, Siri was forced to work in a variety of brothels, each exploiting two hundred or more women. Siri reported that she was constantly under surveillance; armed guards kept a close watch over her.

The criminals did not want the slaves to build any meaningful relationships out of which an escape plan might hatch, so they regularly moved the sex slaves from house to house and brothel to brothel. Siri did have enough conversations with the other victims to learn that the majority had been trafficked from throughout Southeast Asia.

After several weeks of living a nightmare, Siri begged Johnny to send her back to Thailand. He told her that what she was asking was impossible because she owed him $1,500—he listed costs for transportation, a passport, housing, food, and a finder's fee for the recruiter. Siri told Johnny that she could raise the "reimbursement" if he would allow her to make a phone call to her family. He consented, and she called the one person she hoped might take action, her uncle.

Hearing Siri's testimony, the IJM staff based in Thailand started to piece together the reach of this crime ring. "The case touched on every element of human trafficking," says Litton. "Fraud, bonded labor, sex slavery, violations of immigration law, and kidnapping, all woven seamlessly into a single network."

Given the risks of confronting a sophisticated mafia, Litton decided to call in reinforcements from IJM headquarters in Washington, DC. The organization's top-drawer investigator—whom Litton refers to simply as "the Genius," in large part because he doesn't want to disclose the man's identity for the sake of future cases—was sent to the target city to go undercover.

As the IJM investigator made the rounds of the city's high-profile brothels, he confirmed that Siri had not exaggerated the fortresslike security that the trafficking ring deployed. Armed security guards equipped with walkie-talkies monitored the perimeter of the buildings. Steel doors blocked the front entrance of the brothels. A guard checked out potential clients through a small porthole that slides open and shut.

The Genius was able to pass the careful eye of scrutiny at the front gate of the brothel, where a pimp ushered him into a lounge where he could review the women available for his pleasure.

The investigation now reached the crucial moment, when the Genius earned his reputation. He evaluated on the spot which of the candidates would be most likely to cooperate in his investigation. Given the constant threat of violence, some women are too frightened to betray their captors. Others may want to win favor with a cruel master by exposing the investigator. So the Genius had to run the women through his own personality profile; how he does it remains a mystery even to Litton.

Over the ensuing several days, the Genius interviewed a batch of women who were pleased to share their tale of abduction and captivity. Cautious not to raise suspicions of the brothel owners, he carefully recorded their stories and instructed the women to follow their normal protocol. While he conducted interviews, a team of IJM lawyers toiled around the clock to turn the material into a compelling report that would be strong enough to stand up in a court once it came to prosecuting the criminals.

The investigation turned up a great deal about the trafficking syndicate. The women originated in countries throughout Asia: above all Cambodia, Vietnam, Burma, Laos, Thailand, and southern China. Every girl interviewed had been trafficked without her consent. The youngest female interviewed was fourteen years old, though most of the women fell between the ages of sixteen and twenty-five. The women had to complete anywhere from seven to ten tricks a night, with an average charge of $40 per visit. When the women were not working, the trafficking ring distributed them in groups of twenty to homes across the city to make it more difficult for the police to track them. An Asian-based mafia was at the hub of the syndicate that operated vibrant cells throughout Southeast Asia. The johns driving the demand were mostly wealthy Asian businessmen.

Once the IJM team felt like it had gathered sufficient evidence, it took on the ambitious task of engineering collaboration among the appropriate police bodies in Thailand and the other countries involved. Up to that point, these agencies had never collaborated on a trafficking case.

Most critical of all, IJM presented a report of its investigation to senior law enforcement officers in the country where the brothels operated. Once they had reviewed the evidence that IJM had gathered, the police officers were enthusiastic about bringing down the syndicate. Wary of the vacuum in the local law, IJM sought an agreement from them that the police raid follow two essential conditions: 1) the trafficked women should be treated as victims and not as criminals; 2) the traffickers must not only be arrested, they must be prosecuted.

In early April 2005, a large police force raided some of the largest brothels operating in the target city. Unfortunately, the traffickers were tipped off and the police did not arrest a single syndicate member on the day of the raid. On the rosy side, the police rescued ninety-five women from the brothels.

The case turned out to be a revelation for IJM. Up until that point, it had focused its efforts on internal trafficking within Thailand and Cambodia. Now that the agency had exposed the broader regional trafficking, it needed to reassess its operations to address the sophisticated networks that were growing in Asia.

Subsequent IJM and police investigations helped the local police arrest one of the key agents of this Southeast Asian trafficking ring along with seven accomplices. The Thai recruiter who had ensnared Siri was among those arrested. IJM lawyers worked to secure prosecutions of all eight perpetrators, who are now awaiting sentencing.

Pierre Tami—Training Camp

Pierre paid several more visits to Cambodia in 1991 and 1992. The political scene inside the country continued to be tense. The Khmer Rouge advanced its efforts to overthrow the government and had set up camp no more than ten miles outside Phnom Penh. In response to the growing unrest, the United Nations sent in a peacekeeping force to do what it could to prevent all-out war.

While he watched and waited, Pierre began learning the Khmer language. It was a trusted method that went back to his childhood in the south of Switzerland. At the age of eight, Pierre already had his sights set far beyond the Alps. A Catholic priest who was serving the poor in Africa came to visit Pierre's church. The priest shared the story of Saint Francis of Assisi. It made such an impression on the young Pierre that he heard a voice inside him say, "I want to be like Saint Francis." After the mass finished, Pierre approached the priest and asked him, "What can I do in order to devote myself to serving the poor?" The priest replied, "Son, develop a unique skill and learn languages, and God will use you."

Already fluent in Italian (which is widely spoken in the south of Switzerland) and Swiss-German, the young Pierre absorbed English, French, and Spanish. But he admits that somewhere along the path of adolescence he lost the plot. Fast cars and romance captured his teenage imagination. When he turned twenty, he began a fast track to business management at the Zurich International Airport, first with Swissair and later with British Airways.

Pierre lived the high life of travel and opulence in London. "I got sucked into the dreams of materialism," he says. But at the age of twenty-three, he recalled the story of Saint Francis. Francis came from a wealthy family in Italy and became a successful merchant of textiles. Following a religious conversion, Francis dedicated his life to the kinds of riches that accrue from being a peacemaker and practicing compassion to the poor.

Pierre felt a similar conviction stirring in his soul. He decided material gain could never bring him fulfillment. He had started seriously dating a woman, Simonetta, who shared his sense of spiritual purpose. The couple took out a year for study and spiritual reflection, then got married and moved to Japan.

The call to Cambodia now represented another leap of faith. On an extended visit to Phnom Penh, Pierre was paying visits to abandoned women at the city hospital. One day a nurse asked if he would visit in the emergency room a young girl who soldiers had found lying on the streets of Phnom Penh. Naked and unconscious, the girl had practically withered away from starvation. The doctors could do nothing for her. Within hours, she died next to Pierre, a stranger.

"Somehow she got cut off from her family and her community," Pierre says sadly as he recalls the episode. "No one spared a tear for that girl. I felt like God was saying to me, 'Have I got your attention now?'"

Srey Neang—The Difference a Friend Makes

At sixteen, Srey Neang was the old hand at the karaoke club. She provided guidance and comfort to the newly enslaved. Though she honestly did not feel like she had learned too many survival tips, she freely passed along what she did know.

Everything changed once Mei arrived. An uncle had sold her to Chuan; the fact that her mother had blessed the arrangement nearly caused Mei to lose her mind.

Srey Neang and Mei bonded like sisters the moment they met. Somehow they found a way to bring laughter into the apartment. Keenly aware of Chuan's isolation strategy, Srey Neang instructed Mei to hide their blossoming friendship. "Outside this room you must act like you do not even care that I exist," she advised Mei one afternoon while they were locked up in the apartment.

"That miserable wretch," Mei hissed. "Why should he care about our friendship? He rules over every other detail of our lives!"

"That's exactly it," Srey Neang explained. "He fears that we will plan a future that he cannot control."

Inspired by friendship, Srey Neang renewed her quest to escape. She decided her best chance lay with Yuth, a young man who paid to have sex with her every two weeks. His clockwork schedule could be traced to his job: Each payday Yuth rewarded himself with a visit to the karaoke club.

Yuth lived out a fantasy that Srey Neang had become his girlfriend. He often brought flowers or some other small gift. Srey Neang played along; men treated girlfriends far better than they did whores.

Not long after Mei's arrival, Srey Neang threw caution to the wind and told Yuth the truth of her situation. If Yuth betrayed her to Chuan, she could expect a severe beating. In fact, he would lash a girl for showing anything but pleasure while being raped by a man.

"Do you realize that I am kept prisoner here?" she asked Yuth.

"'Prisoner? What do you mean?" he replied with a puzzled expression.

"I am Chuan's slave," she said bluntly. "He forces me to have sex with men each night and locks me up in an apartment when I am not at the club. I did not choose this life, and I cannot choose to leave."

Yuth took a few seconds to digest this information and then said, "That's impossible."

"Why would I lie about something like that?" she replied with a flash of anger. "Don't you ever wonder why you never see any of the girls from the club in the streets of Siem Reap? It's because we are captives."

Yuth then spoke the words that Srey Neang had prayed for: "In that case, I will do whatever I can to help you escape."

"I would be eternally grateful to you," gushed Srey Neang. She then put all her cards on the table. "I want to take one girl with me. Her name is Mei, and she is the only friend I have ever had."

Yuth did not balk at her request and moved into rescue mode. Doing a quick survey of the bedroom, he pointed toward the window. "The wires covering that window aren't really all that strong. With a bit of effort I bet I could slice through them with my wire cutters."

The window opened to an alley between the club and a warehouse. Unfortunately, foot traffic in the alley remained fairly constant over the course of a typical evening. Taking that factor into account, Yuth and Srey Neang decided that they could not pinpoint a date and time of flight. They would prepare the way and wait for the right moment.

Thereafter Yuth increased the frequency of his visits—not too radically lest he raise suspicion. On each visit, he cut a single stretch of wire with cutters that he hid under his shirt. It took him nearly two months to finish the job.

The actual escape relied on careful timing and a bit of luck. Once Yuth would pay Chuan for a visit with Srey Neang, Mei would cajole a john to take her upstairs to an adjoining room. While she suffered her client, Srey Neang and Yuth would closely watch the alley for an opening.

The first attempt failed. Two men casually stood in the alley smoking cigarettes and having a jolly conversation for the entire half hour of Yuth's session.

Fortune smiled on their second try. The alley and the adjoining street were empty of traffic. Yuth and Srey Neang leaped into action. She pounded three times on the wall to alert Mei, while Yuth pried apart the wire mesh. Just as Mei burst into the room, Yuth had tied the last of his clothes together into a makeshift rope. He fastened one end to a radiator that sat directly below the window and tossed the other end out the opening. Though the rope reached but halfway to the alley, it was close enough.

Mei passed through first and in a matter of minutes stood safely below in the alley. Next came Srey Neang's turn. Heights generally made her dizzy, so she simply concentrated on moving slowly down the clothing rope. The coat and pants held her weight fine, but the shirt knotted to the radiator did not. The tearing noise alerted her only a second before she went into free fall. She thudded in the alley with a splash, landing in a pool of water. Unfazed, she rolled over and raised herself on all fours, happy to discover that all her limbs worked properly.

Whatever plans Yuth had made for the girls after reaching the ground no longer mattered. In fact, Srey Neang never did learn how Yuth made his way out of the club dressed solely in underwear. Her only concern was to put as much distance as possible between herself and Chuan.

The girls bolted down the alley into the darkness of Siem Reap.

Pierre Tami—Giving Shelter to the Abandoned

Early 1993 was not the ideal moment for Pierre to move with Simonetta and three young daughters and live in Phnom Penh full-time. Other foreigners actually were fleeing Phnom Penh in droves in 1993 as the country entered the final phase of the UN-run elections. The Khmer Rouge, which had refused to participate in the elections, made threats to launch an offensive that would overtake the capital. Painful memories of the 1975 Khmer Rouge invasion were still fresh in the people's minds. Violence flared up all over the city. "It was like the Wild West," Pierre recalls. "Cambodians of all walks of life had guns, and they were not afraid to use them."

To make matters worse, Pierre had scant funding or institutional support for his mission. His friends accused him of being irresponsible; more truthfully, they considered him downright crazy.

Pierre initially undertook an ambitious project to survey the needs of woman living on the streets of Phnom Penh. He detected several patterns in their individual stories. An alarming number of husbands had kicked their wives out of the home after they had found a younger woman as a replacement. Nearly all of the women had suffered physical abuse at the hands of their husbands. And a large number of women had been trafficked to Phnom Penh for sexual exploitation.

The survey results pointed to a dire need for a shelter for homeless mothers and their children. Other agencies in Cambodia were reaching out to street kids or single women, but they steered clear of mothers. "It's a very costly endeavor," the director of one international aid group warned Pierre. The man then painted Pierre a dreary picture: "Not only do children come along as part of the package, but who takes care of them if the mother finds a job?"

Complicated challenges do not easily discourage Pierre. Despite being a remarkable visionary, he avoids making wild promises that he does not intend to keep. Execution is secondary in his mind; discovering the right mission is paramount. "If I stopped acting every time someone told me, 'Pierre, you can't possibly do that,' I would never have gotten anywhere," he says with a chuckle.

Once again, the Bible provided him with the right mission. He bumped into the story of Hagar, an Egyptian servant in the house of Abraham. Hagar conceived a child with Abraham. But spurred on by the jealousy of his wife Sara, Abraham cast Hagar out into the desert with her son, Ishmael. As they were about to die of starvation, Ishmael shrieked in pain. God heard his cry, saved mother and son, and blessed their future.

Hagar literally means "the one who flees and is afraid." Pierre considered it the perfect name for his new shelter. "Here I was thinking about abandoned mothers and children," he recalls, "and I ran across in the Bible the same story of a mother and son thrown out into the street by her husband."

So Pierre built a home that rescued hundreds of outcast mothers. The prime minister of Cambodia, Hun Sen, attended the opening ceremony for the Hagar Shelter in March 1994. Hun Sen stood up in the middle of the ceremony and exclaimed, "This is not just a story from the Bible; it is the story of the suffering of Cambodian women!"

Srey Neang—The Rooster Crows Thrice

"So, what do we do now?" asked a frightened Mei.

Srey Neang wished she had a good answer for her friend. They had been running through the streets of Siem Reap for the best part of an hour.

"We have to find a way out of town," she told Mei. She steered their path in the shadows, clear of streetlights. If a patron from the club spotted them, he would be sure to inform Chuan.

They came to a park in the center of Siem Reap. Bustling with tourists during the daytime, the park slept peacefully at night. Turning in a full circle to figure out which direction to head next, Srey Neang noted a taxi parked across the street. A single orange glow in the window tipped off the presence of a driver, cigarette alight, waiting for a fare. Using a tall bush for a shield, she moved forward to get a better view.

"Come, let's see who that is," she whispered to Mei as she clutched her right elbow.

Once they moved closer, Srey Neang could make out the driver's face. It was a man who occasionally visited the karaoke club. Everyone called him the Rooster. She had no clue what his real name might be. She had socialized with him over drinks at the club, but never for a paid session. More than once, the Rooster had expressed his disdain for Chuan: "Your boss thinks he's such a hotshot now," he said to her with a scowl. "I remember when he was just a street punk. Someone needs to bring him back down to the dirt."

In the club it would be suicide for a girl to encourage any slander of Chuan. So Srey Neang kept silent, though she secretly enjoyed the dig at her tyrant. Now, in her moment of dire need, she hoped that the Rooster's hate for Chuan ran deep.

"I think this guy will help us," she spoke softly in Mei's ear.

"How can you be sure?" Mei asked anxiously.

"I can't. But we really don't have many other options," Srey Neang reasoned.

Without further deliberation, the two girls broke their cover and walked directly toward the car.

"Hey girls, where can I take you?" the Rooster asked.

"We really need your help," Srey Neang pleaded.

"Hey, I know you girls," he said, as his eyes took their measure. "Aren't you girls from Chuan's club?"

"Yes, that pig has kept me his prisoner for over a year," she poured out in quick confession. "My friend Mei and I just escaped tonight, and there is no doubt that he is now scouring the streets of Siem Reap in search of us. Please, help us get to Phnom Penh."

The taxi driver took a deep breath and whistled softly to himself, "Phnom Penh? That's not just around the corner, you know."

The girls stayed quiet, their fate hanging in the balance. The Rooster broke the silence with a hearty chuckle, "So Chuan finally got one in the gut," he roared. "Wonderful! Two of his prized possessions flew the coop," he added. "We can't let this moment of sweet justice pass, can we? Jump in, girls. Your chariot to freedom has arrived."

The Rooster drove the girls late through the night to Phnom Penh. Exhausted from the drama of the evening, Srey Neang and Mei fell into a deep sleep. Only the bright lights of Phnom Penh could stir them from their slumber.

"OK, we've reached the capital. Where should I take you?" the Rooster asked, as he peered back at them through his rearview mirror.

Once more the girls had reached a confusing crossroads. Everyone Srey Neang knew in Phnom Penh had in one way or another participated in her bondage. Mei had grown up in a rural province and never before had visited Phnom Penh. Her family had sold her to Chuan, so going home was out of the question.

After a pause, Srey Neang replied, "Oh, why don't you just take us to the waterfront near the town center?" Bereft of a plan, at least she had fond memories of sitting along the river with Sovanna.

"Are you kidding me?" the Rooster asked. "It's not even light out yet. Don't either of you have any family or friends who live in Phnom Penh?"

The girls both shook their heads without uttering a word. It took the Rooster a few moments to absorb how two young girls could be so lost and alone in the world. "Listen, I have some relatives who live here in Phnom Penh. You can stay with me for a couple of days until you figure out how to survive in this city."

For the next three days, the girls did little else but eat and sleep. The Rooster's relatives offered polite hospitality and kept to their own business. On the fourth day after their arrival, the Rooster abruptly ended the girls' retreat from reality: "So, where do you go from here?"

"To be honest, we don't have a clue what to do next," said Srey Neang.

The Rooster gave each a hard stare and then proposed an arrangement. "We can't stay on here but a day or two more. Like you, I'm broke. I can earn a bit of money driving my taxi, but it's tough going in this city."

Trusting that the Rooster had come up with a brilliant solution to their shared dilemma, the girls listened attentively. "You girls, on the other hand, can make good money," he continued. "A friend of mine in Phnom Penh owns a karaoke club, and he's agreed to give you both steady work."

Srey Neang did not need to hear more. She rushed toward the Rooster with her arms flailing. "How dare you try to throw us back into a hellhole!" she screamed.

Raising both arms to protect his face, he tried to reassure her. "Look here, it will be different at this club. You will be free to come and go; no locks and chains. And if a john turns out to be a real jerk, you can refuse to go with him. Besides, my friend has offered us an apartment near his club," the Rooster went on unabashed. "I don't see any other option, do you?"

It was not a fair fight. The girls had no place to turn, and the Rooster knew it. The next morning they moved into the apartment, and by that afternoon the girls had started working the tables at the karaoke club.

THE CURSE OF WOMANHOOD

To be born female in Southeast Asia can feel like being brought into the world under a curse. Girls face discrimination from a young age. When family funds turn scarce, girls are the first to be pulled out of school since "they have more important work to do anyway." They bear the burden of family responsibility— caring for younger siblings and chores at home, and bear primary responsibility for the welfare of their parents.

Buddhist religious traditions, woven deep into the fabric of Southeast Asian societies, reinforce the relegation of females to second-class status. In Thai (Theravada) Buddhism, women cannot even reach the highest levels of spiritual enlightenment. The best that they can hope for in this lifetime is to build up enough good karma to be born male in their next life. The reverse logic also holds true: to be born female in this present embodiment suggests that a woman acted sinfully in her previous existence.

These assumptions profoundly shape social roles. Young men of honor are expected to devote a period of their life to a monastery practicing the life of a monk. After fulfilling this religious obligation, males pass along the good karma to their parents and then can move on to become the head of a household. Females, on the other hand, never escape their karmic debt in servitude to their family. If a girl does not tend to her parents well, she will face a future of suffering.

Consider the life of a young Thai girl named Noi. She works in a karaoke club in northern Thailand, in the city of Chiang Mai. When men sit down at a table to have a drink, the seventeen-year-old girl swiftly moves to offer accompaniment. Her job is straightforward: encourage men to buy her drinks and then propose sex at a price.

While the idea of escaping the karaoke club has appeal, Noi ultimately rejects the idea. She explains that her parents eked out an existence in rural Thailand. They had sold Noi to the owner of the bar for a tidy sum, with a promise that more money would come each month that Noi stayed at the club.

"Although I hate everything about this place," she admitted, "I owe a debt to my parents. If I were to run away, my owner would stop making payments to them."

Perhaps if her parents knew the terrible conditions she had to endure at the bars even they might consider the arrangement too much a sacrifice? Noi would have nothing of it: "No, I have learned to accept my fate. As long as I can provide for my parents, it matters little what happens to me. I must sacrifice my body for my family."

In a twisted way, Noi views the owner of the brothel as an instrument of good in her life. The fact that he occasionally abuses her physically makes for conflicted feelings. But he has made it possible for her to fulfill her obligation to her parents.

The sale of a daughter (or less commonly a son) in moments of financial need does not raise an eyebrow in most sectors of Southeast Asia. In times past, a family in desperate straits might sell a child to a wealthy household as a house servant or an agricultural laborer. In recent decades, the sex trade has raised the demand for slave children to a new level, and the general impoverished masses generate the supply.

A research study conducted in mid–2006 reveals that close to 35 percent of the Vietnamese families living in Cambodia sell a daughter into the sex trade, and another 25 to 30 percent seriously consider the option but do not follow through with the sale.[6] The Vietnamese exist as a marginalized minority in Cambodia, so one must be careful to generalize from this set of data. Nonetheless, the numbers reflect how widespread and culturally acceptable the sale of daughters can be.

Annie Dieselberg—"It's Just His Girl"

Annie's friends back in the United States often innocently ask why she doesn't just go to the police and report the coercion of women in the Thai sex industry. Whenever that question arises, a vivid memory pops into her mind.

She was strolling down a major thoroughfare in Bangkok one afternoon when a female's shrieks drew Annie's attention to an assault in progress on the opposite side of the street. The woman had been fleeing a man twice her size, and the man had just caught up to her. With his right hand, he held a sharp shining object against her neck. He used his other hand to drag her back toward an open car door parked along the sidewalk.

Highly agitated by the woman's predicament, Annie turned her head in all directions to see if she could find help. To her relief, a Thai policeman dressed in full uniform stood a few feet behind her. He, too, was watching the scene unfold across the street, but he gave no sign that he might intervene.

Annie does not accept injustice silently. She marched up to the policeman and asked him politely if he could go across the street and help the woman. He gave her a dismissive shrug and muttered, "It's just his girl; they'll work it out."

By now the man was forcing the woman into the back seat of his car. The woman continued to scream for help as the man jumped into the driver's seat and screeched his wheels as he passed down the street.

Annie looked at the policeman incredulously for a moment, and spilled out her righteous anger: "Officer, sir, why are you wearing that uniform?!"

Srey Neang—Freedom Blues

At sixteen years old, Srey Neang had not realized how relative a state freedom could be. She and Mei no longer lived under lock and key, but they nonetheless left their apartment each day faced with the prospect of turning ten tricks. The club owner paid the Rooster their earnings every Friday, minus 30 percent club hosting fees and 40 percent more for the cost of the apartment. The Rooster then took out his "commission" of 20 percent. "If it weren't for me you girls would be out on the street," he told them if they bothered to complain. That left the girls with about 10 percent of their earnings, which did not go far when buying food and other necessities. In many respects, the girls were living more poorly than they had in Siem Reap.

Freedom of movement did offer the girls a chance to make friendships beyond the walls of the karaoke club. In fact, Srey Neang first met Rang at the farmers' market. She was sorting through a pile of tomatos intently when she heard a voice playfully chiding her: "You realize you have to pay for every one you touch." She looked up to see the smiling face of a boy no more than a year or two her senior. They spent the rest of the morning chatting amiably as they moved from one vegetable stand to the next.

That chance encounter led to scheduled activities and a growing connection. Rang hit it off with Mei as well, and soon he was introducing them to his gang of friends.

Early on in the relationship, Srey Neang had decided to be completely honest with Rang about her background. She did not want to pretend that she was someone that she was not. To her relief, Rang took her stories in stride and even expressed admiration for her resilience.

His ready acceptance seemed all the more remarkable to Srey Neang when she considered the stability of his upbringing. In essence, they had grown up in different universes. Rang still lived with his mother and father and had strong links to a large extended family, many of whom resided in Phnom Penh. Not only did he become literate at a young age, he stayed in school until he earned his high school diploma. Though he currently worked with his father at an auto mechanic shop, Rang expressed his desire to study at the university in the capital.

Srey Neang told Rang how trapped she felt at the karaoke club. How she would love to learn how to read and write her thoughts down on a piece of paper. Above all, she dreamed of a day when she would not be for sale to creeps like those who visited her at the club.

"If you hate it so much, why don't you just leave," he asked innocently one day.

"Mei and I both would leave in a heartbeat," she told him, "but we fear that life would be even more harsh on the streets."

Hearing her response, Rang's face turned pensive, but he said nothing.

At their next meeting several days later, Rang could hardly wait to give her "the exciting news."

"What is it?" Srey Neang asked. "I don't think I've ever seen you so giddy."

"I spoke with my parents about your situation," he said, "and they gave me permission to invite you and Mei to come live in our home. We have a spare room that the two of you can share."

Aware that she would have concerns beyond a shelter, Rang continued on: "And it gets better. My mother spoke to her sister, and she can give you both part-time jobs in her restaurant. If she likes your work, she will look at giving you more hours."

She said nothing but leaped immediately into his arms.

"So I guess that means you accept," Rang said with a smile.

"Absolutely," she nearly shouted. "How soon can we move in?"

Srey Neang simply could not walk back to the apartment. She tried, but within moments her legs would start running again. She burst through the door of the apartment and informed Mei of their good fortune. They spontaneously broke into tears and held each other in a tight embrace.

After a good fifteen minutes of celebration, they regained sufficient composure to discuss the logistics of the move. With freedom so close at hand, they agreed that working at the club that evening was unthinkable. Calculating that the Rooster would not show up at the apartment for at least another hour, they set aside thirty minutes to clear out their stuff.

"I could be out of here in five minutes," Srey Neang thought to herself. "I'm happy to leave it all behind."

THE MEN WHO DRIVE THE DEMAND

Every night the streets of Bangkok are filled with middle-aged men who walk hand-in-hand with teenage girls. These sex tourists have traveled from all over the world to be here and play out their own private fantasy. Some men pay for quick sex, but most prefer to buy a "girlfriend' for an entire night or even several days. The johns behave like young adolescents, publicly pawing their "dates," squeezing their buttocks and breasts with little shame.

Specialized travel agencies around the globe promote "exotic sexual adventures" with Asian women "who know how to please a man." After sex tourists experience firsthand how easy it is to buy young girls, they frequently make their own arrangements for return visits.

Thailand, in particular, has been branded internationally as a Disneyland for sexual escapades. A Bangkok-based children's rights group has tracked the country's boom in sexual tourism over the past two decades. Its research shows that 2 million foreigners visited the country in 1984, 4 million in 1988, and more than 11 million in 2003.[7] Out of the total number of foreign visitors, roughly two-thirds entering Thailand were unaccompanied men. In other words, about 7.3 million unaccompanied men visited the country in 2003. Certainly, not all of these men came as sexual tourists, but it's a good bet that a significant percentage did. In fact, according to a survey of travel agents conducted by international aid agency World Vision, 65 percent of all tourists to Cambodia are men and one-fifth of them travel with the express purpose to have sex.[8]

Male clients from Japan, China, Korea, and Taiwan drive the demand for young girls who are virgins. In these Asian cultures, sex with a virgin is thought to bring good luck to a new business venture. Moreover, virgin girls pose less threat of exposure to sexually transmitted disease.

The lucrative market in virgins tempts parents to sell their pre-adolescent daughters to a brothel for a high premium. It's a bizarre business: a john may pay $750 for one night with a young girl, and one week later that same girl may be seeing ten clients a night for $2.50 a session.

The growing demand for virgins has created a niche market outside the usual channels for commercial sex—the bars, karaoke clubs, and brothels. A growing number of parents market their daughter's virginity like an independent talent agent, selling her to the highest bidder for a one-time sexual experience once she reaches the age of twelve or thirteen. As a matter of propriety, the daughter will be sent away "to visit relatives" for a couple of weeks. After a fixed period of sexual exploitation, the girl will return to her normal life at school or work at home.

Though much less common, Japanese and Chinese men are known to pay parents years in advance to "sponsor" a young child. The families receive a regular payment to raise a healthy daughter, and when the sponsor is ready, he will come and use her for sex.

Western sex tourists, on the other hand, tend to frequent the bars and brothels in major cities. Though some specifically request sex with children, most act in an opportunistic way; that is to say, they react spontaneously to what happens once they arrive at a sex bar or karaoke club. Some men may not even initially plan to engage in commercial sex on their journeys to Southeast Asia, but find it easy to do once they are there.

Sexual tourism clearly feeds the beast of sexual slavery. Nonetheless, its contribution to the sex trade in Southeast Asia is vastly overrated in the global media. By far the largest proportion of johns comes from the local population. "Foreigners are not the only ones who exploit our children," confirms Cambodia's former Minister for Women's Affairs. "The real disease comes from within."[9]

Particularly in Cambodia and Thailand, men will visit a brothel together during a night of partying; it's simply a part of the evening entertainment. A number of studies conducted in both Cambodia and Thailand show that approximately 40 to 50 percent of local men pay for commercial sex during the course of a year.[10] Married women quietly accept that their husbands will pay to have sex on a night out with the boys. Men have sexual needs, the wives reason, and at least they will not be in pursuit of eligible single women who could displace them.

Paying for sex has become embedded in many social rituals. Businessmen use paid sex as a courtesy in the arrangement of commercial deals; if a firm does not offer its clients sex, it may risk losing them to competitors who will. Working-class men buy sex for their friends on birthdays and other special occasions. Doting fathers pay for their sons to have their first sexual experience at a brothel.

Sexual tourism could end tomorrow, but it would make only a modest change in the flow of sexual slavery in Southeast Asia. In fact, at the sites frequented by sexual tourists, a minority of the women who work are enslaved. By and large, bar owners consider it too risky to present enslaved women to foreign visitors. While some women may be in debt slavery to the bar owners, most of them work as free agents, paying the bar owner a commission for each trick. Enslaved women, on the other hand, typically are found in brothels that cater to local men.

Srey Neang—Family Honor

When tragedy has been your constant companion, it is not easy to enjoy a turn of good fortune. You half expect your bliss to be snatched away at any moment.

This explains Srey Neang's measured joy after she moved in with Rang's family. Her life seemed too good to be true. Most days she worked the lunch and dinner shifts at the restaurant owned by Rang's aunt. Like most workers, her favorite time of the week was payday. She had labored long and hard in the past, but had never truly been paid for her work.

She came to treasure her bond with Rang. Their conversations, marked by honesty and laughter, often ran into the wee hours of the night. With the passage of time, they began to share a physical intimacy that matched their emotional connection.

While it felt innocent and beautiful to them, their romance released an unexpected fury. Rang's mother and father had showed warm kindness to the girls from the moment they arrived. Most every morning, they would sit around the kitchen table with the girls and casually share conversation over breakfast. But once the parents picked up signs of Rang's growing love for Srey Neang, a cold front descended on the house. The girls found themselves alone at the morning breakfast table. Sensing the sudden change, they compared notes on whether one of them had done something wrong. Their review came up empty.

Several weeks later, Rang finally cleared up the mystery. He entered the girls' room and addressed them in almost a whisper: "My parents say that you are no longer welcome in our home." With tears in his eyes, he looked at Srey Neang and continued, "Basically, they don't want me to have anything to do with you."

"How did I offend them?" she asked forlornly.

"You did nothing," he replied. "But you will always be prostitutes in their eyes, and for that reason alone they are angry that I could fall in love with you."

"That's so unfair," Srey Neang whispered. "Can't we change their minds?"

"No, they are not willing to bend," he said. "I have tried many times and failed."

"But I love you," she offered, pouring out her heart. "I don't want to lose what we have."

"I'm sorry," Rang responded sadly. "I cannot shame my parents. And that's exactly what would happen once it becomes known that my girlfriend was a prostitute."

Rang urged the girls to move out of the house the following day. Given his demeanor, Srey Neang realized it was pointless to put up a fight. Family honor trumps love.

Annie Dieselberg—Total Control

Annie and her team visit the sex bars in Bangkok at least twice each week so they can foster relationships with young women. As long as they keep buying drinks for themselves and the bar girls at a reasonable pace, the owner usually does not mind. Now that NightLight has earned its reputation as "an alternative to the sex club," a few bar owners have warned their girls not to talk to Annie.

It disturbs Annie that so many of the women feel trapped without an exit. The bar managers have intimidated them thoroughly with random acts of violence and threats to their families. The abuse runs the gamut, beyond physical beatings. The bar owners aim to control them emotionally and spiritually as well.

Many managers perform daily spiritual rituals inside the bar, usually early in the evening before the bar girls have left on "dates." On several occasions, Annie has been present to witness the drama and describes a very bizarre scene. The manager arranges the women in a circle and then presents a large wood totem that has the distinct shape of a male penis. The owner sprinkles water on the totem, and then passes it around for each woman to fondle. Once it has moved around the circle, she moves around the bar touching the end of the totem onto each table where customers will be sitting that evening. Finally, he selects a couple of bar girls to finish the ritual. They move to the front door of the bar, place the totem between their legs, and then throw water through their legs out into the street.

The spiritualism deeply affects the women, especially those raised in rural settings where it is widely assumed that spirits could enter inside an individual and take over one's body. Women who had left the sex trade frequently asked Annie how they can break free from these spirits; even if they escape the bar owner, they can never outrun a spirit.

Annie makes it clear that resisting the criminal networks that make money off the sex trade must go beyond the humble efforts of abolitionist groups like NightLight. "We badly need a movement of the Spirit in the global church," she tells me.

Pressed as to whether churches actually can make a dent in the global slave trade, Annie becomes resolute: "I spent most of my childhood in Zaire and in Thailand, and I saw a great deal of injustice. But when I watch the darkness that destroys the lives of women and young children in the sex trade, I feel that I am confronting a profoundly evil force."

For that reason, Annie looks to religious communities to deploy prayer and action against sex trafficking in their own local region, and link those efforts to international movements. "The world badly needs the love for family and bonds of community that the church teaches," she says. "Now we have to go out into the society and live it."

Srey Neang—A New Mother

"There's nothing wrong with you," the nurse told Srey Neang with a big smile. "You are pregnant."

It took Srey Neang a few moments to figure out what those words meant. For several weeks she had felt very ill, especially in the morning time. Once the vomiting came, she decided to visit the clinic to see what was wrong with her. But she never expected this diagnosis. She assumed that she had picked up some awful disease from the men at the karaoke clubs.

Part of her was very excited to be pregnant. She wished there were someone back at her apartment with whom she could share the news. Ever since Mei had left town to return to the province where she grew up, Srey Neang had stayed alone.

Within a few days, she gathered the strength to inform Rang that he would be a father. She knew better than to contact him at his parents' home, so she waited outside his workplace and approached him as he left the building. Though two months before they had shared a deep bond, Rang now looked at her as if she were a stranger.

Following a brief greeting and exchange of pleasantries, Srey Neang got straight to the point. "Rang, I'm sorry to have made contact with you against your wishes," she began apologetically, "but I have some important news to pass along. You and I conceived a child together; seven months from now you will be a father."

For a brief moment, Rang showed a flash of emotion. But he plugged up the dam and spoke coolly to her: "And how do you know that I am the father?"

"Oh, don't be silly, Rang. You know that we shared our love exclusively with each other," she quickly rebuked him.

He looked aside, obviously working hard to avoid direct eye contact. But he spoke harshly: "Given your track record, I imagine it could be any number of men who might have gotten you pregnant."

A disgusted Srey Neang turned on her heels and left Rang at the bus stop. Tears poured from her eyes. She had experienced a great deal of cruelty during her seventeen years, but rarely had the stab come from someone she loved. It made the cut more painful.

Though Rang refused to acknowledge his responsibility, she remained resolute to give birth to her child. Over the next couple of months she continued to work at the restaurant. Rang's aunt had chosen not to fire Srey Neang even though her sister had banished the girl from her home. She told Srey

Neang that she liked her work ethic. But once Srey Neang began to show her pregnancy, her boss immediately dismissed her. The aunt did not want any questions raised about the parentage of this child.

Srey Neang had just enough money saved up to keep her apartment through the course of her pregnancy. Ironically, the day she felt her labor pains coincided with the final day on her apartment lease. Getting the baby born had been her sole goal; she would have to sort out later how she would raise the child.

Somehow she managed to waddle across half of Phnom Penh and admit herself to the hospital. For nearly eighteen hours she endured contractions and then gave birth to a beautiful boy. She thought she would burst from happiness when the delivery doctor placed her newborn son on her breast. Noting her exhaustion, the doctor asked Srey Neang if family would be coming to help her care for the newborn for a few days while she recovered. "I'm the only family that this boy has got," she replied bluntly.

Four days later, Srey Neang and her son were discharged from the hospital. When she walked out the front door of the hospital, she literally did not know whether to turn right or left, since neither direction held any promise.

If her son were to get sick, she reasoned, it would be best to be near the hospital. So Srey Neang turned to the right and sat down on the sidewalk, resting her back against the front face of the hospital. She then carefully swathed her child with a blanket, and tried to get comfortable.

The next morning on his way into work, the delivery doctor was shocked to see the mother and her newborn sprawled on the sidewalk.

"What in the world are you doing out here?" he asked in clear distress. "Is your child sick?"

"No. I don't have any other place to go," she replied.

"Well, if you stay out here too much longer both you and your child risk getting sick from exposure," he said.

"Can't I stay in the hospital until the baby gets stronger?" she begged.

"No, that's impossible," he said. "But I have an idea who might be able to help you. Stay here, and I'll be back in a few minutes."

The doctor walked into the hospital and placed an urgent call to the Hagar Shelter.

Pierre Tami—Entrepreneurial Ventures

Within abolitionist circles, Hagar would be called an "after-care facility." At Hagar, the term *reintegration* gets used more often, which reflects its goal to equip women to return to society as independent, productive citizens. What this goal requires varies according to the individual who arrives at Hagar's door.

In most cases, the women need post-traumatic counseling to help them overcome past abuses. Few of them can read or write or possess a vocational skill. For them, Hagar provides an expansive education program.

Across all of its programs, Hagar delivers the highest quality of social service. That's certainly laudable but mirrors what many fine agencies across the globe accomplish. Where Hagar is unique is in its commercial enterprises.

Shortly after starting the shelter, Pierre created a job placement service. But he quickly discovered that an extreme scarcity of jobs in the Cambodian job market meant that many of the Hagar women would stay unemployed. He was frustrated. What good did it do to provide woman a vocational skill and then send them off to flounder in the ranks of the unemployed? The best way to ensure employment, he realized, would be to create real jobs.

Moving Hagar in the direction of financial self-sufficiency had been in the back of Pierre's mind anyway. Perhaps because of his business background, he feels uneasy in a strictly nonprofit organization. He dreamed to create a range of Hagar enterprises that one day could underwrite a healthy slice of the agency's social services budget.

Hagar's Soya Company is Cambodia's first and only large-scale producer of soya milk. It began humbly in 1998 when twenty-five women staying at the shelter were daily sent out to the streets of Phnom Penh with wooden carts full of fresh soya milk. Pierre relied on his background with the airlines: he had the women dress in flight attendant uniforms! They poured the milk into small plastic bags and sold it for twenty cents. Because the milk only had a shelf life of a few days, the product only had a market inside the capital.

A few years later, the U.S. Department of Agriculture contacted Pierre about creating a milk nutrition program in Cambodia's public schools. At first Pierre had to laugh at the notion of women filling thousands of plastic bags of milk every day for schoolchildren. But the USDA offered to link Hagar up with the International Finance Corporation (IFC), which specializes in supporting small- and medium-size enterprise development around the globe.

With IFC financing, Hagar Soya made the leap from a tiny microenterprise with a production capacity of five hundred liters per day to a significant factory capable of producing twelve thousand liters per day. With mass production came packaging that extends the shelf life of the product for up to one year. All of a sudden, Hagar Soya could ship its products throughout Cambodia—and possibly even export them internationally. The company today produces a variety of soya drinks and is diversifying its product line into fresh juices and green tea. By mid–2006, Hagar Soya had boosted its payroll to eighty-three employees.

Pierre's second enterprise, Hagar Catering, also possesses remarkable potential. The business grew out of a cooking-skills program offered at the shelter. When Pierre launched the soy milk enterprise, he had built twenty-five carts with his own hands and painted them yellow and blue. Now, for his catering enterprise, he constructed an additional twenty carts, embedded cooking pans on the top, and painted them yellow and green. Pedestrians passing through the city center of Phnom Penh were apt to see a woman dressed neatly in a flight attendant uniform standing behind a yellow and green cart and offering to cook them a nutritious meal on the spot.

One day Pierre had the bright idea of consolidating his customer base. He paid an impromptu visit to a garment factory in Phnom Penh that employed seven hundred workers. He successfully persuaded the manager of the factory to hire his catering team to make a midday meal for his workforce.

Hagar Catering today provides quality meals to workers in staff canteens at major hotels, factories, and government agencies in Phnom Penh. Some of its clients include the U.S. Embassy, five-star hotels like the Inter-Continental and Raffles Le Royal, and international companies like British American Tobacco. Not only does it employ seventy-three workers today, in 2005 Hagar Catering delivered a dividend of $20,000 cash toward funding Hagar's social service projects.

Pierre's third enterprise, Hagar Design Limited, was established in 2004 to manufacture women's accessories and home decor products. Still in its infancy, the company designs its own product line and provides outsourced production services for international retailers. The company currently employs eighty-five workers and has healthy revenue growth.

The innovative approach Pierre brings to "aftercare" has not gone unrecognized. In 2004, Secretary of State Colin Powell gave

Pierre an award in a ceremony that took place in Washington, DC. Powell heaped accolades on Pierre's creativity, saying:

> Mr. Tami has brought a Swiss businessman's approach to helping victims of trafficking in Cambodia. His view is that assistance programs must be innovative and financially sustainable so former victims have opportunities to change their lives for good rather than remaining permanently vulnerable to crimes such as human trafficking. ... These enterprises are providing new hope to the people of Cambodia who have been traumatized by modern-day slavery, allowing some of them to receive paychecks for their work for the first time in their lives.

Given his sterling record in Cambodia, the IFC and other international investors have encouraged Pierre to implement the Hagar model in other sites around the globe where the slave trade has left a trail of victims. He is investigating new projects in Africa, Latin America, and other parts of Asia. He's just waiting for a moment of revelation. After all, execution is secondary in his mind. Discovering the right mission is paramount.

Srey Neang—Freedom at Last

On the seventh day of creation, God rested; on the eighth day, God created the Hagar shelter. Srey Neang believes that Hagar's existence could be traced to some such miracle. Without a doubt, the shelter rescued her from destitution. Her chances of survival on the streets of Phnom Penh were dim, and much worse were the prospects for her newborn son. Most likely at some point she would have had to sacrifice her dignity and beg the Rooster for help. The thought of returning to the life of a karaoke girl sent a cold shudder down her spine.

At Hagar she did not feel alone. In fact, dozens of women walked into the shelter with their own harrowing stories of sexual slavery. Samphors, who became one of her closest friends at Hagar, broke down in tears whenever anyone mentioned a mother-daughter relationship. In a group counseling session Srey Neang discovered why. From the time that Samphors was twelve, her mother acted as her pimp, regularly selling her to men in the village. When her mother ran into trouble with gambling debts, she sold Samphors off to a brothel in Phnom Penh.

Listening to Samphors and other women speak during these counseling sessions, Srey Neang realized that every person she had trusted in her life had betrayed her. Painful memories came flooding back. How could her parents sell her to the old woman? The downward spiral started there. Learning how to trust, she realized, would be a long-term challenge.

At Hagar she finally got her wish to advance toward literacy. Once upon a time she had dreamed of attending school. That opportunity never presented itself, but at the shelter she learned to read and write. In fact, she was required to complete a literacy course before enrolling in a vocational program.

Sewing ended up being Srey Neang's ticket to independence. For nearly six months she practiced the craft on industrial machines. To her surprise, she had a real knack for figuring out design patterns. Transforming fabric into clothing did not even feel like work to her. After she completed her apprenticeship, Hagar Design offered her a job as a design seamstress.

Srey Neang recently celebrated her twentieth birthday. She keeps steady hours at Hagar Design, rents a house in Phnom Pehn, sends her son off to school each day and makes sure he is well fed.

Today she feels no shame. She is free.

2
Breaking the Chains
of Bonded Laborers:
South Asia

G ary Haugen gives lawyers a good name.

His pedigree could land him a corporate counsel post at a Fortune 500 company or perhaps secure a coveted appointment in the judicial system. Blue-chip education? Check that box. He graduated from Harvard University and then earned a law degree at the University of Chicago. Stellar career path? Check that box, too. He served a six-year tenure as a trial attorney in the civil rights division of the U.S. Department of Justice (DOJ). The DOJ even loaned him to the United Nations to direct a high-profile war crimes investigation. In short, Gary moves as a professional at the top of his game.

How fortunate for those trapped in slavery that he exercises his talents as an abolitionist. In 1997 he founded International Justice Mission (IJM) and developed it into an extraordinarily effective operation.

Gary may be best characterized as a pragmatic idealist. Like a general immersed in the heat of battle, he can rattle off a detailed strategy. The next moment he can wax philosophical on the nature of good and evil or expound his concept of the state in a civil society. It's a rare mix of talents: driven by big ideas yet acting with surgeonlike precision.

Anyone who gets to know Gary also takes note of his charisma. He makes you feel as if your engagement with him is the most important thing on his calendar that day. The next person who meets him that day will leave with the same impression. Beyond this personal charm, he wears on his sleeve a passion for his vocation that becomes infectious for those around him.

His IJM office, located on the outskirts of Washington, DC, offers more clues to what makes him tick. Positioned on his bookshelf rest two stones, one stacked atop the other. Next to the stones leans a photo of a small girl. Eyes as big as saucers and a beaming smile light up the portrait.

Ask Gary what IJM aims to accomplish, and he turns to the bookshelf. He picks up the stones and tells how troubled he was to discover an entire village in South Asia enslaved to toil in a rock quarry. A cold and callous owner forced young and old alike to break boulders down to a size suitable for construction. He recounts how IJM helped to liberate these slaves. Out of gratitude, one young boy handed Gary these stones as a memento.

Gary sets the stones down and lifts the portrait of the small girl. Her name is Devi, and her family was imprisoned along with sixty-five other laborers inside the walled compound of a rice mill. The owner did not allow the children to attend school; as soon as they were old enough, he pressed them into labor. What age is "old enough"? Devi started working in the rice mill at the age of four.

Gary describes the deep satisfaction of watching Devi and her entire community walk out of the rice mill as free people. IJM subsequently worked alongside prosecutors to bring the owner to trial in a local court.

Once he finishes recounting these redemption tales, Gary confesses that the mementos do not just sit on his bookshelf ready for show-and-tell. Whenever setbacks bog him down, the mementos give him a tangible reminder of the high stakes at play in IJM's work.

Narayan—The First Deception

Karma never ceases to confound Narayan. How could a kind favor result in such a terrible curse?

Narayan had visited Mr. Vasu with the best of intentions. The last words his sister Maya had spoken to him bore the weight of desperation: "Narayan, we have no money; please do what you can to find us work."

Narayan already had a job in a brick kiln. He had taken a loan from its owner so that he could buy a cow. His uncle Amar and cousin Bishnu had taken a cash advance from the same man. Though they had labored together at the kiln for over a year, none of them had made as much as a dent in their pile of debt.

Most of Narayan's kin lived in the same village where he was born. During religious festivals, the owner let Narayan, Amar, and Bishnu visit them. Not that their family celebrated the festivals in a lavish way. They survived on the bare essentials; ending a day with a full stomach was sufficient cause for celebration.

Family solidarity proved to be their best defense against the ravages of poverty. So when the brick kiln owner asked Narayan if he knew of workers looking for jobs, he immediately thought of Maya.

"My friend operates his own brick kiln," the owner told Narayan. "He will provide housing and food on the property."

Narayan and his uncle Amar paid a visit to Mr. Vasu the following day. He showered them with honor far beyond what they might expect as members of a low caste. The men could not recall the last time they had eaten so well—he served them a curry with rice and substantial pieces of chicken mixed into the dish.

Immediately after the meal, Mr. Vasu got down to business. "I need about a dozen workers who can start immediately."

Narayan was equally direct: "My sister and her husband will come, and I am confident that another handful of our relatives will work as well. But they would need a total of $650 up front so that they can take care of some urgent needs."

"Those terms are acceptable," Mr. Vasu replied. "But they will work for me, and solely me, until they pay back every bit of the $650." He paused long enough for Narayan and Amar to nod their heads in assent. Then he added another condition: "And if they run off without repaying my money, I will hold the two of you responsible. You will serve as their guarantors."

Narayan and Amar left the property on an emotional high. Six hundred and fifty dollars spread across the family would provide sweet relief. Moreover, Mr. Vasu seemed like a kind man who would look after their relatives well. Narayan could not wait to tell his sister the good news.

Gary Haugen—A Gift in a Time of Need

Gary has had a wealth of experience in hot spots around the globe. In 1989, as he was completing his law degree, he spent four months in the Philippines investigating atrocities that soldiers and police had committed against the civilian population. During his stay in Manila, he made contact with people who worked in poor Filipino neighborhoods providing health care, literacy training, economic development, and emergency shelter.

As the years passed, Gary stayed in contact with these friends. The truth is he gravitates toward inspired people who want to change the world. His aid and development friends told him that despite their best efforts to make an impact, they faced two major obstacles.

First, they witnessed how the powerful use violence to exploit the poor. When the poor resist, the violent bear them away. Even though laws to protect citizens' rights exist, the police and the courts do not enforce justice consistently. Gary's friends confessed that they felt powerless to act once violence erupted. "So, what should we do," they asked Gary, "when the powerful take advantage of the weak?"

Their second daunting obstacle involved the abduction of children. Young girls between the ages of ten and fourteen vanished from their projects. On a given day, they might ask the kids at their street shelter, "Hey, I haven't seen Rosa around for a while. Do you know what happened to her?" The kids would just shrug their shoulders. The next day brought more disappearances: "Hey, where's Maria? Has anyone seen Flora?" More silent shrugs.

Eventually, they discovered the truth. The girls were being kidnapped and forced to sell their bodies in brothels. When Gary's friends investigated further, they discovered that the police sometimes played a prominent role in running the brothels.

"Now, what are my nice friends who are trying to serve the poor to do?" Gary asks sympathetically. "They can't just write off the girls as casualties of a corrupt system; that doesn't feel right. But they don't have a lot of experience working with the police."

Gary realized that his friends had stumbled into areas of his own expertise. He had to admit that he could tackle these problems without feeling overwhelmed. To take apart a social problem and design a viable strategy—wasn't that in fact what he had been trained to do?

Blessed with a gift in a moment of critical need, Gary established an agency to rescue victims of violence, sexual exploitation, slavery, and oppression. He became employee number one in a small office in Washington, DC. Today IJM has almost two hundred full-time staff in thirteen different offices around the globe.

Grounded in a deep religious faith, Gary interprets IJM's mission as an expression of the Golden Rule: "Do to others as you would have them do to you" (Matt. 7:12).

"If I were trapped in a brothel, what would I want?" Gary asks rhetorically as he launches into a sermon. "I would want someone to get me out! If I were enslaved in a brick factory, I would want someone to end my bondage! If I were being trafficked, I would want to be rescued. That's our work. To love our neighbors and set them free."

Maya—Firing Up the Kiln

Five couples—all related in one way or another—committed to work in the brick kiln. Narayan and Amar had made the opportunity sound very appealing. "Mr. Vasu treated us far better than our own boss does," they reported enthusiastically. "He's also a holy man. He used his own money to build a temple in the local village and devotes himself to its care. You could not ask for a better employer!"

Maya had not expected Narayan to find a job so soon. Financial crises tend to linger in their village. The last drought had wiped out every bit of the cushion that she and her husband, Ajay, had worked so hard to save. Their small plot of mustard green had dried up. Large farmers in the region experienced the decimation of their crops as well and no longer had use for day laborers. Maya saw both sources for her family's meager income vanish overnight.

Yet the number of mouths she and Ajay had to fill did not change. Ajay had an obligation to support his parents. Maya and Ajay had an eight-year-old son of their own as well. All three generations crowded into one tiny hut.

Despite their pressing needs, Maya and Ajay approached the cash advance with caution. The drought would not last forever; once the rains returned, they could stand on their own feet. So when the family sat down to divvy up Mr. Vasu's loan, Maya and Ajay requested only $30 as their share. That amount could sustain Ajay's parents and their son for some time. Surely it would not take too long to earn back such a small sum, they reasoned.

A week later, twelve aspiring brick kiln laborers said their good-byes to the rest of the village. One couple brought along their ten-year-old daughter; another member of the family brought along a five-year-old daughter. The other parents left their young children in the care of relatives. The laborers promised to visit during the religious festivals at least. Based on Narayan's experience, they had no reason to assume otherwise.

It took half a day, and three bus rides, to reach Mr. Vasu's property. Upon arrival, they meekly approached the tall iron gate standing at the front of the compound. After fifteen minutes of passive deliberation, they rattled the bars with a stick. A young man emerged around an inside wall to greet them. As he removed the padlock and motioned for them to enter, he introduced himself as Mr. Vasu's son. His father had gone to town to run errands and would return soon, he explained. In his absence he, the eighteen-year-old heir, would orient them to the facility.

Maya took stock of the fact that the son reset the padlock on the gate once they moved inside. She also noted the high cement walls that surrounded the front half of the property. It connected to a wire fence that ran around the back end of the compound. Beyond the fence, as far as her eyes could see, lay rows of freshly planted rice.

The son guided them first to their living quarters—a small, rectangular building located in the middle of the property. Along the way, he pointed to a house situated along the left fence. "That's where my father and I stay," he said, "but most of the time we live with my mother in the village." As if carefully mulling over his next choice of words, he paused, and then said, "You are not to approach the house; it's off-limits to you."

The "living quarters" where the family would be staying turned out to be a single room. Wood lattices jutted out from multiple points along the back wall, somewhat resembling stalls in a horse stable. (In fact, from that day forward, the family referred to their shelter as "the stable.") The dirt floor had been swept recently, and the mud walls and thatched roof kept the room markedly cooler than the sweltering heat outdoors.

Maya and her kin placed their meager belongings in the room and then rejoined the guided tour. A chimney stretched high into the sky about fifteen feet from the stable. At its base an open mouth gaped, but no fire burned inside. "It will take a while to get the fire to a heat sufficient to dry the bricks," the son remarked.

Just then a voice behind them boomed, "And I trust it will be the last time that any of us will see a cold kiln!"

Startled, Maya and her relatives jerked their necks around to see a portly man standing no more than five feet behind them. He was clothed in saffron-colored pants and shirt, a common dress for holy men.

"Hello, I am Mr. Vasu," he began, "and you are now in my service." As he slowly annunciated these words, the man held up a set of papers that he held in his right hand. "This contract formalizes the terms of our arrangement."

The owner then strutted like a peacock over to Ajay and handed him the papers. Ajay accepted them awkwardly. Being completely illiterate, a failing he shared with all his kin, Ajay simply held the documents to his side.

"As you will read," Mr. Vasu went on as if he were oblivious to the humiliation he produced, "you will be expected to pay back the money that you borrowed, plus interest. I will provide food and add its cost to the amount that you owe. For every thousand bricks you produce, you will earn $4.50. I will deduct what you earn from your debt. Once you have canceled your debt, I will compensate you for your labor in cash, or you may choose to look for other employment. Until that day arrives, you will work only at this kiln. Any questions?"

The laborers stood mute. His speech mirrored more or less what Narayan had explained to them, though they admittedly did not comprehend what "interest" might mean. No matter, they were happy to be in a position to earn some wages.

"It's all written down for you to read," Mr. Vasu repeated, as if he were delighted to be tossing salt into a fresh wound. "I will come back in half an hour, and each of you will sign the contract. Meanwhile, I want you to get started on firing up the kiln."

As he spoke, Maya thought her imagination must be playing tricks on her. She could swear that a hot flame seared through her body.

Work at the kiln began at 6:00 a.m. The family worked collectively. Moving the brick molds in and out of the kiln required tremendous strength, so the men generally assumed that task. Pretty much everyone else manufactured the bricks.

Maya passed most of the day packing wet clay and straw into row after row of wood forms. Once the sun rose high in the midmorning sky, she would start carrying the clay molds atop her head into an open space where direct rays could reach them. For the molds to dry into a stable form usually took a couple of hours in the sun. In midafternoon, the family took an hour break and grabbed a bite to eat. After lunch, some continued packing the molds, others moved them into the sunlight to dry, and yet others brought the dried molds to the kiln to bake the bricks into their final form. They strove to have all the bricks completely baked by sunset.

The men rotated the job of stoking the charcoal fires of the kiln. Working outdoors means facing sweltering heat in normal conditions; standing next to a glowing charcoal furnace can be downright unbearable. The skin, glistening with sweat, becomes an inviting haven for clay dust and soot. Reaching deep into the pores, the dust dries with the heat, causing the skin to crack. At day's end, the man working the kiln looks like a walking briquette of charcoal.

Mr. Vasu drove the work crew with capricious demands. If they produced fewer than a thousand bricks in a day, he would yell, "You lazy dogs; why were you so slack today?" If they worked at a faster pace and produced twelve hundred bricks, he would scream, "You manipulative cheats! Don't expect to be paid for more than a thousand bricks in a day." When reviewing the day's production, he always found a reason to complain. He would pull out bricks with the slightest flaw and decry their "faulty workmanship."

The verbal abuse began the day they arrived. By the end of the first week, it had turned to physical violence. The men he whacked with sticks, the women he struck with an open palm. One day Maya got slapped to the ground as she was walking to the well for a drink of water.

"Why aren't you working?" Mr. Vasu asked gruffly, moments after he had emerged from his house.

"The heat is unbearable today," Maya replied honestly, "and I am dying of thirst."

She did not see the blow coming. His hand struck her hard on her right ear and sent her sprawling. "Maybe that will help you forget about your thirst!" he muttered and walked away.

Power reserves for itself the right to act capriciously. Clay molds could tumble accidentally off a woman's head, and Mr. Vasu would laugh as if watching a slapstick comedy. The same mishap could occur a few days later, and he would lash out ferociously.

One afternoon he clubbed Ajay brutally for overheating the fire, a mistake that caused an entire pallet of bricks to crack. To their utter surprise, the following day Mr. Vasu gave the family a chicken to cook "as a reward for doing such good work."

That day lingered in their memories, for eating chicken was not common at the compound. Three times daily they poured porridge and mustard weed into their bowls. On rare occasions they supplemented their diet with vegetables, though both meat and vegetables cost far beyond their tiny food budget.

Mr. Vasu gave them money to buy food on his own schedule. Occasionally the family would go a day without eating because he failed to provide funds. The first time that occurred, Maya's cousin reminded Mr. Vasu that a week had passed since their last trip to the market. The owner gave him a scowl and walked off. He returned a few minutes later with his stick and struck her cousin forcefully several times. "I will tell you when it's time to go to the market!" he yelled out as he wielded the club.

Mr. Vasu permitted only a few individuals to go to the market and he always forced the children to stay behind and work. A majority of the family had to stay inside the compound at all times. "If you do not come back," he would warn those going off to the market, "I will make this place a living hell for those who are left behind."

Maya initially assumed that greed motivated his restrictions on their movement: he wanted to keep as many of them working as possible. But then Mr. Vasu flatly refused to let them travel to a religious festival back at their home village. "Because you dogs have been so lazy, I cannot fulfill my brick orders," he snarled. "You must stay and work."

Slowly it dawned on Maya that they had not landed a job. They had joined a prison labor camp.

Gary Haugen—Anatomy of a Rescue

Early in the evolution of IJM, Gary and his team conducted an extensive needs survey. Their focus group targeted nearly seventy religious organizations that were operating relief and development programs around the globe. Collectively, these groups supported tens of thousands of workers in over a hundred countries.

Every single agency reported back to IJM that their workers encountered serious situations of abuse in the course of their work. They witnessed forced labor, sex trafficking, corrupt seizure of land, and corruption in the public justice system. When the agencies tried to address the injustice, they received minimal support from the police or the courts.

The survey results confirmed what Gary had experienced in his previous human-rights investigations: oppressors use violence to commit acts of injustice and to discourage potential rescuers from coming to the aid of the victims.

The absence of an effective public justice system blocks every step the poor take to change their social condition. For example, the staff of a renowned aid and relief agency reported to IJM that coercive labor was undermining its efforts in South Asia to enroll kids in school. Young children were being forced to roll cigarettes for seventy to eighty hours per week or to weave carpets in makeshift factories. Though these practices are illegal throughout the region, the guardians of the law look the other way. If they refuse to stop the slave owners, to whom can the children turn for help? Even their advocates in this top-tier international aid agency feel powerless.

Another aid agency working in South Asia reported a completely different problem to the IJM survey. Its health clinic encountered a fresh wave of kids who had contracted AIDS. The children were coming to the clinic straight out of the city's red-

light district. Though the agency gave assistance to those af-
flicted, it realized that more preventive work would be needed to
address the problem. But rescuing kids already embedded in the
brothels meant confronting both criminal elements and an inef-
fective law enforcement bureaucracy.

Given the preponderance of stories like these, IJM adopted an
organizational strategy that focuses on four clear objectives:

1. **Victim relief:** Rescue individuals who have fallen victim to
   slavery, sexual exploitation, and violence.

2. **Perpetrator accountability:** Use the tools of public justice
   to pursue accountability and just consequences for the specific perpetrators of these oppressions.

3. **Victim aftercare:** Give rescued victims access to material,
   emotional, and spiritual aid that can help them transition
   into new lives that they can sustain long into the future.

4. **Structural prevention:** Strengthen community factors
   that reduce the vulnerability of at-risk populations, empower local authorities to stop abuses, and deter potential
   oppressors.

Of these four objectives, IJM has gained notoriety for rescuing
victims. To some degree, its skewed public image can be attributed
to the media. Most Americans became acquainted with the agency
for the first time in 2004 after watching a *Dateline* television show
about an IJM-inspired raid on the Svay Pak brothels in Cambodia.
The intervention rescued thirty-seven girls between the ages of five
and seventeen and led to the arrests of several brothel owners as
well as the dismissal of a few corrupt police officers.

Rescuing victims can be dangerous, dramatic, and glitzy. A
television producer will not give equal airtime to a successful

microenterprise project that reduces a community's vulnerability to sex traffickers.

The fascination with rescuing victims goes beyond entertainment, however. It is a natural and compassionate response to want to save individuals who fall into captivity. When people first embrace the abolitionist cause, they often imagine themselves storming a labor camp to rescue individuals in captivity. More modest dreamers might ponder how they could buy a young girl out of a brothel and give her a new life.

Due to this romanticism, IJM's rescue work is often misunderstood. The agency does not run cowboy posse operations. To the contrary, its interventions are linked carefully to a broader agenda to sustain communities and to strengthen the public justice system.

IJM's efforts must also be distinguished from the well-intentioned efforts of some Western agencies to buy victims out of slavery. Redemption purchases have been deployed "successfully" in the Sudan and among a handful of international groups that free women from brothels.

Certainly, extreme cases may arise when a slave redemption might be necessary. But buying a slave's freedom can lead to several unintended consequences. For starters, it may create an even more dynamic market in the trade of human beings. Slave traders treat humans like any other commodity that has financial value. If the demand increases and there is no shortage of supply, purchases generate recurring revenue. Slave traders will simply go out and recruit other vulnerable people and force them into labor until a Western agency comes along and pays for their redemption.

Buying back slaves also diminishes the prospect of prosecuting slave traders. Police agents rarely show a willingness to get involved in the investigation of a crime that has already been "resolved." If the victim is rescued without the involvement of the police, most court systems are also reluctant to pursue a criminal case.

Gary recognizes the effort to buy back slaves for what it actually is: an end run around the real problem. The concept of paying off criminals would not arise if the public justice system functioned properly. Moreover, slave redemption becomes a self-defeating strategy. If we presume the power of those who act outside of the justice system, playing the game by their rules, they will win every time. "If you do not have the rule of law," Gary argues, "you have the rule of those who wield power at their own whim."

A typical IJM rescue, on the other hand, refuses to presume the legitimacy of the oppressor. Gary recounts a 2004 rescue operation in which IJM freed seventy laborers held captive in a rice mill. An IJM operative met one of the enslaved as he was purchasing food supplies at the market in a local town. It was not easy convincing this forced laborer that a way out of the rice mill existed. Once he did accept the risk, the man then had to persuade the other slaves to sneak out of the compound at night, one at a time, to meet with IJM staff. A team of lawyers stood by to take their testimonies.

Gary recalls that a woman named Vani was one of the first brave laborers to sneak out. During the rainy season, Vani and her husband had run out of money, so they took a loan of $10 to get food for their children. Five years later, her entire family still worked in the rice mill.

In her testimony to IJM, Vani detailed the work schedule at the rice mill. Labor started at ten in the morning with the boiling of the rice. After the first boil, the rice fruit is laid out in the sun until it dries. The laborers then boil it a second time, a process that they begin around eight in the evening. The second boiling finishes around one in the morning. The laborers dry the rice again and then package it in sacks. They finally finish up around five or six in the morning. They go to bed and have to wake up before ten to start the cycle over again.

Vani also reported to IJM lawyers that children in the compound were not allowed to go to school. All ages had to work. If anyone tried to leave the mill, they were chased down, dragged back to the compound, and severely beaten in front of the other laborers.

While the legal team continued recording testimonies, undercover IJM field operatives paid a visit to the owner of the rice mill. The operatives, who were from the local area, pretended to be managers of a faraway rice mill who were searching for fugitive slaves.

"What do you do when your slaves escape?" they asked the owner. The owner proudly related his best strategies for hunting down his laborers. He also bragged about beating them brutally to discourage anyone else from attempting to escape.

The owner's self-incrimination and the testimonies of dozens of slaves made for incontrovertible evidence. IJM, however, does not have any law enforcement power. So its next step is to identify an honest law enforcement official who will arrest the perpetrator.

IJM uses a method it calls the "power-actor analysis" to identify that law enforcement agent. The analysis poses questions like these: How does the legal structure currently operate in the community? How do matters of public justice get resolved in informal ways? Who is the person formally responsible for executing justice? Whom within the IJM network would be the best person to interact with our best law enforcement candidate?

In most cases, IJM does not approach members of the police agency at the bottom of the chain of command. The beat officers are more likely to be socially connected to the perpetrator and more likely to have a family or financial tie. Ideally, IJM finds a senior officer who has the capacity to make things happen without a supervisor's approval.

Once the right "power actor" has been identified, IJM presents its evidence and gives him or her the opportunity to do the right thing and get credit for it. "The best leverage is the truth," Gary stresses, and in most cases that is sufficient motivation for the power actor to apply the law.

The fact that an international legal agency has presented the evidence may serve as useful leverage. Few law enforcement officials will take the risk of being publicly exposed for sitting on the evidence and refusing to act. Playing the foreign card could also backfire, however. The official might consider it a matter of pride to snub his nose at the outsider agency despite the fact that most staff members are in fact from the region. All of these considerations must be weighed in the power-actor analysis.

"Intervention takes a tremendous amount of prep work," Gary says. IJM's job is much easier when it already has a history in a region and has built relationships with highly committed magistrates. When it starts from scratch in a new area, IJM has to perform a lot of meticulous groundwork.

In the case of Vani's community, a local magistrate accepted the evidence and ordered his police officers to raid the rice mill. After local government officials interviewed the victims, they were set free.

In Gary's eyes, the rescue of Vani's community can be deemed "successful" because it met three goals: (1) it rescued the victims from captivity and moved them into an economic restoration program and solid environment where they could build an independent and dignified life; (2) the state offered long-term legal protection for the victims; and (3) law enforcement authorities executed justice, an experience that lays the groundwork for future justice work.

Maya—One Violation Leads to Another

Though Mr. Vasu regularly made reference to their debt, Maya had no clue how much she and her relatives actually owed. It took her almost six months to build up the courage to ask him for a financial accounting.

He once had claimed that they would earn $4.50 for every thousand bricks they produced; in essence, that quantity of bricks represented a day's labor. Spread out over five families, the wage would not be significant. But Maya figured it would at least enable them to chip away at their debt.

So when Mr. Vasu informed her that her debt had actually doubled she was confounded. "That's impossible," she boldly blurted. "We have labored here for six months."

Almost as if he expected this response, Mr. Vasu pulled out a sheet of paper filled with lines and numbers. "As you can see," he began with a sickly smile, "you have incurred interest on your initial loan. I also have given you a substantial amount of money to pay for your food."

Maya stared at the paper, but the numbers made no more sense than erratic scribbles. Certain that she would offer no protest, he offered some advice: "It looks like you are just going to have to work harder."

When she reported back to the family what she had learned, they grumbled in disbelief. One of her cousins voiced what everyone was thinking: "How are we ever going to work ourselves out of this prison?"

It was humanly impossible to, say, double their daily production. Regardless, whenever they did surpass the benchmark of a thousand bricks in a day, Mr. Vasu did not give them credit for their surplus.

To make matters worse, the kiln would shut down for weeks at a time. Mr. Vasu explained that they had caught up with outside orders. During these waiting periods, he pressed the men to labor around the compound—scouring the kiln, sweeping up the straw, mending the fence, and so on. For performing these chores they received no compensation.

The owner likewise entreated the women to clean the temple that he had built for the local village. On the first occasion, he transported to the temple only three women—Maya and two of her cousins. Beginning early in the morning, they scrubbed the floors and polished the statues of divine figures. By midafternoon, they had finished their assigned chores, so they waited for Mr. Vasu to return and take them back to the compound.

When he arrived, he did not come alone. Maya assumed that the five men who accompanied him had temple responsibilities. They held no such holy ambition.

"Maya, I have a chore for you in the back room," Mr. Vasu said, and then barked loudly, "Come!"

She dutifully followed behind the owner and one of his cronies. Once they had passed into the back room, her owner shut the door and calmly ordered her to take off her clothes.

It took Maya a few moments to absorb the shock of his command: could a "holy man" so brazenly act with evil in his own temple? Realizing the vulnerability of her situation, she turned to flee. Her owner's friend already had positioned himself to cut off her retreat and hit her to the ground. He held tightly onto her arms while Mr. Vasu tore off her clothes and raped her. He then switched positions to assist in his friend's own act of violation.

"Get dressed. We will return to the compound in ten minutes," Mr. Vasu said once they had finished their assault. He spoke in such a casual tone that she wondered, Why do I feel so awash in shame while he apparently feels none?

Once dressed again, she returned to the main temple and understood immediately that her cousins had undergone the same torment. The women did not say a word to each other, nor did they speak of their violation once they returned to the compound. Fearful of further humiliation, they held on to their secret.

DIGNITY BEYOND THE WALLS

Rescuing slaves does not end the moment they are freed from captivity. To abandon the rescued and expect them to fend for themselves would leave them vulnerable to falling back into a forced labor relationship with a different owner. Abolitionists therefore must answer the question "What next?" before they rush into a rescue plan.

That solution probably will not be as simple as "sending them back home." In some cases, enslaved individuals were trafficked across borders, perhaps from even an ocean away. Even if the brothel owner or pimp can be brought to justice, the victims may be ongoing targets for the original traffickers who extracted them from their home village.

Though social workers throw around terms like *reintegration* and *restoration,* the process of aftercare often turns out to be far more complicated. Teenage girls freed from a brothel may decide that a pattern of shame and abuse awaits them in their home village, so they elect to build a new life elsewhere. Because they are likely to experience intense emotional trauma from repeated episodes of sexual abuse, they may need a supportive environment free of recrimination.

Interviews with forced laborers that IJM helped rescue from a rice mill reveal yet more complexity. Among the rescued, twenty-five of the laborers have a kinship relationship.

When the matriarch of the family was asked where she was from originally, she gave a puzzled look and replied, "The rice mill." She explained that her father had been pressed into labor when he was in his twenties, so she had worked in the rice mill her entire life. She raised her own children as laborers in the same mill.

As the matriarch recounted the saga of four generations of servitude that began with a $10 loan, her thirty-five-year-old daughter offered pieces of her own story. She too had met her husband at the rice mill. They were raising three children, ages eleven, thirteen, and eighteen, who had a long future of boiling and drying rice ahead of them. IJM and a local magistrate teamed up to alter their destiny overnight. What would "sending them back home" mean to this family and to millions of forced laborers with similar histories?

IJM today helps sixteen hundred people, former slaves and their families, in a broad array of aftercare programs. For the period immediately following a rescue, IJM collaborates with a network of relief partners to provide ex-slaves with shelter, food, emotional counseling, and protection from vindictive owners. Except in extreme circumstances of imminent violence, the agency will delay executing a rescue plan until it has a long-term support structure in place.

IJM assists former slaves in obtaining loans or grants from local authorities and available government land for houses. Additionally, IJM helps former slaves enroll their children in public school, often the most important tangible right that those in slavery so desperately want.

How critical is effective aftercare? Monitoring the results of its own programs, IJM learned that 93 percent of the former slaves it places in a supportive environment do not return to bondage.

Maya—The Bold Escape

Like jackals that have tasted blood and return to their prey, Mr. Vasu and his friends sexually assaulted the females at every opportunity, acts that included beating and burning their bodies. Usually, the owner and his son acted alone. With increasing frequency, Mr. Vasu announced to the women, "It's time to clean the temple." He said it in front of their husbands in a hushed tone, as if they were joining him in a sacred duty.

Though the women maintained their secret, they did hatch a plan for a mass escape. Their husbands rejected out of hand such "desperate measures." The consequences of a failed escape frightened them far more than the daily mistreatment they received at the hands of Mr. Vasu. If they were to run away, he would leave no stone unturned to find them.

Then one evening, Mr. Vasu brought his temple friends back to the compound after a wild drinking spree at a local tavern. The rowdy gang burst into the laborers' living quarters and started dragging the females outside. When their husbands put up a fierce resistance, the gang beat them mercilessly with sticks and tied them up to prevent their interference. Writhing in pain on the dirt floor of the stable, the men could only listen to the ribald chatter of the marauding herd as they violated their wives.

Sunk deep in humiliation, the pieces of the puzzle finally fell into place: now they understood why their wives so desperately wanted to escape. Once the horrible ordeal drew to an end, the bruised women stumbled back into the stable. Out of respect, their husbands did not say a word. But the next morning, as the entire family stood at the table throwing clay and straw into wood forms, they mapped out a plan.

Ajay had overheard the owner telling his son about a festival they would attend in the local town. The Vasu men set off one afternoon several days later, and that evening the family scaled over the iron gate. Though negotiating the spikes at the top of the gate was no easy feat, they helped one another make it to the other side safely.

Knowing that Mr. Vasu would interrogate local residents, the fugitives used the cover of darkness to get as far away from the compound as they could without being seen. Then, at the first hint of dawn, they jumped on a bus that would take them toward their home village.

The fugitives received a hearty welcome from their village kin, who had wondered whether they had vanished off the face of the earth. "Why didn't you ever visit us?" they asked innocently. To a horrified audience, Maya and the others shared the tale of their days in captivity.

The fugitives soaked in the familiar warmth of their homes, but they realized that here would be the first place that Mr. Vasu would send bounty hunters to look for them. Distant relatives lived on the other side of their province. They all agreed that it would be best to hide out there. They would do whatever was necessary to avoid capture and a return to the brick kiln.

IS THIS SLAVERY? TRUE OR FALSE

When slave owners become subject to criminal prosecution, they usually cloak their activity in a number of falsehoods. IJM has created a handout that aims to straighten out the record. It lists the most common rationalizations that slave owners have used and counters those falsehoods with the truth. The following list is paraphrased from the handout:

Falsehood: "My loan helped these people in an emergency."
Truth: While the initial loan may have brought immediate relief, forced labor puts them in a far more vulnerable position. Because the victims are paid very low wages and are often charged high interest rates, they are never able to repay the lender and may suffer a lifetime for a single loan.

Falsehood: "The worker asked me for the advance."
Truth: Whether or not workers wanted an advance, the employer cannot take away their freedom.

Falsehood: "If it weren't for me, these people would be homeless."

Truth: The provision of housing, which is often substandard, does not mitigate the injustice of enslaving victims. Moreover, relevant law states that freed laborers are not to be evicted from their homes.

Falsehood: "If you release these people, they'll be jobless."

Truth: In addition to the rehabilitation to which victims are entitled upon release, they are freed from debt, removed from an abusive labor situation, and allowed to find a better source of income.

Falsehood: "If I'm not repaid for the loans I gave, I'll lose a substantial amount of money."

Truth: Because the loan was illegal in the first place, it is null and void. To accept payment on such a loan is to be subject to criminal penalty. Regardless, in most cases victims have repaid the loans multiple times over and the owner has already made astounding profits on the loan.

Falsehood: "The industry would fail if it couldn't use forced labor."

Truth: Fair labor practices are necessary for legal, moral, and economic reasons. It is true that the cost of eradicating slavery might be borne largely by wealthy classes. But it will also lead to the modernization of industry practices and may boost the country's economic progress.

Falsehood: "The workers are free to go if they pay the advance first."

Truth: Relevant law specifically prohibits employers from preventing individuals from pursuing employment elsewhere. An inability or unwillingness to repay an advance does not abrogate that right.

Falsehood: "You are just picking on my operation. Every other business in the industry does the same thing."
Truth: The law is binding. An industry's failure to follow the law does not give any employer the license to deny workers their fundamental rights.

Falsehood: "Brokers brought me these people. I didn't know how they were paid or what freedoms they had."
Truth: The law assumes that those in charge of a company know its operations. On that basis, the law deems those in charge of a company guilty when an offense occurs, regardless of their personal knowledge.

Falsehood: "No one will work if I don't give them cash advances."
Truth: Advances are not illegal. The issue is whether or not the laborers are forced to work.

Falsehood: "Even if the law says the advance must be canceled, the workers still have a moral obligation to repay the debt."
Truth: As well as having no legal obligation to pay the debt, laborers have no moral obligation. A moral obligation cannot arise from an immoral act.

Narayan—Temple Hostages

Narayan thought it was strange that his sister and Ajay did not return home for religious festivals. He knew that Maya disliked being under anyone's obligation. Maybe she and Ajay had decided to work extra hard to cancel their debt. Narayan made a silent pledge to visit them at their brick kiln soon.

Then early one morning Narayan caught a glimpse of Mr. Vasu as he passed through the gate of the brick kiln. Within the hour, Narayan's boss emerged from his office and told him that Mr. Vasu wanted to speak with him alone. Narayan's curiosity turned to dread; surely the man had not come to report good news.

Mr. Vasu was pacing across the middle of the office when Narayan entered. He rushed toward Narayan and thrust his head forward so that only inches separated their faces. "Your family has failed to fulfill their obligation!" he screamed. "They have run away. If you know what's good for you, you will tell me where they have gone."

Narayan could not believe that his sister would behave so rashly. "I am sure that they will return," he offered. "They probably went on a brief visit to our home village."

"I didn't think you would cooperate," Mr. Vasu replied. "I warned you and your uncle that I would hold you responsible for their actions. Go fetch your uncle and your cousin—you will be leaving with me now."

Mr. Vasu spat his words out with such venom that Narayan reckoned it was useless to argue. He nodded his head and walked out the door.

Outside the office Narayan's boss awaited him. "Don't worry, Narayan," he whispered. "You can come back in a few days. Mr. Vasu will turn over every rock until he tracks down your family."

A chill ran up Narayan's spine, yet he held his composure and gave his boss a polite nod. He headed directly to where Amar and Bishnu were working and explained to them the troubling circumstances. A few moments later, they shuffled out of the gate behind the determined strides of Mr. Vasu. The man pointed to the rear bed of his pickup truck, and they jumped in.

As the pickup barreled along the highway, the men went over likely scenarios. Where else would their relatives go but back to their home village? And why would they act so outrageously against the wishes of their boss?

They took a break from their earnest conversation to figure out why the truck had come to a halt in front of a village temple. They presumed that Mr. Vasu would transport them back to his compound.

Half a dozen men emerged from the temple as soon as they arrived. Two of the larger men leaned over, gruffly jerked Amar out of the flatbed, and carried him toward the temple. The remainder of the men moved Narayan and Bishnu in like manner.

The brutes made a circle around the laborers and beat them brutally with sticks, clenched fists, and boots. Narayan passed out after a fist knocked him square in the nose. When he regained consciousness, both his relatives were lying next to him, passed out in a sea of red.

It was just turning dusk when Mr. Vasu returned with his thugs. "Are you ready to talk now?" he asked in menacing tone.

"As I've said all along, we didn't even know that they had left your property until you came to the brick kiln this morning," Narayan said with his head down, not daring to look at his tormentor directly. "I would guess they went to our home village."

"Wrong!" Mr. Vasu screamed as he gave Narayan a hard kick in the ribs. "I already sent some of my men to the village this morning, and they weren't there. No one there will admit to having seen them. So where else could they be?"

The captives had run out of answers. So the thugs tore off their clothes, pinned them down, and shaved their scalps bald. Then Mr. Vasu instructed his men to hold each one upright while he took a photo to capture their humiliation.

The men slept that night naked on the concrete floor of the temple. Narayan twisted to find a part of his body that did not feel tender so that he might be able to rest comfortably. As he struggled to fall asleep, his eyes scanned the temple. Since he was a young boy he had attended a temple ceremony every week. He now wondered: Did the gods who watched over this sacred place not see his distress? Why didn't they intervene now and offer him protection?

Gary Haugen—Pursuing Justice

Gary has discovered time and time again that the perpetrators of injustice deploy two tools to get their way: coercion and deception. Coercion, forcing an individual to perform an act against his or her will, usually involves the threat or act of physical violence. Perpetrators use deception to mask their true intention and to cover up their crimes. The combination of coercion and deception makes it difficult to bring slave owners and other violators of human rights to justice.

Gary's previous work as a human-rights investigator prepared him well for his abolitionist work. In 1989 the Lawyers Committee for Human Rights commissioned Gary to devote four months in the Philippines investigating abuses. The country had recently emerged from the long shadow of dictatorial rule. A new populist leader had assumed control of the government, and the Filipino people had high hopes for a new era of justice. Unfortunately, violations against the poor did not end, and the perpetrators were going unpunished.

Once Gary had settled in the Philippines, he elected to focus first on a high-profile massacre that had taken place in the village of Lupao. Soldiers from the Filipino army had been charged with the murder of seventeen unarmed villagers; among the victims were six children. Most of the evidence that Gary reviewed, including the testimonies of seven survivors, indicated that the soldiers had indeed executed the unarmed civilians. Despite the preponderance of evidence, a military court had acquitted all of the accused soldiers. Gary wanted to find out how this could have happened.

Immediately following the acquittal, the new democratic president of the country tried to justify the results to the public, announcing that witnesses to the event had chosen not to cooperate with the court. Her justification matched the story of military prosecutors and the presiding judge of the court trial, who all reported that without the help of witnesses, they could not prove the guilt of the accused soldiers.

As he pored over the case review, Gary smelled a rat. In his experience, individuals who witnessed the murder of a loved one deeply desire to testify against the perpetrators and bring them to justice. So why hadn't they showed up for their court date?

Rather than rely on official reports, Gary elected to take a nine-hour bus ride out to Lupao and get to the bottom of the mystery. There he met with a number of the witnesses and learned that all seven survivors actually had testified at the court-martial and had clearly identified four of the defendants. As Gary suspected, the official reports of the trial had been an outright lie.

Though the faces and places change, Gary experiences the same dynamics in his IJM work. The powerful everywhere use coercion and deception to abuse the rights of the poor. They can deploy their own security forces and resolve disputes in their own way. The poor and the weak, on the other hand, cannot provide their own security or execute their own justice. The rule of law, properly executed, is their only source of security and the only place where they might find justice. The powerful can work around a corrupt system; the poor cannot.

Narayan—Family Obligations

Mr. Vasu interrogated the laborers at the temple for two days. Though they never altered their story, the torture continued unabated.

On the third day, Mr. Vasu moved them to his compound and changed tactics. He gave them ill-fitting clothes and forced them to perform meaningless tasks of hard labor. For an entire day, they shoveled sand out of a dump truck and piled it high on the ground. The next day they shoveled the sand off the ground and filled up the dump truck. The purpose behind these chores only Mr. Vasu knew, for he continued to take photos of their activities.

On day six of captivity, Mr. Vasu woke Amar early and ordered him to jump into the back of the truck. He drove him back to the temple. Amar feared that he was entering a renewed phase of torture. Instead, Mr. Vasu told Amar that he was to go and search for the runaway slaves. Mr. Vasu said that he would continue to torture Narayan and Bishnu until Amar returned.

"But I honestly do not know where to look for them," Amar complained. He was sure that he was being set up for failure.

"You will call me by phone each day to let me know what progress you are making," Mr. Vasu replied, unmoved by his protest. "And Amar, if I do not hear from you on a given day, I will take your punishment out on your poor relatives. And if you attempt to run away, I will kill both of them."

The owner gave Amar a small sum of money to cover the cost of bus fares and phone calls and sent him forth on his mission. He ordered Narayan and Bishnu to jump back into the rear of the pickup, and they headed back to the compound.

Mr. Vasu did not receive a call from Amar that day, nor the next day, or any day after. When it came to threats, he was a man of real integrity, always following through. Each night he beat Narayan and Bishnu harshly. "Where is your Amar?" he would taunt them as he brought down his stick. "Your entire family is making you pay for their failure to keep promises."

Gary Haugen—Structural Prevention

In late 1994, the U.S. Department of Justice put Gary on loan to serve as the director of the United Nations genocide investigation in Rwanda. Only months before his appointment, tribal Hutus had butchered complete villages of Tutsi women and children as a senseless hysteria swept the country.

Gary started with a list of one hundred mass graves where witnesses and UN military intelligence personnel indicated a massacre might have taken place. It's hard to imagine a more gruesome task. At each site, he and his team sorted through the bodies and looked for evidence that might lead them to the perpetrators. They would learn that no fewer than eight hundred thousand Tutsis were killed in an eight-week span.

Gary and his team found one mass grave situated behind a Roman Catholic church in the town of Kibuye. In April 1994, nearly 450 people sought shelter in the church after they heard reports of hostile militia activity in the region. When the troops arrived, they killed every single person they could find, including those who prayed for mercy in church pews.

As Gary's feet sank in the mud of the mass grave and his nostrils filled with the stench of rotting bodies, he was tempted to sink into despair. What could *justice* mean here? And what good would it do to convict the perpetrators now that the violence had ended?

He came to a profound conclusion: the pursuit of justice creates a social legacy. It did mean something that the International Tribunal for Rwanda used the evidence his team documented to indict the leaders of the Kibuye massacre—the governor of the region, the mayor of the town, and their accomplices. Holding perpetrators accountable for their crimes against humanity not only dignifies the suffering of the victims, it instills in the survivors a confidence in the rule of law. Moreover, the criminal convictions sent a strong message to the next generation of Rwandans that abuses do not go unpunished. "Never again" must be the motto that guides future generations, and it begins with enforcing justice today.

This dogged pursuit of justice has informed Gary's work at IJM. Not that he hasn't faced his share of legal disappointments: despite the fact that IJM has pressed hard with local prosecutors in South Asia to convict slave owners for their crimes, not a single owner has served a day in jail.

So he is not surprised when social "realists" tell him to give up his quest for public justice in countries where the rule of law is anemic. "They are just way too corrupt," they say. "It's just the way those people are, and they'll never change."

Gary does not accept that argument. When he reads political history, he appreciates that Western democratic societies are the result of a long experiment to restrain violent behavior. Our public justice systems aim to ensure that citizens do not sort out their disputes through the exercise of brute physical power. That should not imply that people in democratic societies are inherently nicer or more reasonable. The reason we enjoy civil rights and freedom of movement is because we have a functioning public justice system. Though far from perfect, it offers a better solution for violence.

Gary recalls an episode when he went undercover in an investigation of child sex trafficking in Cambodia. A pimp led him to a room where he presented a dozen girls between the ages of five and ten years old. For a few dollars, these children will perform any sexual act requested by customers.

"Keep in mind that the sexual exploitation of minors is completely against the law in Cambodia," Gary says, shaking his head.

"But here I am very openly engaging in a negotiation to violate these young girls!" He adds, with frustration, "This transaction could happen because the law is not enforced. Slavery flourishes in the world because it is tolerated by law enforcement!"

For that reason, Gary believes that pursuing the conviction of criminals is one of the most effective tools to deter future crimes. Only then will individuals who are trafficking or abusing people get the message that they must stop or face the consequences.

In that respect, the agenda for modern-day abolitionists stands apart from that of the nineteenth-century abolitionists who confronted the transatlantic African slave trade. At that time, the slave trade was state-sanctioned and intricately tied to the financial interests of the state. Abolitionists like William Wilberforce and Frederick Douglass appropriately channeled their energies to make slavery illegal.

Today, however, there is not a country in the world where slavery could be considered legal. Yet slavery still thrives. If the laws that already appear on the books were enforced, the slave trade would end tomorrow. But the laws are not enforced, and slave owners know they can rely on a broken public justice system to escape prosecution. They count on the apathy of local authorities, they create delays in the courts, and they leverage family ties and social influence.

"At the moment, slave owners and sex traffickers are not afraid," Gary laments. "Victims of sex trafficking, on the other hand, are afraid. Families trapped in forced labor are afraid. Our challenge is to reverse the equation. In that sense, our work has only just begun."

Maya—Family Reunion

Maya saw the strange man with the shaved head heading across the field toward her hut. As he drew closer, she suspected that the man had been in a bad accident: black and blue bruises discolored almost every inch of his swollen face.

"Peace to you, Maya," his familiar voice said when he reached the hut. He noticed her confusion, so he gently added, "I am your uncle Amar."

Maya gasped, then rushed to give him a hug. "Oh, my dear uncle! Whatever happened to you?"

"It is not a pretty story, my niece," he said in a sad voice. "Could you bring Ajay and your cousins? A single telling of this tale may be all that I have the strength to do."

Maya left him to rest at the hut while she ran out to a rice field where most of the family labored. They debated whether Amar had come by himself or whether Mr. Vasu might be using him to lure them into a trap. They decided to send a team around the perimeter of the village to make sure that no bounty hunters were lying in wait. By midafternoon, the family had gathered back at Maya's house.

A ghastly silence gripped the family as Amar painfully recounted what had happened to him, Narayan, and Bishnu over the past few days and passed around the photos that Mr. Vasu had sent with him. It was awkward for the family to bear witness to the humiliation—and worse still that their escape set these events into motion.

Just when it felt as if the air could no longer hold the tension, Amar spoke: "We do not hold you responsible for what has happened to us. In many ways, we are responsible. Who could have imagined that Mr. Vasu would turn out to be such a tyrant?"

As everyone murmured agreement, Amar continued. "But now we have a real dilemma. Mr. Vasu pledges to kill Narayan and Bishnu if we do not return, and we all know not to hold his threats lightly."

Amar paused to check if anyone wanted to speak, but everyone in the circle remained silent, with eyes cast down to the ground. He decided to press forward: "As badly as I feel for Narayan and Bishnu, I cannot return. My guess is that you will refuse to go back as well. But we cannot abandon our relatives. We must do something."

"Yes, we wholeheartedly agree, Amar," Ajay spoke softly. "Here in this province the people are fortunate to have very good leaders. Yesterday I met with one of them and recounted to him our experience. He told me about an agency called International Justice Mission that protects enslaved people like us. I think we should ask him to connect us right away. Maybe the agency has the means to fight Mr. Vasu. Acting alone, I know that we cannot."

Operation Rescue

After Maya and Ajay went to the village leader to plead for help, events moved swiftly. They visited the leader's home in the morning, and by early afternoon the man offered them a solution. It involved eight members of the family traveling to a secure location where they would give their testimonies to IJM. The village leader was confident that the hostages would be set free as long as the family members did their part.

"You can fully trust the people in this organization," he told the couple. "In the past, they have freed many laborers in my district, even from some of the most violent owners."

IJM used undercover investigation to confirm that they were dealing with a hostage situation. In normal circumstances, the agency would give itself several months to gather evidence on a slave owner—a more thorough case increases the chances for a successful conviction.

Despite the rush in this case, one factor worked in IJM's favor: only a dozen or so laborers appeared to be involved. Some of the slavery cases they investigate involve anywhere from 100 to 150 laborers.

The family did not need much convincing to cooperate. Surely Narayan and Bishnu were living on borrowed time. Moreover, they knew that Mr. Vasu would never surrender his claim on their own lives. If they did not stop him now, they would always be looking over their shoulder.

In her testimony to IJM, Maya did not have to rehearse a single detail; painfully, every moment of the past ten months was as fresh as if it had happened yesterday. She had initially not planned to mention the sexual assaults. But when the lawyer asked if she had been violated sexually, she surprised herself when she answered, "Yes, many times on the floor of the temple."

Within forty-eight hours, IJM staff accompanied local government officials on a raid of the kiln. They had trouble finding the hostages at first—a search of the living quarters turned up nothing. An IJM backup team monitoring the raid from afar with binoculars observed one of Mr. Vasu's cronies moving toward a small shed in an adjoining field. They radioed the ground team and alerted them to the suspicious activity. When the IJM team members approached the shed, they heard muffled cries. They forced open the locked door and found Narayan and Bishnu crouched on the floor, too terrified to speak.

IJM brought all of the freed slaves to the office of the district magistrate the next day. He issued to each of them a document stating that they owed no obligation to Mr. Vasu and were free to pursue their own destiny. The magistrate's office explained to them that the certification made them eligible for many benefits, including a lump sum of cash. The family happily returned to their home village that very afternoon.

Despite the evidence against Mr. Vasu, the police who conducted the raid declined to take him into custody. IJM persisted and presented to the police a list of criminal offenses that the owner of the brick kiln had committed, including wrongful confinement, physical abuse and torture, rape, and forced labor. Despite thorough documentation and credible testimonies from multiple victims, the authorities would not file charges. After two years, Mr. Vasu was finally arrested and released on bail. He now awaits trial, which may take years to commence. He has not spent a day in jail for his crimes.

Maya and Ajay today work hard to make ends meet. When they are lucky, they both find fieldwork at one of the local farms. They have been able to buy a few cows and sheep. Though they cannot save much money, they make enough to feed and clothe their family and have some savings. They vow never to take another loan again.

Despite a much better life, Maya admits that she still feels unsafe. Mr. Vasu could pop back into her life at any moment and take her back to the brick kiln. For that reason, she stays close to home. Who knows who might see her if she visits one of the larger towns in the region? Maybe one of Mr. Vasu's cronies might see her at the market. Though the government recognizes her freedom, she still lives in fear.

Rescuing the Child Soldiers: Uganda

For over two decades, a rebel army in East Africa has been enslaving children. The children, some as young as seven, are forced to perform as soldiers, sex slaves, and baggage porters. Human-rights groups estimate that as many as forty thousand children have been taken captive.

It is called "the forgotten war." Most westerners know next to nothing about it, and our governments do little to stop it. Frankly, the region holds no strategic geopolitical interest for us. We treat it as just another story of Africans killing Africans in endless guerrilla warfare—a Darfur in slow motion. Perhaps if the rebels were stealing oil rather than children, the world would pay more attention.

The prime perpetrator of this atrocity is the Lord's Resistance Army (LRA), a guerrilla militia that, since its inception in 1986, has terrorized the northern region of Uganda. What began as a rebellion against the ruling government has turned into a messianic military cult.

Its commander, Joseph Kony, claims that he will create a society based on the Ten Commandments. Ironically, he and his troops seem hell-bent on violating every one of them. Kony, a former Catholic altar boy, stirs verses from the Old Testament and Koran together with traditional tribal rituals to mix a bizarre religious cocktail. As the years pass, his political objectives become less clear and his tactics more brutal.

Child abductees comprise as much as 80 percent of the LRA ranks. Senior commanders press them to raid villages, execute unwanted prisoners, and square off against the Ugandan national army. Former child soldiers report that senior commanders regularly placed them on the front lines of the battlefield. When they set up camp, the children stand watch in an outer ring while senior commanders rest securely in the center.

Jan Egeland, the UN undersecretary-general for humanitarian affairs, visited northern Uganda and declared that it must become a top priority for international action:

> It's a moral outrage, frankly, to see thousands of children that have been abducted, that have been maltreated, that are going through the most horrendous torture by the rebel movement. . . . I cannot find any other part of the world having an emergency on the scale of Uganda with so little international attention.[1]

Since Egeland's visit in 2003, the humanitarian crisis in Uganda has only deteriorated.

Charles—The Abduction

News reached the Achana household that a detachment of the Lord's Resistance Army was circulating the province. The previous evening, LRA rebels had attacked a village nearby, no more than a twenty minutes' walk.

Betty Achana would not take any chances. When malaria had stolen away two of her daughters as infants, she felt totally powerless. She would not let fate fix the destiny of her two sons as well.

She instructed her older son, Charles, to lead his younger brother out to the bush that night and sleep a safe distance from the village. She shared her plan with neighbors, and they saw its wisdom. So at the first hint of dusk, the village boys, each toting a blanket and a schoolbag, headed off to a familiar hiding spot.

Charles felt like any other ten-year-old child might in his situation: he was embarking on an adventure. Sleeping under the stars did not trouble him. On hot, dry nights he regularly ventured outside the family hut. He loved to lie still and identify the creatures by their night calls. This night, however, he chatted with his friends until his eyelids turned heavy.

Morning arrived without warning. Charles initially rolled over and turned his back to the sun, but then he recalled that it was a school day. Aware that the other boys did not share his enthusiasm for study, he did not stir them. He quietly rolled up his blanket and headed off in the direction of the school.

Charles strolled along the path, lost in his thoughts. He was practically on top of the soldiers before he noticed their presence. They sat casually around a smoldering fire, eating a simple porridge. Charles was not terribly alarmed; he often encountered national army troops as they made their rounds in the province. Skirting to the side of the soldiers, he kept his pace.

The shout startled him: "Hey, you! Stop right there!"

Halting in his tracks, Charles turned and took his first good look at the soldiers. Something was amiss: they did not dress smartly like national army soldiers. Though some wore army shirts, none had pants to match. And now that he had a closer look, he noticed that some of the soldiers were about his age. A wave of nausea swept over him.

"Where are you going, boy?" asked one of the men who cradled a gun in his right arm. Most of the younger boys, he noted, held a machete in their hands.

"I asked you why you were in such a rush!" the man screamed.

Charles realized he had failed to answer. "I'm headed to school," he said, almost in a whisper.

"Not anymore you aren't," said the commander with a hearty laugh. "Boy, you just joined the Lord's Resistance Army."

Florence Lacor—The Painful Road to Abolition

When discussing the crisis in northern Uganda, it is hard not to focus exclusively on the child slaves of the LRA. Once you meet Florence Lacor, you can no longer overlook the pain of the parents.

Since 1997 Florence has worked as a counselor at a children-of-war center in Gulu, the largest town in northern Uganda. Parents often go there looking for abducted sons and daughters. More times than not, their kids are still held captive out in the bush. Florence tries to help the parents deal with their loss. She knows their pain: her own daughter was missing for over eight years, enslaved by the LRA, and Florence knew little of her whereabouts. It is the uncertainty, she realized, that leads to madness:

> Parents suffer so much when their children are abducted and held in captivity. When it's night, you know your child is out in the cold. When a thunderstorm comes, you can feel your child getting soaked. When you hear bombing, you think of the bombs dropping on your child.
>
> When your child dies, at least you can mourn. But when she is abducted, you always wonder what is happening. You can never forget.

Florence's daughter was kidnapped in one of the most infamous LRA raids ever conducted. In October 1996, the rebels attacked Saint Mary's College, a private girls' boarding school located in Aboke in northern Uganda. The assault became a public sensation in part because 139 girls were abducted in one fell swoop. Of equal significance, these girls were regarded as the best and brightest of northern Uganda. If the girls of Aboke town could be taken, no one was safe.

On the night of the abduction, the director of the school, Sister Rachelle Fassera, heroically trailed the rebels into the bush and refused to relent. She begged them to release the girls, offering medicine, money, and even her own life. "Take me and release the girls, or kill me and release the children," one of the abducted girls recalls the nun telling the commanding officer of the raid.[2]

Incredibly, the LRA officer appeased her. He sat all the girls down and directed the senior commanders to carefully select out the thirty most beautiful girls. Some of the girls tried cutting their faces with rocks or any other sharp objects they could find. Others posed as if they were crippled—anything to avoid selection.

Once they had completed their selection, the senior officer released the remainder of the girls into the nun's care and bid her leave quickly before he changed his mind. He then warned the chosen thirty that if any one of them escaped, he would summarily execute her twenty-nine peers.

Once news of the abduction reached Florence, she rushed to the school. She waited anxiously for Sister Rachelle's return; along with the other parents, she prayed that her daughter had been released. Alas, her daughter had the misfortune of being among those schoolgirls selected to become sex slaves for the senior commanders.

Although Florence had read newspaper accounts of abducted children in the rural areas, she never imagined that her daughter would be a target in a private school. "I frantically wanted to do something, anything, to rescue my daughter," she says, "but every action I could think of seemed futile."

In an effort to educate herself about the LRA and what it does with abducted children, she visited the children-of-war camp run by World Vision, a Christian relief and development organization that helps children and their communities worldwide. World Vision operates two of the most effective camps for freed slaves in northern Uganda. One of the camps attends to females and younger boys, and the other focuses on young men over the age of eighteen. At both camps, victims receive medical care, counseling, and vocational training. Since its launch in 1995, World Vision has helped about fifteen thousand freed slaves put their lives back together.

After only an hour at the World Vision camp, Florence had heard enough. "I couldn't bear to imagine my daughter living through the experiences that I heard the former child soldiers relate," she recalls. "So I walked out and vowed that I would never return."

For months Florence alternatively grieved, prayed, got angry, and generally felt sorry for herself. She constructed her own internal prison, where any happiness would be soundly punished with lashes of guilt and shame.

Then one day she had an inspiration. She had learned at the World Vision camp that when the LRA abducts children, they frequently force the kids to kill their own parents. "Maybe I can't save my own daughter," she heard herself saying, "but I can be an advocate for those child slaves who are now orphans."

Florence returned to the World Vision camp and joined in its abolitionist efforts.

Margaret—Marching Orders

Two o'clock on a sunny afternoon in November.

How strange that she can recall the exact time. Margaret spent eight and a half long years in the bush, where time had no meaning. But the moment of her capture stands frozen as a monument to her innocence.

When the rebels raided the village, she was nine years old. No one stood watch: rebels do not attack during the day. But here they were, announcing their arrival with gunshots and hollers.

Margaret scampered into her family hut, praying that the grass walls might offer miraculous protection. She heard a ruckus at the vocational training center that an international aid agency had built in the village; of course, the rebels would covet its equipment. The melee shifted to a neighbor's home. She hardly had time to hold her breath before a shaft of light crashed through the door.

A boy about her age stood in the passageway, slowly scanning the hut as if he were looking for something in particular. Then his eyes fixed on her. He lifted the machete that hung down his right side and pointed its end to punctuate an order: "Get up and follow me. *Now!*"

He escorted Margaret to the middle of the village. Her heart sank when she saw her brother captured along with almost every neighbor child. The soldiers guarding them carried crude clubs— actually, they were no more than slightly whittled tree branches. Margaret shuffled to a spot alongside the other prisoners.

Satisfied that they had gathered every item of value in the village, the rebels piled their booty into a single heap. They then ushered most of the adults into the training center. A handful of the village men were pulled out of the crowd and ordered to sit back-to-back next to the children.

The commander in charge yelled through the door to the prisoners inside the training center. "If I hear even a whisper coming out of this place, I personally will set it on fire," he warned. "And I assure you that no one would make it out alive."

Once the troops had sealed the door, the commander made his way to the children. He stopped abruptly several yards from where they huddled and cast a hard look. "You no longer belong to this village; you belong to the Lord's Resistance Army!" he shouted.

He then fell into a speech that sounded well rehearsed: "If today, tomorrow, or any other day in the future you try to escape, we will hunt you down and kill you. Know that we will also return to this village and eliminate every last person. Neither the young nor the old will receive mercy."

The commander then ordered the children to divide into two camps, boys and girls. As soon as the boys had shifted to one side, a soldier pulled out several lengths of rope and tied their hands together tightly behind their backs.

The commander instructed the girls to walk in a line past the pile of loot. Soldiers distributed to each girl a load commensurate with her size. A teenage rebel wearing a tattered army shirt handed Margaret a set of cooking pans bound together with string. Margaret slung the pans over her shoulder and shuffled forward quickly, not giving the rebel a chance to add to her load.

The sun still hung high in the sky when they departed the village. The captives marched in a single file, with watchful soldiers ambling up and down the line. The column stayed on the move through daybreak. Margaret felt sharp stones and ragged elephant grass cut into her bare soles. A rebel rewarded those who paused along the path with a swift jab from his club.

Finally, at four o'clock the next afternoon, the commander halted the march. Margaret joined the other captives in a collective collapse to the ground. Suddenly released of body weight, her feet pounded. Despite the ache, she desired only to sink into a deep sleep.

"Hey, you lazy misfits, get up!" the commander's voice blared, ending her brief respite. "You've got work to do!"

He threw bright-colored jerry cans at three of the girls, Margaret among them. "There's a well down that path a few minutes," he said, pointing a finger toward a clearing. "Go fill these jerrys." Once the water crew had risen, he turned to the other girls. "The rest of you gather small sticks and build a fire for cooking."

Margaret moved slowly down the path. Ahead she saw what appeared to be an abandoned homestead. The roofs of the main huts were missing; the top of the walls bore the charred scars of a recent burning. She made her way to the water well situated just beyond the ring of huts. Testing the pump, she was a bit surprised that it worked. It did not take her long to fill the jerry can.

She had not figured on the challenge of getting the water-laden container back to the camp. At first she tried holding it to her side, but after a few steps her light frame nearly tipped over. She next tried lifting the can up so that it rested on her right shoulder. That technique worked for a few steps, but her limbs, already weary from the long march, did not cooperate. As she entered the thick brush, her feet stumbled over a tree root. The jerry went flying off the path into the brush, and her body followed close behind.

For several seconds she lay on the ground, stunned. The stream of water poured from the upturned jerry and worked its way beneath her. Once she realized that the flow was soaking her clothes, she jumped up on her knees and stretched out her hands to right the can.

It was in that position that the child soldier found her. "Come back here on the path," he said with a whistle, as if scolding a disobedient dog.

Margaret quickly grabbed the jerry and scurried to stand alongside the boy. He guided her back to the camp and directly to the commander, who at that moment rested against a tree chatting with a few senior soldiers.

"I caught this girl attempting to escape," said the boy rebel, "but she didn't get far."

Margaret wanted to defend herself, but fear had captured her tongue. It was as if she were standing outside herself, a bystander curious to find out what would happen next.

"Well done, Samuel," said the commander with an approving smile. Once his eyes shifted to Margaret, his face lost its warmth. "So, you don't like your new family, is that it?" he asked.

Margaret kept her gaze to the ground, not daring to face her tormenter. He grasped her arm with a tight squeeze and dragged her forward. "Let's show your friends what happens when you try to escape the Lord's Resistance Army," he said.

"Samuel, go get Taylor and Walter, and bring your machetes with you," he yelled over his shoulder to the boy.

The commander shoved Margaret toward the girls who were trying to coax a band of tiny twigs to ignite into a respectable fire. The village boys sat bound with rope some fifteen feet from the stone ring that the girls had fashioned into a fire pit.

"It's time for a reckoning," the commander barked. The startled girls jumped back from the fire and spun around to give the commander their full attention. His audience secured, the commander threw Margaret roughly to the ground.

"You will learn that we do not tolerate betrayal," he began in an even tone. "When you try to escape our camp, we consider you *traitors*." He spoke the last word as if he had swallowed venom. "This foolish girl was caught trying to run away with one of our jerry cans," he went on, looking directly at Margaret. "She is lucky that we did not have to work hard to capture her; otherwise, she would be dead."

He paused for a few seconds to let the message soak in. He then swung around and addressed the child soldiers who stood with their machetes poised for action. "Samuel, you captured this stupid girl, so you get the honor of the first strike."

The boy walked proudly forward until his feet nearly touched the top of Margaret's head. He raised his arm high and, with the flat side of the machete, delivered a slap against her back.

The blow gave Margaret such a horrific shock that she forgot to scream. Hot coals placed along the length of her spine could not have caused such pain. She found her yell once the other young rebels joined in raining down machete slaps on every part of her body.

Margaret blacked out long before they stopped beating her.

THE NIGHT COMMUTERS

The LRA typically raids rural villages at night. Given the risk, many families living in northern Uganda send their children off to seek safety in city centers before night falls.

As many as thirty thousand "night commuters" journey on foot—some walk for five to ten miles—to reach a shelter that lies near a national army garrison. Not all of the children are fortunate enough to find a formal shelter. Many sleep in bus terminals, in parks, under shop verandas, or in abandoned buildings. The kids walk back to their home village at dawn.

Noah's Ark is one of twenty shelters in Gulu for night commuters. On a single night in the summer of 2006, about one thousand children sought shelter there. Several dozen new mothers showed up as well. If their villages were attacked, they could not hope to outrun the rebels with an infant in their arms.

Before the sun had set, hundreds of kids had already arrived and were playing games and singing songs in a central courtyard. The scene bore the markings of a school recess.

As the skies darkened, more kids came from every direction, walking down roads leading to the shelter. Some carried little brothers and sisters on their back. A guard stood at the front gate, welcoming each child. A chain-link fence surrounded the

entire compound, with barbed wire running along its top to discourage would-be intruders.

Most of the younger kids behaved as if they were on a fun
sleepover with friends. About one out of ten, however, walked
around shell-shocked, obviously craving to be at home with their
mother.

Several of the teenage girls expressed relief that they had made
it to the refuge unscathed. Gangs of young men commonly lie in
wait along the side of the road for girls to pass on their night
commute. The girls all have stories of friends who were raped
and left battered and bruised.

Noah's Ark can afford to pay only a handful of staff,
which explains its "lord of the flies" environment: a village
populated wholly of children. Some of the more disciplined kids
sat in a lighted hall and did their schoolwork. The majority sat
clumped together in the central courtyard, chatting with their
friends.

As the night wore on, kids strolled in small groups to their
sleeping quarters. They needed no shepherding. The younger
kids moved into classrooms, one for boys and the other for girls.
The teens, also separated by gender, slept on concrete slabs covered by an enormous canopy.

Blankets hung clumsily over rope lines that had been strung
across the width of each room. As the children entered their respective quarters, they grabbed a blanket and found a space to
stretch out on the hard floor. Before long all the rooms were
covered with small bodies lined up like sardines in a tin can. The
stench of urine and body odor was overwhelming.

The flow of night commuters rises and falls in response to
rebel attacks. The summer of 2006 was a slow period for night
commuters. During the first half of the year, the LRA had made
few attacks; rumor had it that its troops had retreated to south-

ern Sudan and the Congo. The director of Noah's Ark claimed that in 2004, when rebel raids reached a peak, around seven thousand children flooded into her refuge each evening. During that same period, Saint Joseph's Mission, a shelter located in the town of Kitgum, reported an average daily population of five thousand night commuters.

Charles—The Initiation

After the rebels captured Charles, they seemed in no rush to break camp. Their resting spot, situated at the crossroads of several paths commonly used by local villagers, served as the perfect trap. They merely had to wait patiently for their prey to come to them.

By midmorning, they had snared half a dozen boys and three grown men. The prisoners dared not speak to each other; they sat quietly by the fire, staring blankly at the dying flames. One of the boys appeared to be around the same age as Charles, ten, and the rest a couple of years older. Charles did not know the boys, but he knew two of the men from his village.

Once the rebels started to pack up their camp, the man with the gun—who gave most of the orders—told the adult captives to move to an open space about ten yards from the fire. The men obediently shuffled to the spot where he pointed his gun. The commander then ordered the men to kneel in a straight line.

With a surly bark, the commander let the men know that they had positioned themselves too closely together. After arranging them more to his liking, he addressed the boys: "You pups, listen closely to me because what I have to say is a matter of life and death."

He pointed to a pile of tree branches that had been cut into approximately six-foot lengths. "Each of you will grab a club, and you will use it to beat these ignorant men to their death," he announced. Then, as if further explanation might be warranted, he added, "They are traitors to the Acholi people."

One by one the boys got to their feet and walked over to the woodpile. After selecting a club, they moved behind the men, who stayed silent in a praying position, like lambs before the slaughter.

"Now strike these traitors over the head," yelled the commander. When not a single boy moved, the rebel leader snatched the club out of Charles's hand, swung it back, and whacked one of the older boys square in the back. The boy let out a blood-curdling scream and thudded to the ground. Cocking his club back for another swing, the commander glared at the next boy in line. He needed no further urging. The boy raised the club and brought it down hard on the man kneeling directly in front of him. Blood came pouring out of the man's head as he crumpled sideways. The unthinkable breached, the other boys immediately joined in the slaughter. The commander put the borrowed club back into Charles's hand and gave a satisfied smile as Charles put it to work.

In a matter of minutes, the three bodies lay lifeless at the boys' feet. Charles felt numb, like he wanted to cry but could not pull out the tears.

"That's it boys, but there's still one thing left to do before you are worthy to be LRA soldiers," the commander announced. "To gain the strength of a warrior, you must lick your victims' blood so that it will run through your bodies."

After what the boys had just done, this request seemed simple. At least Charles thought so until he tasted the blood on his tongue. The sensation made the whole episode turn suddenly real; he could no longer pretend that this was a bad dream. His stomach lurched as if to vomit.

"Well done, boys. Welcome to the LRA," the commander said after each boy had completed the gruesome task.

In case they might overlook the full meaning of their initiation ceremony, he added, "There is now no going back to your home village. You are murderers; the families of the men you killed will seek revenge. You would be foolish to attempt escape. Where would you go?"

Florence Lacor—An Unexpected Joy

Florence is "a presence"—there is no better way to describe her. The actor Morgan Freeman has a knack for conveying a similar kind of gravitas in his films. Maybe it's the quiet confidence or the regal elegance or even the way her eyes seem to look straight into your soul. Whatever it is, Florence uses it powerfully to give comfort to the rescued children who come to the center in emotional tatters.

Early on, she found it tough going to hear rescued child soldiers describe how they had raided villages and abducted other children. They could be talking about her daughter! "I felt my blood boil," she confesses. "But then I realized that I had to get beyond my anger. These kids were innocent; they had been forced to assume the role of a soldier."

Florence eventually turned that corner. In many respects, she serves as a surrogate mother to boys and girls of all ages at the camp. They look to her for advice, for scolding, and for love.

She never stopped hoping that one day she might find her own daughter, of course. Whenever the national army alerted World Vision that they would be delivering a new batch of escapees, Florence asked if her daughter might be among them. Over an eight-year period she received the same reply: "No, Florence. She's not here."

Occasionally an ex-slave would acknowledge having seen her daughter, so at least Florence knew that she was alive. Such reports came irregularly, however, and Florence could not help wondering if her daughter might have fallen victim in the meantime.

One morning, early in 2004, as she was deep in prayer, Florence felt a wave of joy. "I was puzzled because nothing special had happened to warrant my happiness," she recalls, "but the feeling stayed with me all morning."

Once she arrived at work, she got the word that a number of children had been rescued. She journeyed out to the military airport in Gulu to meet them. A couple of the escapees informed Florence that her daughter was in the rebel camp with them when the national army had attacked. They did not see where her daughter had run, and she was not with them when the national army captured them.

"After I helped get the kids settled at the rehabilitation center, I went home and continued praying," she says, recounting each detail of the day. "The feeling of joy had not left me, which was very strange because usually any bit of bad news about my daughter broke my heart."

The next day she received a call at home from a friend in the national army. The troops had picked up her daughter in southern Sudan, and she was alive and well. Over the phone that evening Florence talked to her daughter for the first time in more than eight years. They were reunited in Gulu two days later.

Florence's long, dark night was over. Despite her personal celebration, she grieves for the mothers whose children will never return from the bush. "The pain a mother feels for her lost child never stops burning deep in her soul," she says, and her eyes well with tears.

NORTHERN UGANDA AND WAR—
HISTORICAL BACKGROUND

Violent coups and armed rebellions have been all too common in Uganda's postcolonial history. To most westerners, the name of former dictator Idi Amin elicits images of torture, extrajudicial killings, and mass murders. The military general led a coup in January 1971 and for the next eight years ran Uganda like a military garrison. In a short span of time, he quadrupled the size of the military and manipulated ethnic divisions within the ranks as a means to maintain control. During his reign, an estimated three hundred thousand people were murdered, most of them civilians.[3]

Idi Amin unfortunately represents a succession of regimes that have ruled Uganda with an iron fist. The pattern is tragic: after a violent overthrow, the new regime takes revenge on the soldiers and civilians (or tribes) that provided the support base for the ousted regime. They carry out these crimes against their own people with impunity.

When it formed in 1987, the Lord's Resistance Army seemed like another armed rebellion acting on behalf of its tribal interests. The year before, a militant strongman from the western region of Uganda, Yoweri Museveni, had led a bloody overthrow of the regime of General Tito Okello Lutwa.

No event in Uganda transcends tribal politics. Okello was an ethnic Acholi, a tribe that is most prevalent in the country's three northernmost districts—Kitgum, Gulu, and Pader. The Acholi people have long felt abused by the more prosperous tribes in the south and west of Uganda. It's a legacy that goes back to nineteenth-century British colonial social policies that unevenly disadvantaged northern tribes. So when Museveni rose to power and his troops carried out violent raids against northern

villages (or so the Acholi charge), the embers of old tribal grievances reignited.

Surviving members of Okello's armed forces and civilian dis-
sidents from the north rallied around the leadership of Alice
Auma, a spiritualist with political ambitions. Alice claimed that a
spirit named Lakwena had possessed her. In the Acholi language,
lakwena literally means "messenger." Lakwena gave Alice a message ordering her to cleanse the Acholi of their "sins" and to
mobilize a military rebellion against the Museveni regime. The
spiritualist assumed the name Alice Lakwena and called her militia the Holy Spirit Movement. As bizarre as the whole story
sounds, the Holy Spirit Movement marshaled a stiff military
challenge to Museveni's forces before retreating into Kenya.
Alice Lakwena lives there in exile to this day.

After the defeat of the Holy Spirit Movement, Joseph Kony, a
first cousin to Alice, assumed the mantle to finish her divine mission. He fully expected the Acholi people to rise up behind his
leadership, but that did not happen. He felt rejected by his own
people and blamed it on their sinful nature. He turned his wrath
on the Acholi people and undertook a campaign to "purify"
them. If adults would not join his movement, he would raise up
the Acholi children himself and teach them the meaning of liberation. The new generation would be faithful and would not
betray him.

Margaret—The Sacrifice

Once the commander ordered Margaret to be beaten, every one
of the rebels scurried to watch. They neither cheered nor
laughed, yet they drew close to the violence like moths to light.

In Uganda, freedom usually costs the suffering of another.
The village boys did not waste Margaret's sacrifice. With the
rebels distracted, they worked as a team to loosen the knots

binding their hands. Within moments, Margaret's brother and five of his friends slinked quietly off into the brush. Another dozen boys dared not move a muscle, even though the ropes no longer bound them. The severity of Margaret's punishment had made a solid impression.

Perhaps they chose wisely. Once the commander realized that the boys had escaped, he sent his best hunters in pursuit. They captured four of the boys and killed them on the spot.

Margaret's brother and one other boy made it safely all the way back to their home village. The adults doubted they would ever see their children again, so the sight of two of the abducted boys emerging from the bush became cause for great celebration.

Their happiness was short-lived. The boys relayed the commander's dire threat and told the adults that they had no doubt that rebel soldiers would soon descend upon the village and murder every living soul they found. The villagers immediately ran to their huts, grabbed a few valuables, and made haste for the provincial capital.

Within the hour, the rebel hunters crept quietly around the outskirts of the village. Their stealth proved unnecessary. They found the huts completely abandoned. The rebels freely spent their fury all the same. By day's end, only smoking embers remained of the village.

THE FIRST DAYS OF FREEDOM

On a sunny afternoon in June 2006, three girls, all around sixteen years old, walked into the children-of-war center in Gulu. The girls looked like skeletons, and a hollow gaze flattened their eyes. Friends they had known in captivity within the LRA gave them an animated greeting, and the girls responded with hardly a flicker of emotion.

The three arrived with their heads completely shaved, and one had a terrible burn on the top of her head that exposed part of her skull. When the national army had launched its attack on the LRA, the rebel camp was preparing its dinner. A commander forced this girl, in retreat, to pick up a boiling pot and carry it on her head. When she tripped and fell, the commander kept running and left her behind. Shortly thereafter, the national army captured her.

One further peculiarity stood out about these three girls. The majority of the teenage girls at the camp are young mothers. Not one of them held a baby in her arms.

The LRA does force some girls to fight as soldiers, but the senior commanders divide up the majority of the girls to be their sex slaves. It is not unusual for a commander to maintain four or five concubines, while Joseph Kony surrounds himself with a harem of sixty young sex slaves.

Sometimes child slaves successfully escape LRA captivity using their own ingenuity, while others are rescued during a national army offensive. In recognition of the fact that the child soldiers did not join the rebels voluntarily, the Ugandan government passed an amnesty law in 1999. The amnesty safeguards from prosecution any LRA fighter—even Kony and his senior commanders—who surrenders to the government.

Once the national army takes child soldiers into custody, it brings them to a "child-protection unit" that it houses in its garrison in Gulu. The army holds them there for several days of questioning in an effort to gain intelligence on the rebels. National army officers urge the older boys to join the fight against the LRA, and a good number accept.

Some human-rights groups have criticized the length of some detentions and the coercive recruitment of older boys. The national army does not permit civilians to participate in the unit, a move that would offer better protection for children's rights.

The national army eventually releases the prisoners to a rehabilitation center. Aware of this protocol for processing rescued
child slaves, parents regularly visit the World Vision camps desperate to find their abducted children. Their happiness may turn
to distress when they see sons and daughters without limbs or
daughters holding their own babies.

Most of the child slaves already know the name World Vision.
To dissuade their ranks from attempting an escape, LRA commanders (mis)inform them that World Vision will feed them
poison or give them potatoes laced with shards of glass.

To ease the fears of new arrivals, the World Vision staff organizes a welcome celebration. When they walk into the camp, the
freed child soldiers encounter a sea of open arms ready to give
them an embrace. Often they find old friends, also rescued from
the LRA, singing and dancing.

Immediately after the welcome party, a World Vision health
care professional assesses the health of each child. Some children
manifest serious injuries and require medical attention in a hospital. Nearly all are malnourished and suffer from scabies, worms,
and damaged feet.

As the days pass and newly freed slaves become more comfortable in their new surroundings, they enter into rehabilitative
counseling. The majority of children do not want to talk at first.
To help them express painful memories, counselors at the camp
will use drama, dance, song, and art. Most kids will draw the
odious acts they participated in before they will talk about them.

Margaret—Becoming a Child Soldier

Until she turned eleven, Margaret could join the boys in military
training. They learned how to assemble an automatic weapon
and then take it apart; how to hold a gun, aim it, and shoulder
its kickback. The commanders also taught them battle tactics and

the art of retreat. Slowly but surely, the abducted children evolved into child soldiers.

The LRA uses the adult men they capture, on the other hand, as pack mules. The adults carry large weapons, the tents used by commanders, and other weighty items. How these porters could shoulder their burden day in and day out never ceased to amaze Margaret.

Early one morning, one of the porters made a break for it. The night security team had returned to camp and was focused on grabbing a bit of breakfast. The porter crawled for nearly the length of a football field, then jumped to his feet and sprinted. A child soldier who was out collecting twigs for the morning fire saw the man running and sounded an alert.

The sleepy camp transformed into a whirl of commotion. As commanders barked out orders, waves of child soldiers scampered out of the camp in pursuit. One of the girls—whom Margaret recognized from her school—took advantage of the chaos to bolt in the opposite direction.

Neither the porter nor the girl enjoyed more than ten minutes of freedom. The child soldiers quickly tracked them down and dragged them back to camp.

A slave "could commit no greater crime than betrayal," a senior commander announced. Several junior commanders then commenced to pierce the porter in the buttocks with their bayonets. They treated it like a game; the man's yelps only enhanced the entertainment. Several sharp kicks flipped the man over, and the young men sliced off the man's penis. Finally, apparently tired of his squealing, one of the soldiers brought his bayonet down hard into the man's chest.

The torture shifted next to the girl. The young commanders stabbed her breasts repeatedly. As they prepared to expand the scope of their torture, the senior officer stopped them. "She must be punished by one of her own," he declared with authority.

He scanned the newly abducted girls and selected two to approach him. Then, as if an idea had just popped into his head, he looked directly at Margaret, saying, "You, come here. I trust you have learned a few lessons from your own beating."

He ordered boy soldiers to lend their clubs to his handpicked assassins. At first, the girls aimed blows at their victim's body, but it only prolonged her suffering. So one by one they crashed their clubs down on the girl's skull until she breathed no more.

Florence Lacor—The Burning Ritual

Within hours of their arrival, just freed from the LRA, Florence gives the children a set of new clothes. She gathers the clothes they arrived in—along with knapsacks, bandanas, hats, and anything else they wore as soldiers in the LRA—and stores them away for safekeeping. Often the children "won" the old clothes off a body they had killed. Surprisingly, they show some reluctance to give up these clothes to Florence. They had meager belongings in the bush, so these clothes had turned into a "security blanket" of sorts.

About once a month Florence presides over a very symbolic ritual. She gathers the children into a circle and places into the center a bundle. She asks the children if they recognize anything in the pile. One by one, they yell out recognition of a personal item that had been part of their uniform in captivity.

Florence instructs them that they do not have to be bound to the past. "No one had the right to force you to do so many awful things," she shares with compassion. "And now that you are free, you can make choices that will lead you on a different path."

After finishing this short homily, she asks one of the young girls to pour kerosene over the pile. She hands a set of matches to the young boys, who gleefully set the clothes on fire.

Charles—The Controller Ritual

Supreme commander Kony took away their fears. Shortly after their abduction, Charles and the other new recruits were taken to Kony's camp. He prayed over them and performed a ritual involving the oil that comes from the shea nut.

"When you cover yourself with this oil, the bullets of the enemy cannot pierce your body," he said. As he smeared on the oil, he added, "My spirit now is part of your spirit, and I know all of your thoughts. If during a battle you consider escape, or your thoughts turn to your family at home, my spirit will no longer protect you, and you will be killed by our enemies."

Kony also revealed to the children that they had been chosen for a special purpose to purify Uganda and usher in a new kingdom. God had cursed Museveni and his troops; it was only a matter of time before they would fall. "We are fighting to bring peace to the Acholi people," he declared, a slogan that Charles would hear often during his captivity.

Mystical rites and spells infused almost every aspect of rebel activity. Charles was placed under the charge of a "Controller." The Controller took his "spiritual children" to the river and poured a solution of water and leafy herbs over their heads. As he did so, he prayed that the children "would be cleansed of impure thoughts of disobedience."

SUDAN AND THE UGANDAN CONFLICT

Sudan. The same government that foments war in Darfur has played a heavy hand in the conflict in northern Uganda.

The LRA agreed to help the Sudanese government fight its civil war against the Sudan People's Liberation Army (SPLA) in exchange for a steady supply of weapons and food. By the mid-1990s, the Ugandan national army had improved its capacity to track down rebel forces. The LRA was constantly on the run in the Ugandan countryside, so it decided to move its base into southern Sudan.

Sudan's involvement in the Ugandan conflict made the war more relevant to western nations in some respects. The most significant shift occurred after September 11, 2001, when the United States stepped up its campaign against terrorism. President George W. Bush declared the LRA "a terrorist organization." Pressed to demonstrate that it did not support terrorism, the Sudanese government claimed that it had cut off supplies to the LRA. If that did in fact happen, the weapons and food started flowing again in 2002 after the LRA helped Sudan take over the strategically important town of Torit from the SPLA.

Also in 2002, Ugandan President Museveni unleashed a major offensive against LRA bases located in southern Sudan. Code-named Operation Iron Fist, the national army geared up to completely wipe out the LRA. Instead, the campaign stirred up a hornet's nest.

The Ugandan army's attack on LRA bases in Sudan became so intense that the rebels divided into small operational units and infiltrated back into northern Uganda. Over the next eighteen months, the LRA abducted ten thousand children and wreaked havoc on the civilian population. It was not until the end of 2004 that the national army regained some semblance of military control in Uganda, and LRA bands trickled back into southern Sudan.

Then, in August 2006, the Ugandan government and the LRA signed a truce to the war. Under the terms of the truce, the rebels would leave their bases throughout Sudan and the Congo and establish bases at two sites in southern Sudan. The government of southern Sudan has pledged to the LRA its protection, and the Ugandan government promises that it will not attack the rebels.

The International Criminal Court (ICC) further complicated the political situation in Uganda, however, when it issued warrants for the arrest of the LRA leadership. The court would make Kony and his top four commanders liable for war crimes. Some political bodies argue that ICC indictments need to be kept in place in order for justice to be done. Others argue that they deny LRA leaders any incentive for giving up their fight and only prolong the war.

Joseph Kony says that he will not surrender as long as he and his top commanders risk prosecution by the ICC. The rebel chief also has refused to release captive child soldiers and sex slaves.

Margaret—The LRA "Wife"

Once she turned eleven, Margaret could no longer join the boys in combat. "It's time for you to become a wife," a senior commander informed her.

She had no precise idea what it meant to be a wife. Observing the older girls, she supposed it involved doing a commander's cooking and laundry.

The next day she was given to Michael, a twenty-year-old commander who had served in the LRA for almost nine years. He already had one "wife," and she gave Margaret a brief orientation to her domestic duties.

That first evening, Michael told his first wife, "Leave and don't come back for an hour." He then ordered Margaret to come into the tent. As soon as she entered, he grabbed her by the back of the neck and pulled up her shirt. Margaret squirmed away from his hold, stumbled backward, and ran out of the tent. He did not pursue her, so she stayed out in the bush and slept on the ground that night.

In the morning, she returned cautiously to the tent. Michael's first wife, who was busy washing pans, did not look up from her chores. Margaret sat down next to her and picked up a dirty pan. Neither spoke.

Margaret was relieved that she could not see Michael's boots outside the tent. He must have departed already, she thought.

A few hours later, a senior commander strolled into their campsite and told Margaret that she "had need of instruction."

"Michael has taken a group of boys to check out rumors of enemy movements on the other side of the river," he began. "I do not expect him to return until tomorrow evening."

Margaret shook her head dutifully, but inside she felt a wave of joy—one more day of reprieve had just been granted to her.

"Michael told me what happened last night," the man continued. "Your behavior was unacceptable; no one refuses sex to an LRA commander."

He spoke this last sentence with such force that Margaret dared not give any response other than a nod. "You will do anything that pleases your husband," he declared. "Do I make myself clear?"

Though Margaret offered another nod, the officer did not leave the door open for further rebellion. "You will not eat again until you have slept with your husband," he said. "If I hear you have violated my order, your punishment will be worse than you can imagine."

Margaret went hungry for the rest of that day and the day that followed. On the evening of Michael's return, she entered his tent, and without any words being exchanged, he raped her.

She quickly came to understand what "wife" meant in the LRA. For the next six years, she was a slave to Michael's every whim.

Florence Lacor—A Community of Survivors

Seventy-five young women performed a traditional dance in the main courtyard of the World Vision center. Each woman had in her hand a ceremonial wood hatchet, and they moved their feet and hands in collectively coordinated motion. At the front of the formation, two women squatted low on their haunches and fervently banged drums with the base of their palms.

Florence stood in the middle between the two drummers, her body swaying back and forth slightly. Though she is of average height, at that moment she looked eight feet tall. She periodically yelled out an Acholi word, and the women changed the direction of their stance. Slowly and in rhythm, Florence shuffled to the front of the new configuration.

The dance continued in this fashion for about an hour. Their endurance was astounding, especially given that the temperature boiled to well over 100 degrees and the dusty courtyard offered zero shade.

The young women performing the dance have "graduated" from the center and now live an independent life in Gulu. They return one day a week for assistance with food, clothing, and emotional support. Activities like the dance remind the women that they are not alone. They belong to a spiritual clan of survivors.

The women are sixteen to twenty-four years old, and maybe 80 percent carry an infant or have a toddler running around their feet. At one time these young women were sex slaves to the senior commanders of the LRA.

The LRA educates males to view women as creatures that exist to serve their pleasures. When women do not submit to the authority of the men, they are handled violently.

The testimony of one ex-slave dramatically illustrated this dynamic. She witnessed Joseph Kony order the death of two young commanders simply because they showed too much kindness to their concubines. The supreme commander declared that their "poor example" would be a cancer that would destroy "natural relations" in the camp. Following the execution of the two commanders, Kony redistributed their property (their concubines) to "more worthy" officers.

The rebels assert that sex is a man's right, and they practice neither birth control nor protected sex. As might be expected, most girls in the LRA face pregnancy at some point. The commanders do worry about contracting HIV, which makes enslaving young virgin girls all the more appealing.

At the World Vision camp, the women receive education about HIV/AIDS and safe sex. All the same, many women refuse HIV testing. Revealing to anyone that you have contracted the virus is simply not done in rural Uganda. The women would feel far too much shame to admit it.

Young mothers stay in Gulu because they find it very difficult to reintegrate into their home communities. The stigma of being defiled—a victim of constant rape—carries enough shame. The assumption that the absent father is a commander of the hated LRA adds to a young woman's isolation. When ex-sex slaves do meet a man who expresses romantic interest, the potential suitor fears that an LRA commander will one day return to claim his "wife."

Florence does not sugarcoat the rough road these women have to navigate after liberation. She reports that as many as one-third of the young women will return to the father of her children—yes, the very LRA commander who raped and enslaved her—once he has been captured and granted amnesty. These women would rather live with the devil they know then confront alone the twin demons of poverty and social isolation.

The LRA commanders in turn are apt to consider the sex slaves their rightful property. One captured commander arrived at the World Vision camp and demanded to be reunited with three of his "wives" who had taken up residence there. When the women said they would have nothing to do with their tormentor, he became belligerent. Florence had a hard time getting him to understand that abduction does not translate into ownership.

Charles—The Young Corporal

Murder and pillage replaced reading and arithmetic in Charles's life. He learned how to shoot a gun, follow military commands, scout enemy movements, and obliterate a civilian target.

Raids on defenseless villages had two priorities: bringing back food and kidnapping new child recruits. When the rebels approached the village, they stretched out in a long line to prevent any civilian from escaping. Returning to camp without food would be the only failure that would give a child soldier cause for trepidation. The murder and mayhem that accompanied the attack merely came with the territory. Charles and his companions became killers without a conscience.

It was hunger and thirst that preoccupied Charles. Even after a successful village looting, the commanders reserved for themselves the bulk of the food. They would apportion a single serving to a group of twelve child soldiers. The kids sat in a circle and took turns taking a bite. Anyone who took more than his fair share got tossed out of the group and missed the rest of that meal.

The scarcity of water made for even more desperate straits. At least in Uganda, the rebels could find running streams. In Sudan, Charles would sometimes go three days on a single gulp of water. On more than a few occasions, the child soldiers had to drink their own urine. The weakest literally died of thirst in the Sudanese desert.

Over time LRA commanders began to take note of Charles's prowess as a soldier. When he was only thirteen years old, a senior officer rewarded him for "strong leadership in the field" and promoted him to the rank of corporal. Charles began leading raids on smaller villages. He could even select the boys whom he wanted to accompany him.

Whenever high-ranking commanders spent the night in a camp, the rebels enacted a sophisticated defense. The child soldiers dug trenches in concentric rings around an inner circle where the commanders' tent had been pitched. The newest abductees slept in open-air trenches in the outer rings, while those boys with longer service positioned themselves in the inner rings. Following his promotion to corporal, Charles moved to an inner ring. On occasion, he even joined the security detail for chief commander Kony.

It filled him with pride to be leading boys far more senior in age. He even had authority over the porters; it did take a while to get used to ordering adult men around. The day would come, he was confident, when he would become a commander and be given wives to cook his meals and wash his clothes.

As Charles saw it, you stayed weak and got beaten, or you became strong and did the beating. He knew which path he planned to take.

Idan Lagum Lumoro—
Breaking the Slave Mentality

Sadly, the constant physical and psychological abuse that the LRA uses against child slaves yields results. Most current LRA commanders were once abducted boys in whom a devotion to Joseph Kony was nurtured.

After their capture and release to a World Vision camp, the LRA officers usually attempt to reestablish a chain of command and order younger boys and girls to perform chores for them. Likewise, when they meet women at the camp who had once served as their concubines, the ex-commanders expect the relationship to continue.

Hence in 2003, World Vision created a separate rehabilitation camp for young men who had reached eighteen years old. Idan Lagum Lumoro serves as its director. Not many individuals could be called "a force of nature," but Idan merits the title. She does not ask for respect; she commands it. Placing Idan in charge of these young men who have been trained to disrespect women was an ingenious choice.

Idan's role surpasses administrative tasks. She holds a weekly counseling session with each ex-child soldier. In these sessions, she walks a tightrope between compassion and accountability. The LRA abducted these young men as boys and rewarded them for brutality. They cannot be blamed for that legacy. But if they do not accept responsibility for their behavior in the camp, Idan delivers a stiff rebuke. "The past happened to you," she instructs, "but you happen now."

In early June 2006, Idan gathered all the residents at the center to discuss the prospects for ending the war. To appreciate their comments, four factors have to be kept in mind: (1) most had emerged from the LRA within the previous two months; (2) most had spent over five years in captivity; (3) most had become ranking officers; and (4) most believe Kony has a vast spiritual power and if they speak poorly of him, he will know and will punish them.

"Slave mentality" is an inability to think outside of the box into which an individual has been forcibly packed. After years of strict LRA discipline, it was hard for any of these young men to escape their indoctrination.

One young man expressed his conviction that only Kony can interpret God's plan for Uganda. Others blamed President Museveni for prolonging the conflict; on each occasion that Kony agreed to peace talks, Museveni violated the cease-fire and attempted to destroy the rebel movement. All wholeheartedly agreed that Kony would never accept unconditional surrender or subject himself to judicial prosecution. Because "Museveni cannot be trusted," the young men indicated that only international intervention could resolve the conflict.

The slave mentality was also apparent when the discussion turned to their own experiences in the LRA. Yes, it was horrible to be ripped away from their family at a tender age. Yes, they lament the travesties they were forced to commit against their own people. But if given the chance, many admitted that they would return to the LRA. At least they felt they belonged in the rebel world. Now they feel like a lost piece of a puzzle. They fit nowhere.

Margaret—Playing the Numbers

Michael continued to find favor with the senior officers. They gave him two additional wives. To own a total of four girls, as he did, enhanced a commander's status significantly in the LRA.

Margaret privately celebrated Michael's advancement in the ranks for her own reasons. With four concubines to choose from, Michael called her into the tent at night far less often. And though he treated all his wives cruelly, he vented his aggression on one girl at a time. The sheer weight of numbers worked in Margaret's favor.

Her chores increased once the older wives in Michael's harem started to bear children. All the girls shared the responsibility for child rearing. While it was always difficult to shift camps every couple of days, doing so with toddlers became much more complicated.

For nearly a year Margaret's rebel detachment had settled in southern Sudan. Beyond occasional skirmishes with the SPLA guerrillas, life passed without too much drama. Thirst and hunger became their principal enemies. They could pass two days without a meal. They chewed on leaves and dry cassava in an attempt to satisfy their grumbling stomachs.

Hunger at times drove Margaret's detachment to desperate measures. They would ambush vehicles—on one occasion they scored a crate of beans by surprising an SPLA truck on a road near the border. They became so desperately hungry at one point that they attempted to raid a heavily armed Sudanese village. Many child soldiers were killed, and the raid yielded no bounty.

Then the Ugandan national army unleashed Operation Iron Fist, and Margaret's detachment infiltrated back into northern Uganda. For the next two years, her band was constantly on the move. The commanders kept their wives and children close by their side. They were paranoid that the girls would try to escape otherwise, and they were right.

Margaret did try to escape once during a raid on a village. Michael had tasked her to loot the homes during the attack. When she entered the first home, she found a young woman in her twenties cowering in the corner. Acting spontaneously, Margaret told the woman that she would not be harmed if she would help her escape. The grateful woman hid Margaret under a blanket on the floor and anxiously waited out the raid. For nearly fifteen minutes they heard no noises in the vicinity of the hut, and they thought they were home free.

Their illusion was shattered when Michael and two child soldiers burst into the hut. They came on a mission, and they soon found what they were looking for hidden under a blanket. Michael pulled Margaret up with such force that she thought her arms would tear off. He shoved her roughly out the door of the hut. She could hear the woman inside the hut scream as the boys hacked her to death with their machetes.

Once they returned to their camp, Michael beat Margaret within an inch of her life. It would be the last time she would try to escape.

THE RUINS OF WAR

Childhood slavery should give the international community sufficient cause to intervene and put an end to the war in northern Uganda. The effect of the war on the entire population reinforces the moral obligation to do so without delay.

According to the United Nations, over 1.7 million people—roughly 85 percent of the population of northern Uganda—have been driven from their homes and today live in camps for internally displaced persons (IDPs). Children account for over half the residents in these IDP camps.[4]

The Pabbo camp, located just outside of Gulu, is home to more than sixty thousand displaced persons, making it one of the largest IDP camps in all of East Africa. At Pabbo, a single source for drinking water exists for every fifteen thousand people. People wait in a line the length of four city blocks just to get fresh water.

The huts at Pabbo are stacked extremely close together, which makes it a ticking time bomb. These dire social conditions yield high rates of epidemic illness and AIDS. Of more immediate concern, a fire in one hut spreads to the others like wildfire. In early 2004, a fire at this IDP camp destroyed three thousand homes.[5]

The elected leaders of the Pabbo camp do the best they can to cope with a hopeless situation. But until the LRA and the Ugandan government reach a settlement, they admit that little can be done to alleviate misery at the camp. "We have almost forgotten what it feels like to be human," remarked the camp's senior leader.

Charles—Burying the Rifle

Once Charles became a corporal, more opportunities to escape presented themselves. He and his fellow combatants were often separated in the middle of a battle. The commanders taught them how to regroup once the fighting ended. It would have been just as easy, however, to walk the other way.

Charles had lots of reasons to feel cautious about attempting an escape. The commanders had warned repeatedly that the national army slices captured child soldiers up into small pieces. At times boys had disappeared, and they were never heard of again.

Even if he were willing to risk those consequences, Charles did not know where he would go. Before his abduction, he had not known a life beyond his home—and because he had participated in the murder of two men from his village, he could not go back there. He would be an alien no matter where he landed. So he stayed and endured his misery.

Then one afternoon, at age fourteen, he just snapped. The faces of those whom he had killed—above all the civilians who were defenseless—flashed before his eyes. He wanted to erase the acts, to return to the innocent village boy he once had been. Yes, he would go back. Maybe his old neighbors would kill him, but at least they would give him a decent burial. As it stood, if he died in an armed conflict, only the vultures would value his bones.

Charles hid his knapsack in the brush, slung his rifle over his shoulder, and walked briskly away from the rebel camp. He kept moving until nightfall and then laid down for a rest under the open sky. Rain came down in heavy sheets throughout the night. He made no effort to find shelter, but let the cleansing water pour over him and bless his journey.

At dawn the rain clouds passed, and he resumed walking. He did not encounter a soul in the bush until about midday. He heard the high-pitched voices of women off the path ahead. Hiding carefully behind some brush, he crawled forward to assess the danger. He saw three women bringing their hoes down hard on a patch of garden.

Aware that he might frighten them, Charles buried his rifle and sauntered out into the open casually. The women greeted him warmly though they could not hide their puzzled expressions. Why would an unfamiliar young boy be out here in a remote region all alone? He did not prolong the mystery.

"Could you take me to one of your village leaders?" he asked politely. "I have escaped the LRA, and I want to turn myself in."

At the very mention of the LRA, terror struck the women. "I don't know how we could help you," one of them spoke up, her voice shaking.

"I don't want to hurt anyone," Charles said, reassuring her. "I want to put an end to it."

"OK, I will take you to my husband," the woman said. "Maybe he will know what to do."

Charles jogged back to the brush and uncovered his rifle. Throwing it back over his shoulder, he returned to the spot where the woman waited. Though the sight of the gun made her all the more nervous, she forged ahead.

They found her husband digging a well on the outer edge of a circle of huts. Alarmed to see an armed child walking behind his wife, his grip on the shovel tightened. A shovel may not be the best weapon, but at least the boy appeared to be alone.

His wife quickly defused the tension, explaining to him Charles's mission. The man narrowed his eyes and gave Charles a long look while he pondered the best course of action.

"Well, before we go anywhere, you need to get rid of that gun," the man said matter-of-factly. "Just about anyone who gets a glance at you carrying that rifle will run the other way, and the ones who don't run . . . well, who knows what they are apt to do."

Though he was reluctant to part with the rifle, Charles agreed to hand it over. The man received it, then immediately threw it down behind a pile of dirt that he had spent the morning building.

"Alright, I think it's best to take you to the head of our village council," he said. "He lives no more than ten minutes' walk from here."

Now that it was clear in his mind what he needed to do, the man moved swiftly to a narrow path that ran past the huts. Charles practically needed to run to keep pace.

They did not get far. After having traveled no more than a quarter mile, they met two national army soldiers on patrol coming the other way. The man let Charles offer his own surrender.

The soldiers did not speak much as they led him back to their local garrison. Charles had braced himself for torture, so he did not expect joviality. But once they arrived at the army base, a senior officer extended him a warm welcome. "Congratulations on having the courage to leave the ranks of the LRA," he said, shaking Charles's hand.

Charles spent two days at the garrison, mostly sleeping on a cot and voraciously eating all the food put before him. On the third day, an army truck transported him to the regional garrison in Gulu.

Once there, he spent another couple of days answering a battery of questions about LRA activities. As the intelligence officer wrapped up a final series of questions, he mentioned that Charles would be transferred the next day to the World Vision facility.

He knew that name. LRA commanders often told the child soldiers about the wicked spells that World Vision placed on captured rebels. The spirits to whom they pray can infect a child with AIDS, they warned.

Despite his apprehension, Charles's transfer to the World Vision camp turned out to be the happiest day of his life. When he entered the gates, a cadre of boys and girls met him with hugs and slaps on the back. Many he recognized from the LRA; he had assumed they had died in battle. After the hearty greeting, a

boy flipped on a music box, and everyone broke into spontaneous dance. The party was on.

Four years of brutality cannot be danced away magically, unfortunately. For the first few months at the rehabilitation center,
Charles had recurring nightmares of the killings he had done.

He spent hours pouring his heart out to Florence. "Every day
you watch people around you die, and death loses its grip on
you," he shared after many sessions with her. "My Controller
told me to climb above my feelings; whether I murdered another
or was killed myself, it was always the will of God."

"No," Florence responded, "it is the will of God that you
should know love, and it is only love that will set you free."

Idan Lagum Lumoro—Tough Forgiveness

How can the cycle of terror in Uganda ever come to an end?
Idan Lagum Lumoro works hard to address that challenge. She
reaches out to the communities out of which the kids have been
abducted and against which many have committed atrocities.

She first has to reconcile current events to traditional tribal
law. When a murder is committed in the tribal culture, it is a violation against a particular family and an entire clan. A restitution
must be paid for the death. If that restitution is not fulfilled, then
a murderous revenge will be sought against the clan of the killer.

Idan reasons with tribal leaders that it would be impossible
in Uganda today to balance the score with traditional restitution. Murder has ruled for decades, and every clan could find a
just cause for seeking vengeance. She points them instead to
the tribal reconciliation tradition of *mataput,* which literally
means "drinking a bitter root from a common cup." To avoid
bloodshed, tribal chieftains might bring warring enemies together to put aside their grievances, share a meal, and drink
from the bitter cup.

Idan has received support from several tribal leaders. "In our culture, we don't like to punish people," says Collins Opoka, a chief in the Acholi tribe. "It doesn't really get you anywhere."[6]

To illustrate the complexity of reconciliation, Idan refers to the experience of Mary, a Ugandan woman who had her nose, lips, and ears sliced off, a signature torture of the LRA. The rebels use the macabre practice to intimidate the civilian population, a visible threat to those who might share information with the national army about rebel movements.

Mary was tilling soil in a communal garden alongside five other women when a small band of rebels arrived at her village. Mary was eight months pregnant at the time.

A young rebel commander led three boy soldiers to the garden and ordered the women to sit on the ground. He then raised a walkie-talkie to his mouth and delivered a report to his superior on what he had discovered in the village. A voice came back over the walkie-talkie instructing him to assign a boy to guard the women while he took the rest of the soldiers on a raid of the village.

After completing the looting, the commander escorted his band back to the garden. He relieved the boy assigned to guard duty and prepared to depart the village. As the rebels reached the edge of the village, Mary saw the young commander lift the walkie-talkie to his ear. To her horror, she watched the boys retrace their steps back to the garden and viciously hack away at her friends with machetes. They killed all five of the women, but they did not touch Mary. The commander told the boys to spare the life of "the pregnant one."

"We will use her as a sign," he said, and then added, "To kill her might bring us bad luck." Two boys held her down while a third boy sliced up her face.

Several months later, when Mary came to the World Vision center for medical aid, she was horrified to encounter the young commander who had ordered her torture. He had been wounded and captured in a battle with the national army. He, too, now received World Vision's help. Mary wanted justice and complained to Idan: "No help should go to this criminal!"

In his own defense, the ex-commander claimed that he was following the orders of his superior officer to kill all the women. "But I showed mercy by not having this pregnant woman killed," he argued.

The husband of one of the women murdered in the garden massacre confirmed the ex-commander's story. The husband was taken captive in the raid and tied up at the feet of the senior officer. He heard the senior officer order the execution of all the women over his walkie-talkie.

Regardless, one can imagine how difficult it would be for Mary to forgive the young ex-commander. On the office wall at World Vision hangs a picture of Idan leading a "reconciliation ceremony." On one side of Idan sits Mary, and on the other sits the ex-commander, and all three hold hands in a sign of peace.

A year has passed since the ceremony, and Idan admits that Mary still harbors some bitter feelings toward the ex-commander. *Mataput* never tastes sweet. But Mary has dropped all her demands for tribal vengeance. That is a huge leap toward reconciliation in traditional tribal culture.

Nearly every child abducted into the LRA has been forced to participate in some kind of atrocity. For example, the twelve-year-old child soldier who wielded the machete on Mary's face also resided at the World Vision camp when Mary arrived. She did not recognize the boy, however, and the child did not share the truth of his role in the event. Only after he had left the camp and had been reunited with his family did he share his secret with Idan.

Idan urges every child soldier who comes to World Vision's camps—victims and torturers alike—to reach a place of forgiveness.

It's an extraordinary mountain to climb, but Idan believes that Ugandans have no alternative if they are going to have a future: "Only in unity can we rebuild our land with peace and development. If we do not forgive, our communities will explode."

Margaret—An Army Rescue

After five years of rape, the biological lottery caught up with Margaret. At the age of sixteen, she became pregnant.

Her rebel unit had recently returned to southern Sudan. She was grateful at least that they would settle in one camp for a while. Morning sickness does not go well with a nomadic existence.

Early one morning when she was more than seven months into her pregnancy, rebel advance scouts breathlessly ran into the camp. They had observed Ugandan national troops moving rapidly in their direction. The soldiers would reach their camp in half an hour, the scouts predicted.

The commanding officer ordered preparations for a swift retreat. Just as he finished his command, she heard the first mortar hit. It was followed by a second blast no more than twenty-five yards from where she stood.

Michael appeared from nowhere and yelled for his wives to leave their belongings and start running. He then sprinted off, clearly demonstrating that he would not be waiting around to help them.

LRA commanders had spoken of the terrible things that would happen if national army troops captured them. Soldiers with AIDS would rape the girls, the LRA commanders warned. A pregnant girl had even more to fear. Soldiers would cut open her stomach and tear out the fetus. Due to her advanced pregnancy Margaret could not move very fast, but she did her best.

A mortar exploded fifteen yards in front of her and put an end to her retreat. A fragment flew into her knee, and she dropped immediately to the ground. Her one attempt to lift up her weight proved fruitless, so she lay still, hoping that the onrushing soldiers would overlook her.

Five minutes later a soldier detected Margaret lying injured on the ground and took her into custody. Two soldiers carried her on a stretcher to a heavily fortified army position no more than a twenty minutes' walk. Another young LRA girl, perhaps two years younger than Margaret, was already sitting on the ground holding a baby when they arrived.

The prisoners were in for a pleasant surprise. At midafternoon, the soldiers brought them a full plate of hot food and as much water as they could drink—two luxuries that they had not enjoyed for years. A medic attended to Margaret's knee, extracting the embedded shrapnel and pouring a red solution over the wound.

The prisoners were then brought one at a time to speak with three men dressed in crisp uniforms. "You are older than the other girl," they said to Margaret. "You have a responsibility to tell us everything you know."

And that's exactly what Margaret did. She divulged everything she knew about where the LRA stashed weapons and how many senior commanders resided in her camp. She also told them what little she knew about Kony's whereabouts—she had heard the other commanders mention that he had moved his camp to the Congo.

The army officers seemed pleased with her information and told her not to be afraid for her life. They transferred her to the army garrison in Gulu the next day. Following a second session of questioning to see if she could recall any additional intelligence, they released her into the care of World Vision.

Florence Lacor met her at the front gate and greeted her with a big embrace. "My sister, you have made it to freedom," she told Margaret with a beaming smile. "The road to reclaiming your life is not as long as you think."

A month later, Margaret gave birth to a strapping son. She named him Daniel, for he had been rescued from the mouths of lions.

"THESE CHILDREN NEED FUTURES"

Ending the enslavement of child soldiers around the globe will require abolitionists to adopt a broad range of strategic initiatives and skill sets.

Agencies like Noah's Ark are needed to create safe environments that reduce the likelihood that vulnerable children will be abducted into slavery. Heroic individuals like Florence Lacor and Idan Lagum Lumoro of World Vision are needed to provide material aid and emotional support to slaves who find their way to freedom. And though it may not sound as romantic, we sorely need individuals and organizations that will focus on advocacy and public policy.

In April 2006, World Vision played an instrumental role in persuading members of the U.S. House of Representatives to hold a public hearing on child soldiers in Uganda.

On that occasion, Grace Grall Akallo, an ex-slave, gave her personal testimony. Grace was one of the renowned abductees from Saint Mary's College in Aboke town. She told the House subcommittee, "Unfortunately, my story ... has become so common that abduction is now a fear that daily defines the lives of children who live in the war-affected areas."[7]

Responding to her testimony, Rep. Diane Watson asked Grace, "Do you feel they'll ever be normal again? You've learned to use a gun to kill. And I'm wondering how we could really impact on that?"

Grace told the congressional representatives exactly what the children of northern Uganda long for: "These children need love. These children need peace. These children need concrete futures. A matter of counseling a child for only six months doesn't help. ... [We need you to] mobilize the international community ... to protect children and to end the conflict."

Undermining the Sex Syndicate: Europe

San Foca, a fishing village situated at the tip of the boot of southern Italy, seduces you with its charm. The azure waters of the Adriatic Sea perfectly offset the grayish white rocks that dot its shores. In the late afternoon, boats bob lazily in San Foca's harbor while fishermen meticulously mend their nets. Off in the distance—just beyond eyesight—lies the dramatic Albanian coastline and the port town of Vlorë.

Though it may be a romantic vista, it marks one of the most trafficked routes in the modern sex slave trade. Late each night Albanian mafiosi rev up their motorized rafts and transport refugees across the forty-four nautical miles that stretch between Vlorë and San Foca.

Some of their passengers pay smugglers a hefty price to chase their dreams for a more prosperous life in the West. Many on-board, however, do not choose to make this trip. Crime syndicates in Europe maneuver through an intricate patchwork of routes to move girls across international borders. Originally created to smuggle drugs and weapons, today these routes serve to move human cargo as well.

The "Balkan Trail" has emerged as the most notorious of these smuggling routes. Each year thousands of young girls from eastern Europe are forcibly trafficked along this channel to brothels all over the globe. A victim typically originates from a country that was once part of the Soviet Bloc. From her home country, she will be transported through Romania to Serbia, Montenegro, or Croatia, then to Albania, and on into Italy. The final destination for the victim will likely be the European Union, though a significant number of girls will be trafficked to the United States, the Middle East, or the Asia Pacific.

On the streets of Bangkok, Thailand, one sees evidence of just how far these trafficking routes extend. As soon as night falls, a flood of blonde girls wearing miniskirts and heavy makeup ambulates the Muslim quarter. It's a bizarre scene to watch these eastern European women weave along the sidewalks amid a sea of Muslim women wholly covered in black burkas. The Muslim men, meanwhile, don white pants, white shirts, and white hats—the white is meant to represent purity of intention and action. The fact that sexual exploitation can brazenly thrive in such contradiction to a people's deep religious values indicates the immense challenge abolitionists face in their campaign to end sex slavery.

Cesare Lo Deserto—The Crossroads of Poverty and Wealth

An unlikely abolitionist, Padre Cesare Lo Deserto has emerged as a formidable obstacle for the crime syndicates that run the Balkan Trail. A Roman Catholic priest and veteran of work with the poor in Brazil and Rwanda, Padre Cesare established a shelter for refugees in the town of San Foca in 1995.

Born and raised in the south of Italy, Padre Cesare walks where angels fear to tread. Yet he's not exactly an Indiana Jones–type figure. A heavy-set, balding man in his midforties, he could pass as a parish priest in a sleepy village. Nonetheless, he deploys every bit of intellect and guile to navigate the turbulent waters of sex trafficking.

Regina Pacis—"queen of peace"—is the name Padre Cesare gave to his shelter in San Foca. The name stands as a symbol against the violence and greed that tears young women from their homes. He created the shelter to accommodate a maximum of 250 people, but the need quickly outpaced the space. At its peak in the late 1990s, more than six hundred refugees crammed into its rooms and hallways each night.

In its early phase, the refugees who reached Regina Pacis ran the gamut—extended families, single mothers, teens, and even young children traveling alone. Around 1999, however, Padre Cesare detected a shifting trend in his demographic. A wave of young girls from eastern Europe showed up at his door seeking aid and protection. At the same time, he noticed a dramatic rise in the number of Slavic girls selling their bodies on the streets of San Foca and the nearby coastal towns of Lecce and Brindisi. The girls he encountered shared horrific personal testimonies of abduction, rape, and commercial exploitation.

Padre Cesare dedicated a wing of Regina Pacis to cater to the plight of trafficked women. Little by little, he tracked the trail of the traffickers back to eastern Europe. As he explains, geography gave him a unique vantage point to understand the mechanisms of the modern slave trade: "San Foca is the destination where the poverty and wealth of the world collide."

Nadia—The Offer

Saying good-bye to Stefan turned out to be harder than Nadia had imagined. At the tender age of six, Stefan could not comprehend why his mother had to leave.

"Mommy, are you mad at me?" he asked when she came into the room with her suitcase in hand. The words cut her like a knife.

"No, Mommy's not abandoning you. She loves you," she whispered through sobs. "I'll make some money, and then I'll be back home." She moved hastily to the door before she fell apart completely.

Initially, Nadia did not seriously entertain Katrina's offer to arrange a restaurant job for her in Italy. Nadia knew plenty of girls who had left Chisinau to work in the West. But she did not know how she could manage Stefan on her own in a foreign land. At least here in Moldova, her family could take care of him whenever she found the odd bit of work.

But she had a change of heart the day she failed to get Stefan enrolled in school. Nadia could not afford to pay the school's enrollment fees or buy a school uniform. Her family could not help her. They had no savings; every penny went to put food on the table.

Following that depressing day at the school office, she sought out Katrina at the café. The two had met long ago in grammar school. Though they had never been the best of friends, they continued to bump into each other at the occasional party. When they last met, Katrina had mentioned that she had a connection in Italy who gave jobs to teenage girls. "Let me know if you are ever interested."

She found Katrina exactly where she hoped, at the corner table of the café. Following a bit of small talk, Nadia moved the conversation to her agenda. "Hey, remember you told me about jobs in Italy? If they're still available, I'm interested."

"You bet," said Katrina, pleased to help out her friend. "I just talked with my contacts, and a few more jobs just opened up. But they need to fill the positions really fast. Do you think you could be ready to travel a week from tomorrow?"

Now faced with the moment of truth, Nadia had to swallow hard. Could she bear to live apart from Stefan? Maybe she could make enough money in a year's time to come back home with a bit of savings in her pocket. "OK, count me in," she blurted out.

"Fabulous," Katrina said, beaming. "We'll have such a good time together in Italy."

She told Nadia to arrive at her flat in eight days' time with her bags packed, ready to travel.

Cesare Lo Deserto—Answering the Call

Set on the grounds of a former summer camp, the Regina Pacis facility could be mistaken for a high-security prison. High chain-link fences crowned with barbed wire circle its rectangular, block building. The few windows that do grace the building are covered in iron bars. Only the front entrance conveys the slightest hint of invitation. The security measures have proven necessary; on occasion, traffickers come to Regina Pacis expecting to reclaim their "property."

Each girl who comes to the shelter can relate a unique tale of how she was trafficked. The most fortunate girls escape on the trip across the Adriatic to Italy. The Italian coast guard monitors smuggling operations and from time to time intercepts a boat full of immigrants. Albanian traffickers will go to any lengths to avoid capture, however. When hotly pursued, they've been known to throw young children overboard, forcing the coast guard to give up the chase in order to rescue the kids from drowning.

Padre Cesare encourages trafficked girls to press criminal charges against their abductors. Under Italian law, individuals who have been forced to migrate and agree to testify against their exploiter can gain legal status to stay in Italy and work. The law does not treat trafficked individuals as criminals but as victims of a crime. It is a significant piece of legislation—similar to the T-visa program in the United States—that ought to be emulated in countries around the globe.

Most of the girls, nevertheless, fear going to the police. The mafiosi threaten to kill them or harm their families if they testify against members of the syndicate. Moreover, police officers back in eastern Europe may have played some role in their abduction. A trafficked girl therefore does not easily place her trust in the police.

Padre Cesare does not minimize the danger of pursuing legal action, but he stresses that the traffickers will ruin the lives of other innocent girls if they are not stopped. A spontaneous reading of the text messages on Padre Cesare's cell phone suggests why he feels such a burden to take down the traffickers. A sixteen-year-old girl from Romania writes, "Please help me! Only a dog would be treated in this world like I am. Only you can help me!"

Another message comes in from a girl living in Moldova: "I'm dying here! Help me! You're my final hope!" Her plea arrives without details.

A Bulgarian girl who reports being enslaved in a massage parlor in Milan sends a third text message: "Padre! I am one of four girls stuck in this pit of hell. We plan to escape soon. I hope you will take us in."

After reading these text messages aloud, Padre Cesare shakes his head sadly and remarks, "I am praying for a new generation of abolitionists who will open up their hearts. Traffickers get away with murder because good people won't answer the calls of these young women crying out for help."

THE PERFECT TRAP

The collapse of the Soviet Union in 1991 did not deliver the lofty benefits that many of its freed republics envisaged. The early intoxication of self-government and individual liberty gave way to depression once economic realities hit home. The liberalization of the financial markets had promised to open a porthole for new investment. Instead, the reforms turned into convenient escape hatches for a massive flight of capital.

Life under the communist regime was no bed of roses, of course. But at least jobs—however menial—could be found, and few people starved. While a small elite amassed wealth at an astounding rate in the 1990s, the masses faced skyrocketing unemployment and disappearing social services. Under this pressure, families struggled to stay intact. The dramatic rise in alcoholism among men did not make that task any easier. Orphanages sprang up across the region to support abandoned children.

The disintegration of Moscow's iron rule left a power vacuum in its former republics. Organized crime quickly moved in to seize ripe opportunities. Often the criminals turned out to be former communist officials who used their powerful connections for personal enrichment. A new breed of crooked capitalists who held no scruples about their business transactions also arose. The rule of law became a sham, for sale to the highest bidder.

Almost immediately in the post-Soviet era, mafiosi turned a huge profit selling guns and drugs. It did not take the syndicates long to realize that their republics had another gold mine worth exploiting: educated, healthy young women who suddenly found themselves destitute.

Women got hit with the brunt of unemployment after the fall of the Iron Curtain. In the Ukraine, for instance, females comprised 80 percent of the population who lost jobs in the 1990s.[1] Unemployment rates for women ranged between 70 and 80 percent in most of the former Soviet republics. Yet despite the difficulty of finding a job, women were often expected to shoulder responsibility for the survival of their family.

Human traffickers had the ideal candidates to trade in the global sex market and the perfect ruse to recruit them. Eastern European youths have grown up with a fascination for the West. They watch its movies, listen to its music, and crave its consumer luxuries. To be offered a job and an apartment in western Europe would be a dream come true for many young people.

Even the threat of danger would not dissuade them. By the end of the 1990s, sordid tales started leaking back home about what happened to girls who migrated to the West. Despite these red flags, golden dreams of emigration persist. A study conducted in the Ukraine in the late 1990s revealed that three out of four girls between the ages of ten and nineteen expressed a strong desire to work abroad.[2] Some girls fall for the glamour of a luxurious lifestyle, while others hope to become the financial savior of their family. Whatever the allure, traffickers use it for their deception.

Nadia—The Judas Kiss

When she arrived at Katrina's flat, Nadia was surprised to find six additional girls with baggage waiting there. She had assumed that she and Katrina would be traveling alone.

Katrina did not bother to explain the circumstances. After a brief greeting, she asked Nadia in business-like fashion, "OK, you brought your passport along, right?"

Nadia nodded her head, dug the document out of her purse, and held it up.

"Great," Katrina said. "Let me have it, and I'll give it to the guide for safekeeping."

Once Nadia handed it over, Katrina scurried off to speak with a middle-aged man who paced across the flat. They had a short conversation while the man's eyes fixed on Nadia. He handed Katrina what appeared to be a roll of money.

Uncomfortable with the man's glare, Nadia turned her attention to the other girls. She noted at once that she had at least five or six years on them; none of them had yet reached eighteen, she guessed.

One of the girls wandered over to Nadia and, with a hint of anxiety in her voice, asked, "Do you know where we're going?"

"Katrina found me a job working in a restaurant in Italy," Nadia reported as a matter of fact.

"Oh, she told us that too," the girl said. "But I was wondering whether you knew exactly where in Italy we would be traveling?"

Before Nadia could answer, the man whom Katrina had presented as "the guide" spoke up. "We will be leaving in a few seconds." He paused and then proceeded with instructions. "Outside we have three vehicles waiting. I will assign you to one of the cars. Don't worry which one you end up in because we're all going to the same place."

Katrina picked up her suitcase and led the way out the door of the flat. Nadia followed and climbed into the backseat of her assigned vehicle. She settled down next to a girl whom she had not yet met. The driver started the engine once the lead car lurched onto the road.

The three cars moved along as a caravan for several hours. Nadia did not speak a word. She passed the time thinking about Stefan. In a panic she second-guessed herself. Shouldn't she be at home raising her son? Who cares if she can't afford all the things that she wanted for him? But what kind of future would he have without an education? With the droning wheels of the car sounding the backbeat, her internal debate rapped on for some time.

As they neared the border with Romania, the caravan came to a sudden halt. It seemed to Nadia as if they were in the middle of nowhere. After ten minutes, she could see three pairs of headlights approach slowly from the other direction. The cars stopped directly across the road from where they were parked. Nadia saw "the guide" swagger over to them and speak into the window of the first car. He then returned to her vehicle and opened the back door.

"Grab your bags, girls," he ordered. "You're shifting cars for the next leg of the journey."

Once Nadia had moved to her newly assigned seat, she peered out the window. Across the road she could see Katrina sitting in the backseat of one of the cars that the girls had just departed. The first whiff of trouble reached Nadia's senses. Why wasn't Katrina coming along with them?

Nadia rolled down her window and waved her arms to get Katrina's attention. Having failed at that, she yelled out her friend's name. Katrina did not flinch, keeping her gaze dead ahead.

A minute later the caravan was driving across the border into Romania.

TRAFFICKING ORPHANS

Orphanages have become one of the few (legal) growth industries in eastern Europe over the past two decades. The collapse of the family led to massive numbers of abandoned children with nowhere to turn.

Imagine the impact of emigration on the family in a country like Moldova, where an estimated one in four people emigrated between 1991 and 2002.[3] It is not uncommon for parents to leave their children behind when they leave the country. Other children lose parents to alcoholism, death, or outright destitution.

Despite the proliferation of orphanages, the need is still greater. Nearly every orphanage in eastern Europe overflows its capacity and has a line of kids waiting to get in. To deal with overcapacity, the orphanages usually force the older children to leave once they reach the age of seventeen. Few of these kids have savings or vocational training that might lead to a job. Quick to identify their vulnerability, sex slave recruiters view these children as ripe pickings.

Recruiters have started pursuing children who live inside the orphanages as well. Sadly, the recruiters find willing collaborators inside the orphanages who will betray children at the right price. Human-rights groups report that orphans in the region are sold and trafficked internationally for use in child pornography rings. For instance, in its 2003 report card on human trafficking, the U.S. State Department exposed orphanage directors in Moldova for selling background information on children to traffickers and in some cases arranging their abduction. The report details similar travesties in Romania, where "many orphanages are complicit in letting girls fall victim to trafficking networks."[4]

Cesare Lo Deserto—Infectious Compassion

Like many of San Foca's residents, Enzo can attest to the legend of Padre Cesare. Enzo operates one of the most vibrant sidewalk cafés in the village. On warm summer nights in August—when the whole of Italy seems to be on holiday—the plaza in front of Enzo's café fills with people looking to enjoy musical entertainment and a cold drink. The girls who wait on the tables might speak Romanian or Russian or Moldovan. They were trafficked to San Foca for another kind of labor, but Padre Cesare rescued them.

Enzo relates that one blustery winter day he had gone over to Regina Pacis to lend a hand preparing meals for the refugees. Several young boys burst into the shelter yelling frantically that they had witnessed a small boat capsize not far off the shore. Enzo threw on his coat and reached the shelter's front door at the same moment as Padre Cesare. They jumped into Enzo's car and rushed to the location where the boys indicated they had last seen the boat.

Glancing out at the sea as they drove along, Enzo shuddered. In the off-season—when tourism dies down in San Foca—he works as a fisherman. He knows the sea all too well; once a swell kicks up, the angry waves can easily consume a small craft.

Enzo parked the car off the road, and he and Padre Cesare ran along the beach in opposite directions. A gale blew sheets of rain horizontally, making it difficult to see.

Five minutes of searching yielded nothing. Enzo began to fear that the anonymous passengers might be lost at sea. Suddenly he heard a high-pitched cry over the sound of the crashing waves. At first he mistook the noise for a howling wind, but after a pause he distinguished a baby's wail.

Turning in all directions, he detected movement along the base of the cliffs. He motioned to Padre Cesare far down the beach and then ran for the rocks. He found twenty-five Iraqi refugees of all ages—elderly men and women, young mothers, children, and three babies—huddled in a crevice cut into the cliffs, trying to find shelter from the wind and rain.

Enzo stood motionless ten feet away from the refugees, unable to speak their language and unsure what action to take next. The Iraqis stared back at him equally confused, fretting over whether Enzo might be a friend or a foe.

Padre Cesare broke the stalemate, sprinting past Enzo to approach the huddled mass. Throwing off his coat, he wrapped it tightly around the young children. The priest addressed the Iraqis in Italian; though they did not understand a word of what he was saying, the compassion in his voice expressed his intention. He pointed up the beach and started walking. The Iraqis followed him as one.

A caravan of vehicles from Regina Pacis pulled up just as the ragged assembly reached the road. The refugees piled in and were given safe haven at Regina Pacis.

"It was just another day in the life of Padre Cesare," says Enzo, reflecting on the event, "but for me it became a special memory to cherish."

Behind the bar at his café, Enzo keeps pinned to the wall a photo of Padre Cesare with his arms around two of Enzo's children. The priest is practically a patron saint of the establishment. Enzo honors Padre Cesare's example of embracing the foreigner by providing jobs to trafficked girls.

Padre Cesare has touched many lives in San Foca and has inspired them to acts of extraordinary kindness. Young women who escaped sex slavery work at local restaurants, fruit shops, and bakeries. They have married locals and are raising children. "Padre Cesare's girls"—as they are sometimes called in the village—do not walk the streets in shame.

Nadia—The Border Crossing

The caravan of cars traveled for several hours across Romania before pulling up behind an old country house. Though Nadia could see the lights of a small village in the distance, she had no clue where they had stopped.

The drivers barked out orders to move swiftly into the house. They ushered the girls into a dimly lit room and locked the door behind them. Three young Romanian girls sitting on dingy sofas already inhabited the room. They stood up expectantly when the door opened, but dejectedly slid back down onto the chairs once they heard the click of the lock.

"Can you tell me where we are?" Nadia asked.

"I really couldn't tell you," replied a blue-eyed girl of exceptional beauty.

"How long have you been here?" Nadia charged on, hungry for information.

"Oh, I'd say two weeks," the blue-eyed girl replied, "but to be honest, it's hard to keep track."

"Two weeks!" Nadia exclaimed. "Has anyone explained to you what's going on?"

"They're having trouble securing tourist visas for us," the Romanian reported.

That's the only explanation Nadia ever received about their incarceration. A man brought them simple meals twice a day but would not let them step outside the room.

"Why are you keeping us here?" Nadia yelled each time the man entered with the food tray. He invariably grunted that she should "shut up" and departed.

After seven days in confinement, a well-dressed man entered the room, trailed by three scary-looking goons. "Good news," the elegant man announced. "We have your travel visas. So we're off to Serbia!"

Almost as an afterthought, he said, "From there we'll put you on a bus that will take you to Italy. Your new employers have secured apartments for you there, so you can start earning money right away."

The rosy announcement lifted Nadia's spirits for the first time since she had left Chisinau. The goons led the girls outside the house, where two white vans waited. The girls stepped up into the vans and immediately hit the road.

For the rest of the day the vans negotiated narrow mountain roads that cut across desolate wilderness. Late in the evening, the vans veered off the road into a sheltered cove of trees. The goons ordered the girls out of the vehicles.

The elegant man then shared a part of the travel plan that he had conveniently omitted that afternoon. "Girls, we have visas for you to work in Italy, but we failed in our attempts to obtain tourist visas for you to enter Serbia. So you are going to have to sneak across the border under the cover of darkness."

The girls unleashed a cacophony of complaints and queries. The elegant man brusquely cut them off. "I'm sorry. It's the only way we can get you to the bus that will transport you to Italy."

Cars would be waiting for them on the other side of the border, he explained. The drivers would blink their lights three times every two minutes until they all arrived. He went on to warn that if captured going across the border, the girls would be thrown into prison, maybe for years. "And trust me," he said, lowering his voice ominously, "you do not want to serve time in a Serbian prison."

The men guided the girls for nearly half a mile until they reached a clearing. They rested until they could see lights flashing amid a line of trees on a ridge in the far distance.

"There, that's it," the elegant man said, pointing his finger. "Go now, and don't stop running until you reach that ridge."

TRAFFICKING AND GLOBALIZATION

Sex trafficking simultaneously exploits both the best and the worst aspects of globalization. The champions of globalization tout the growing ease of conducting business across national borders. Sophisticated communication tools and relaxed banking laws make it possible to exchange assets internationally with ease. Virtual enterprises can operate everywhere and nowhere, making themselves known only when and where they choose.

Organized crime syndicates take advantage of these tools to create more efficient overseas networks. Although most trafficking originates with local operators, they deftly connect to an international sex industry looking to fill slots in brothels, massage parlors, strip joints, and lap dance bars.

A club owner in Chicago can pick up the phone and "mail-order" three beautiful young girls from eastern Europe. Two weeks later a fresh shipment of three Slavic girls will be dancing in his club. Though a number of quasi-independent traffickers were likely involved in moving the girls, the operation would appear seamless to the Chicago client.

The critics of globalization point out that capital flows wherever it can most easily exploit cheap labor. The owners of capital will abandon a specific location quickly once one of two conditions occurs: (1) the assets it exploits are depleted, or (2) those assets can be obtained more cheaply in other markets.

Sex trafficking also manifests itself in this form. Over the past three decades, the prime area for recruiting sex slaves has shifted rapidly from one zone of economic depression to another. In the 1970s, traffickers targeted girls from Southeast Asia—above all Thailand and Vietnam—as well as the Philippines. After ten years or so of mining in Asia, traffickers shifted their focus to Africa— girls from Nigeria, Uganda, and Ghana flooded the international sex bazaars. In the mid-1980s and spilling over into the early 1990s, Latin American girls from Brazil, Mexico, the Dominican Republic, and Central America (especially El Salvador and Guatemala) became the favored pool.

Traffickers move opportunistically to prey on vulnerable populations. In the 1980s, the trafficking of girls out of eastern Europe hardly registered on the radar screen. Following the economic and political collapse of the Soviet Union, that situation changed dramatically. The International Organization for Migration (IOM) estimates that roughly a quarter of a million females were trafficked within Europe alone—from East to West—since 1991.[5]

Even within eastern Europe, the prime recruitment zones for trafficking shift rapidly to exploit opportunities. In 1992, the vast majority of trafficked victims came from Poland, Romania, Hungary, and Czechoslovakia. By the mid-1990s girls in those markets had been depleted, so traffickers started targeting Russia, Ukraine, Bulgaria, and Moldova. After the turn of the century, the prime recruitment zone shifted to central Asia—Uzbekistan, Kazakhstan, and Kyrgyzstan—and Georgia.

Wherever the greatest profit can be extracted, there the traffickers move. In an impassioned speech delivered in Brussels, European commissioner Anna Diamantopoulou aptly characterized the "ruthless efficiency" of these modern-day traders in human property:

> They know their business inside out and respond to changes in the market with a speed unmatched by even the most competitive corporations. Their expertise and ability to exploit the market are surpassed only by their disregard for human life. Women are bought, sold and hired out like any other product. The bottom line is profit.[6]

Nadia—The Livestock Market

The girls started off across the border in a sprint. The elegant man had not mentioned how hard it would be to cross the terrain. Unable to see their own feet, they repeatedly tripped over sharp rocks and brambles armed with pointy thorns. By the time they reached the ridge, most of the girls had lost at least one shoe. All had deep cuts and bruises up and down their legs. Nonetheless, they managed to track the flashing lights and reached the destination with their entire band intact.

Now safely in Serbia, they piled into three cars and wove their way through a seemingly endless succession of mountain passes. They finally came to a remote stone house that seemed to be planted in the middle of a forest.

Upon entering the house, the girls once again merged with more trafficked victims. A dozen girls, also battered and bloodied, sat on the floor in the entry foyer, leaning their exhausted bodies against the walls.

The woman in charge—who appeared to be in her early thirties and blessed with gorgeous blonde locks—spoke in flawless Russian to the assembly gathered in the foyer. She seemed genuinely concerned with their condition and instructed her staff to bring hot, wet towels so that the girls could clean their cuts.

The Russian woman then divided the girls into groups of five or six and assigned them to an upstairs bedroom. As it was now well past midnight, she urged the girls to get some sleep. "You need your rest because you have a big day tomorrow," she remarked cryptically.

The depleted girls slept to nearly noon the next day. Caretakers woke them up with loaves of bread, butter and jam, and steeping hot tea. It had been a couple of days since they had eaten a scrap of food, so Nadia and her roommates devoured the bread.

After their meal, the girls lay back down on their mattresses and shared details of their escapades. The Romanian girl with the deep blue eyes, whom Nadia had met at their last stop, was a roommate. Two girls told of their journey together from the Ukraine, and the fifth girl told of her trek from Bulgaria. Like Nadia, they had all been promised jobs in Italy.

The woman with the golden locks opened the door and interrupted their peaceful interlude. "OK, girls, I need you to perform well for me," she sang out. "Downstairs in the parlor an important group of men is waiting to evaluate you. We'll go down together as a team, and before we enter you will take off your shirts."

At first Nadia thought she must have misunderstood her Russian hostess. "Sorry, but what do you want us to do?" she asked, trying her best to stay calm.

"Undress to your waist, with your breasts bare," the woman said as casually as if she had asked them to kick off their shoes and walk in with bare feet.

"You must be joking!" Nadia said incredulously.

"Don't worry. Nothing will happen to you," the woman said in an effort to reassure her. "It's just a check. Your employers in Italy have sent these men to ensure that you are healthy."

Noting their puzzled expression, she added, "Sometimes re-cruiters beat their cargo, and the girls are unable to work. We just need to prove to them that you are in good shape."

Despite her misgivings, Nadia went along with the pageant. Her group descended the stairs and halted at the double doors leading into the parlor. They then shed their shirts while the Russian woman clucked, "Alright, alright, that's it, that's it. We're ready. Let's go."

Passing through the doors, the girls spotted a dozen or so men seated in a circle around the four walls. The Russian woman asked the girls to stand apart from the pack one at a time, an-nounce their names, and rotate slowly in a full circle. The men eyed them carefully as if they were examining livestock at the county fair.

Once this humiliating exercise ended, the girls returned up-stairs to their bedrooms and rested. Within the hour, the Russian woman swept into the room and called out Nadia's name and that of the blue-eyed Romanian. "You two will be leaving with your courier in five minutes," she stated curtly.

The two girls hurriedly arranged their bags, wished their roommates good luck, and scampered downstairs. A slight-framed man with black, greasy hair awaited them at the foot of the stairs.

"You work for me," the man said in halting Russian. "You go with me now."

He led them out the front door to where a car stood idling. He directed the girls to the backseat and addressed the driver in a language that Nadia guessed must be Serbian.

They drove in silence for a couple of hours until they reached Belgrade. Their "courier" delivered them to an apartment lo-cated in a residential district. "You wait me here," he instructed them in his broken Russian. "I be back in few minutes."

Half an hour later, the girls heard the apartment door open. It was the courier, accompanied by two portly men, both of whom sported soiled brown leather jackets. The men eyed the girls lustily as they spoke to each other in a thick Serbian dialect. Once they appeared to reach an agreement of some sort, the courier grunted, "OK, you work now."

"What do you mean?" asked a befuddled Nadia.

"You cost me much money," he replied angrily. "You give good sex to these men."

Both girls took several steps backward, and Nadia spoke strongly: "No way! You have the wrong idea about us!" Desperately searching for a way out of this mess, she offered an alternative. "We will work very hard for you in a restaurant, but we cannot do this kind of work."

The Serbian man had no patience for negotiation. He reached inside the right side of his jacket and pulled out a flat instrument. Nadia could not make out what he was holding until she saw the blade flick out from its shell. He deftly grabbed her by the hair and pressed the blade against her throat.

"You show men good time, or I cut throat," he threatened.

Shaking with fear, the girls went into separate bedrooms, where the portly men raped them.

Over the next month, this script was played out countless times. Four simple words—"You go work now"—transported Nadia into a living hell.

THE RUSSIAN MOB

Illicit activity as pervasive and lucrative as sex trafficking in eastern Europe could not happen without the machinery of organized crime. The structure of those syndicates and how they work remain somewhat of a mystery. The criminals work hard to stay clandestine.

It's clear that the Russian mafia has its stamp on practically every facet of the sex trafficking trade in eastern Europe. Its home base within Russia is massive, linking thousands of organizations, including otherwise legitimate businesses. And the mob's influence goes far beyond the region: Russian organized crime is thought to control sex trafficking in Israel and much of western Europe and has a strong presence in the United States, Canada, and Southeast Asia.

The Russian mafia's greatest strength might be its ability to forge profitable alliances. For instance, it coordinates closely with autonomous syndicates in both Albania and Italy to transport girls into western Europe. For the Russian syndicates to build their own smuggling operation in these two countries—along with a protection racket of paid police and government officials—would be far too costly. Instead, the Russian mob outsources the costs of "product distribution." Each link in the chain earns its share of the revenues, realizing that they can do far more commerce working together than they could operating alone. The Russian mafia can therefore decentralize its operations while remaining the puppet master.

The Russian syndicate also has a reputation for the ruthless use of violence when it feels threatened or betrayed. Add that intimidation factor to its effective, clandestine networks, and they become a daunting foe for abolitionists in eastern Europe.

Cesare Lo Deserto—The Danger Zone

Wherever Padre Cesare goes, an armed bodyguard hovers nearby. He does not request such protection. The Italian government unilaterally decided to give him around-the-clock protection whenever he works inside the country. By order of the president of Moldova, he receives the same security measures when he flies into Chisinau.

Their concerns for his safety do not arise from an irrational paranoia. More than a few mafiosi would like to see Padre Cesare six feet under. His commitment to undermine sex trafficking has become costly to their operations.

Early in 2001, two thugs paid Padre Cesare a visit to deliver a warning—or possibly to take more serious action. After dinner, the priest had elected to take a walk on the beach that lies in front of the Regina Pacis property. The mafiosi, who took no pains to hide their identity with masks, were awaiting him on the beach. They calmly suggested that he accompany them to a grove of trees just off the beach. One of the men had a gun tucked into his belt, openly displayed. Under the circumstances, Padre Cesare could not refuse their suggestion.

Once they reached the woods, the thugs turned more menacing. "Padre, you are in deep trouble. Our boss wants you to know how much he dislikes having his property stolen."

Padre Cesare put up a crafty defense: "Gentlemen, you know that I would never take anything that rightfully belongs to another!"

"Don't play coy with us, Padre," one of the men replied in perfect Italian. "If you take one more of our girls off the streets, you will not live to tell the tale."

By this time, the security guards who watch Regina Pacis had grown worried. Padre Cesare had been absent from the compound longer than usual on one of his evening strolls. The guards frantically dispatched a makeshift search party. Their yells for the missing priest sent the thugs scurrying away, and he escaped harm.

Padre Cesare relates the story as if he might be recounting the plot of a film that he had watched at the theater. Asked how he can treat this threat so lightly, he replies, "There's nothing these men can do to me that could compare to the suffering that trafficked girls undergo."

Unable to scare Padre Cesare off his mission, the mafiosi have more recently tried to tarnish his reputation. A few young girls—who were former residents of Regina Pacis—have made formal accusations against him. They presented themselves to the court as "victims of psychological abuse," charging that Padre Cesare runs the shelter like a prison and tries to control every movement of their lives. How ironic—the rescuer charged as an abductor.

The staff who work at Regina Pacis staunchly defend Padre Cesare and are convinced that mafia chiefs coerced the girls to bring charges. Before a judge's careful questioning, one of the supposed victims recanted her entire testimony, according to the staff.

Padre Cesare, on the other hand, does not care to expend energy defending himself. When asked directly about the accusations, he gives one of his characteristic shrugs and remarks, "I can tell you that I am neither a saint nor a criminal, but beyond that I will let my work speak for itself."

LEGAL EFFORTS TO CURB TRAFFICKING

For more than a century, sex trafficking has been a concern of international leaders. In 1904 twelve nations, including the United States, ratified a treaty called the International Agreement for the Suppression of the White Slave Trade. Responding to the widespread abduction of girls for the purposes of sexual exploitation in Europe and Asia, this agreement urged governments to prohibit "procuration of women and girls for immoral purposes abroad."

After World War I, the League of Nations adopted a broad-reaching document against slavery that essentially affirmed the 1904 treaty but added children to the agenda. The League also replaced the term "white slave trade" with the term that enjoys currency today: "trafficking in women and children."

Then, in 1949, the United Nations General Assembly set out to establish a legal framework to stop the traffic. Known formally as the Convention for the Suppression of the Traffic in Persons and of the Exploitation of the Prostitution of Others, it declared that the enslavement of women and children for the purposes of sexual exploitation was incompatible with fundamental human rights. It called on governments to adopt procedures for punishing any person who sexually exploits another individual or who runs a commercial enterprise that profits from such activity.

Under the terms of the convention, the consensual contract between two individuals would be honored as a matter of free choice. All the same, the convention deemed prostitution to be unfitting the dignity of a human being and encouraged nations to offer public education and material assistance to persuade individuals not to sell their bodies for sex.

Unfortunately, the convention was ratified by fewer than half of the member states of the United Nations (72 out of a total of 185). Today, nearly half a century later, its translation into policy yields widely divergent legal strategies.

The United States took a very narrow interpretation of the convention. All of the states except Nevada criminalize prostitution and make all parties liable for prosecution—prostitutes, customers, traffickers, and commercial exploiters. In actual application, the U.S. public justice system has addressed the supply side of the equation (prostitutes and brothel owners) much more aggressively than the demand side (johns).

Rather than seek to prohibit sexual commerce, western European nations make a more concerted effort to regulate it. The best policies for accomplishing that goal, and their consequences for sex trafficking, are matters of heated debate.

The Netherlands, for example, has historically maintained an open tolerance for the commercial sale of sex. In October 2000 it went a step farther and officially legalized prostitution. The German government followed suit two months later.

The lawmakers of these nations were persuaded that exploitation thrives in environments of illegality. If prostitution will always be with us—and lawmakers in Germany and the Netherlands presume that to be the case—then criminalizing it will create a black market where the mob underworld makes the rules. The fact that 70 percent of prostitution in the United States is linked to organized crime would seem to support that argument.[7]

In Germany and the Netherlands, sex workers are offered legal protection from commercial exploitation and receive social service benefits. But these laws do not apply to individuals who are not residents of the European Union. To the chagrin of lawmakers, a booming underground sex trade has emerged in both countries. A 2003 survey found that foreign-born women make up 65 percent of the sex market in the Netherlands and 50 percent of the market in Germany.[8]

Most abolitionists vehemently argue that legalizing prostitution engenders a broader social acceptance of brothels for sexual entertainment. That kind of cultural environment, in turn, leads to a greater demand for young girls that will be filled by sex traffickers. Ongoing research should be able to determine whether prohibition or legalization does spawn higher levels of sex trafficking into a country.

At the very least, the legalization of the sex trade makes the prosecution of traffickers, pimps, and brothel owners almost impossible. They can use the defense that the girl consented to work as a prostitute, and the burden of proof will be on the girl to prove otherwise. If at any point the girl actually did consent to work as a prostitute, all subsequent forms of coercion will find legal cover.

Sweden has moved in a unique direction. In 1999 the Swedish government became the first in the world to prosecute the buyer of sex, the john, while legally treating the woman as a victim. The Swedish government also established a comprehensive outreach program that encourages sex workers to change their livelihood.

The maximum sentence in Sweden for a convicted john is six months in prison. In the first five years following passage of the law, about 750 men had been charged, and two-thirds were sentenced. As a result, street prostitution in Sweden has dropped dramatically, as has the influx of trafficked women.[9]

"What differentiates us from the Netherlands and Germany ... is that we link the 'slave trade' with prostitution and pornography," explains Marianne Eriksson, a Swedish member of the European Parliament and a strong proponent of her country's legal strategy on sex trafficking. "Everyone in the European Union is against human trafficking, of course," she clarifies, "but we know that 90 percent of this commerce has to do with sexual exploitation."[10]

Nadia—Passage Through Hell

Just when Nadia concluded that she would never get out of Serbia, the Russian woman with the golden locks turned up in her life again.

"Oh, look at you two. These Serbs are real pigs," the woman remarked as she reached out and caressed the face of the Romanian girl. "Let's get out of here," she added. "Looks like you both could use a hot meal."

Though Nadia had been deceived once before by this woman's faux compassion, she could not help herself from appreciating any warmth that might come her way.

"It's taken a while, but I finally got you visas to work in Italy," she announced once they settled into some seats at a nearby restaurant. "Soon you will be working a normal job in a café in Rome."

She held open Nadia's passport and showed her an official stamp as proof. "Now you'll be protected if the police in Italy ask you for documents. You'll leave in two more days."

From that point forward, Nadia counted the minutes until her departure. The Serb continued to bring a steady flow of paying customers to the apartment. She did not understand the business arrangement the Serb had with the Russian woman, and she feared him too much to ask. But Nadia mouthed a quiet curse on the apartment two days later when she walked out the door for the final time.

Two burly Russian men transported Nadia, along with the blue-eyed Romanian and three young girls from the Ukraine. They stopped in Montenegro for a few days at a place that the Russians called a "safe house."

On the evening of the third day, they left the safe house and drove to the edge of a very large lake. The driver stopped the vehicle but left the headlights beaming out on the water. Before long, a small rubber dinghy appeared in the headlights. The Russians ushered the girls to the lake's edge and instructed them to jump into the boat.

Nadia asked one of her burly escorts if the boat would be taking them to Italy. "No, first you will go to Albania," the man replied. Her heart sank. She wondered whether her trek would ever end. The Russians left the girls in the care of the Albanian pilot.

As soon as they moved away from the shore, he throttled the motor at full bore for well over an hour. He spoke Russian fairly well and tried to strike up a conversation with a few of the girls.

None of them felt chatty, though, and they kept their contributions brief.

Eventually they could see a cluster of lights off in the distance. The Albanian indicated that their destination lay just beyond the lights, and then he unexpectedly cut the motor. Nadia initially thought the engine had run out of gas.

"Now I'm going to choose one of you to screw," he said bluntly. "If my selection refuses to cooperate, I will drown all of you right here. I don't give a damn."

The girls exchanged frightened glances. "I can't swim," one of the girls from Kiev said in a small voice. One by one, the girls admitted to being completely helpless in these deep waters.

"OK, let's give this bastard what he wants," the Romanian girl said in a resigned voice. Saying this, she instinctively grabbed Nadia's hand, and Nadia did the same to the girl next to her, and so on, until the five were all linked together.

They braced themselves for the selection. The pilot squinted his eyes as he scanned the circle, and then he pointed at Nadia: "You come here."

Nadia looked at her companions with dread.

"Please, go on," the Kiev girl pleaded. "Don't be ashamed. You'll be doing it for us."

Nadia stood up in the raft and moved toward the pilot. He undressed her and then raped her in front of the other girls. After he finished, he declared, "You were really good. If you didn't perform well, I was going to drown you and your friends." He let out a loud laugh and restarted the engine.

When they floated toward Albanian soil fifteen minutes later, an unexpected welcoming party awaited them. All of the men standing on the shore hoisted machine guns. Nadia was even more surprised that some of the men wore uniforms. Her concern heightened once she lifted her eyes to the road above the beach and saw "POLICE" written on the side panels of two vehicles. How ironic. After getting so close to Italy, it looked as if she would end up languishing in an Albanian prison.

The police took the girls into custody and drove them in their squad cars to the city of Shkodra. But they never reached a police station. The officers brought them to a private home, and before departing each took a turn raping the girl of his choice.

POLICE CORRUPTION

Why don't the police in eastern Europe do something about sex trafficking?

Some do—by opening border crossings for traffickers, by shielding them from arrest at the hands of their more conscientious colleagues, by issuing licenses so that the traffickers can operate as a legitimate business, and by capturing girls who escape and returning them to their "owners." In sum, trafficking syndicates depend heavily on the police to sustain their operations.

Corruption makes a mockery of the concept of public justice in the former Soviet states. The vast majority of girls who were trafficked along the Balkan Trail report encountering at least one police officer who abetted their abductors. In some instances the girls testify that the police raped them—and did not feel the need to hide their identity while doing so.

The strategic location of Albania for the transit of young girls from East to West has been well documented. A country report on Albania by the U.S. Bureau of Democracy, Human Rights, and Labor confirms that police are "often directly or indirectly involved" in these operations. The report goes on to critique the public body charged with oversight of the police, the Albanian Ministry of Public Order. Despite strong evidence of police complicity in high-profile trafficking cases, the ministry failed to take any punitive action against officers. Whenever a law enforcement group in Albania does muster the courage to confront the traffickers, "local police often tip off the traffickers when raids are scheduled."[11]

Imagine how powerless it must feel to be the target of a crime and have nowhere to turn for justice. Police officers and government officials more than look the other way when a crime occurs: they are apt to be active participants. Citizens in eastern Europe cannot trust public officials and are unlikely to file a complaint against a bogus agency that has abducted one of their family members. This is especially true for girls already involved in the sex trade: the police treat them as if they deserve whatever maltreatment comes their way.

The complicity of law enforcement authorities in sex trafficking is not peculiar to eastern Europe; it is a worldwide phenomenon. Given the public nature of the industry, it must be so. Narcotics and weapons can be smuggled and sold in a clandestine fashion. The sex trade, however, must be transparent to those who ultimately pay for the freight. It stands to reason, then, that if the johns can find the illicit "product"—openly marketed on a street corner or in a published advertisement—so could law enforcement authorities. The fact that they do nothing to fight sex trafficking demonstrates an apathy to the problem, an ignorance of its prevalence, or a financial stake in its continuation.

All the same, abolitionists will need the help of the police to stem the rising tide of sex trafficking. If the police in eastern Europe—or anywhere else in the world—are written off wholesale as the criminal element, the antislavery campaign will never gain traction. The poor and vulnerable cannot stand alone and survive the onslaught of potent criminals who deploy whatever means are necessary to maximize their profits. Abolitionists must build alliances with honest police officers and support their efforts to establish a credible presence locally.

Cesare Lo Deserto—Moving Upstream

Padre Cesare operates like a sage environmentalist who finds poisoned fish at the end of a stream. As concerned as the environmentalist might be for the ill fish, he would go upstream and eliminate the source that pollutes the waters.

In that token, Padre Cesare realized that by the time trafficked girls arrived in San Foca seeking safe haven, most had already been incorporated into the commercial sex trade. So he followed the trafficking trail back to eastern Europe and tackled the problem at its font. "I could no longer accept our position; essentially, we were waiting for girls to become victims," he says.

In 2003, he began winding down his refugee service and reformulated the core mission of Regina Pacis. A number of factors contributed to his decision. The war in the Balkans had reached a peaceful resolution, and the gush of refugees from that region had slowed to a mere trickle. A more stable political situation in Afghanistan also cut the flow of refugees. Given these developments, Padre Cesare could focus his attention more exclusively on sex trafficking. From a shelter that had become Italy's largest refugee-processing center, Regina Pacis morphed into an international abolitionist network.

Regina Pacis still operates a modest lodging program in San Foca. The staff aims to find stable solutions so that trafficked girls do not fall into dependence. After an initial period of recovery, girls are ideally placed with a healthy foster family. Foreigners get help sorting out their immigration status with the government: trafficking victims have rarely kept possession of their passports. The girls may learn a new vocation. If they already possess special skills, the staff helps them find a job that provides a sense of dignity and self-determination.

These days, one is more likely to find Padre Cesare in eastern Europe. He has established Regina Pacis centers in Moldova and Romania to carry out a broad range of antislavery activities.

Regina Pacis promotes a compelling billboard campaign to girls in eastern Europe: "Your dignity is in your hands. Take care of it!" It does not, however, put the onus on young girls to resist the slave trade alone. "We address three main enemies in sex trafficking," Padre Cesare explains. "First, poverty; second, the john who drives demand; and finally, the trafficker. We create programs that reduce the influence that these enemies can have on the lives of young girls."

Poverty is the most pervasive and invisible "enemy" of the three and therefore the most difficult to fight. In Moldova, for instance, over half of the population struggles below a subsistence-level income, and only one in four people hold what could be considered a steady job. Though the entire population of the country is less than five million, nearly ten thousand girls between the ages of fifteen and twenty-two emigrate each year without any formal guarantee of school or work.[12]

During one of his first visits to Moldova, Padre Cesare met a thirteen-year-old girl who had accepted a "job offer" in Rome. She was the oldest of three daughters in a destitute family. The girl shared with him stories of how her father beat her mother when she asked him for money to buy milk or bread. She also told him how it tore her insides apart to watch her younger sister fall seriously ill. The girl was determined to earn money to buy her medicines.

She saw a billboard in Chisinau advertising job openings for "teenage models." When she went to the audition and participated in a photo shoot, the recruiter told her, "You would be perfect for an advertising campaign in Italy." He gave her a small cash advance and told her, "There is much more to be made once you go to Rome."

Regina Pacis has launched an education program in the schools in Moldova to warn children of exactly this kind of predatory offer. Padre Cesare fortunately met this girl at her school before she departed on her "modeling adventure." He investigated the agency and discovered, as he suspected, that it was a front for a trafficking syndicate. He intervened and saved the girl from a terrible fate. "The girl looked for a radical solution to her family's crisis because she did not have any other options," he explains.

Regina Pacis places prominent billboard ads in Romania and Moldova as another tactic to warn girls and their families that criminals use false promises to lure potential recruits. Its staff scours daily newspapers for suspicious ads announcing overseas jobs. Once they identify a front, they expose it as publicly as possible.

Padre Cesare can attest to the large numbers of girls that these collective efforts have saved. Nonetheless, he admits that poverty all too often holds the upper hand. A girl struggling for her family's survival may suspend her better judgment and assume higher risks. "Prevention. Yes, that's a major goal of our operations in eastern Europe," he says. "But before I can persuade a girl to stay close to home—or, in the case of a girl already in the sex trade, to leave her bondage—I have to appreciate the danger of her family situation." He pauses reflectively for a moment, then adds: "Don't forget, poverty kills too!"

Some girls willingly elect to become prostitutes or strip club dancers, assuming that the lifestyle could not be as hard as their current financial strife. More than a few have the image of Julia Roberts in *Pretty Woman* dancing around in their head. Recruiters tell the girl that she can make lots of money, live luxuriously, and perhaps even meet a wealthy man who might marry her. It may not be until the girl is working in a brothel in Paris or Barcelona, being forced to have sex with twelve johns a day, that she sees the folly of that dream.

Now that Padre Cesare has immersed himself deeper into the eastern European scene, he has uncovered how traffickers use young girls for other purposes beyond the brothels. He has met several girls who traveled to western Europe—some forcibly and others willingly—to serve as surrogate mothers for wealthy couples who cannot conceive a child. Prospective parents pay around $6,000 for the service. Typically the surrogate will live close by the customers during the course of the pregnancy and the delivery, after which time she may return to her home country. In most cases the paying clients have no clue that the girl might have been coerced to serve as a surrogate mother.

Padre Cesare has recently initiated a few experiments in microenterprises—offering small loans at low interest rates to individuals who want to start their own business—in order to offer young girls more financial options. He also tries to persuade wealthy Italian entrepreneurs to invest in the future of the former Soviet republics. He sees it as a simple formula: "If we create new jobs and stimulate economic development, it will proportionately reduce the risks that girls must take that lead to trafficking."

Regina Pacis works on a parallel track to reduce the demand for sex workers. Padre Cesare happily reports that his group played a key role in shutting down a sex tourism agency in Chisinau that was supplying fifteen- and sixteen-year-old girls to Turkish men. A well-placed "mole" tipped his staff off to a stream of older men holding the hands of very young girls as they moved in and out of a downtown hotel. Upon further investigation, Regina Pacis found that the agency was openly promoting in Turkey full travel packages for "Moldovan sex holidays."

Padre Cesare delivered the evidence to the vice director in charge of trafficking in Moldova, who promptly arrested the owners of the travel agency. He does not want to give the impression that the law always stands up to traffickers, however. "If we had taken our evidence to the run-of-the-mill police department, they would have thrown us in cages with bars," he remarks, only partly in jest.

All the same, Padre Cesare does report positive progress in his collaboration with government officials and legal authorities in Moldova to counter sex trafficking. Some police units, in fact, have invited the Regina Pacis staff to run workshops on how to identify girls who may be a victim of trafficking.

The most dramatic sign of how far Regina Pacis has come in Moldova occurred in July 2006, when the president of Moldova granted national citizenship to Padre Cesare "in honor of his heroic work against human trafficking in our country."

LEVERAGING INTERNATIONAL DIPLOMACY

In October 2000 the U.S. Congress passed a vital piece of legislation. The Victims of Trafficking and Violence Protection Act commits the U.S. government to use its political and economic influence to impede human trafficking around the globe. Though legislation of this sort often turns out to be just highfalutin rhetoric, this act comes with sharp teeth. More details on the piece of legislation and its contribution to abolitionist work within the United States is provided in chapter 6.

On an international level, the legislation directs the U.S. State Department to issue an annual report evaluating the performance of individual governments as they confront and prosecute human traffickers. The report charts the incidence of trafficking within each country and examines the specific laws, policies, and practices that the government implements to resolve the problem. The country's performance is then ranked into one of three "tiers":

Tier 1: a country whose government complies fully with the act's minimum standards.

Tier 2: a country whose government does not comply with the act's minimum standards but is making significant efforts to bring itself into compliance with those standards.

Tier 3: a country whose government does not comply fully with the minimum standards and is not making a significant effort to do so.

The "teeth" of the act come into play in two ways. First, the State Department publicly releases the report for the entire world to see. It does so with the hope that inactive or offending governments will be sufficiently embarrassed to change their behavior. Second, those countries ranked on Tier 3 are subject to stiff sanctions, including cuts to foreign aid and U.S. opposition to its applications before the World Bank and the International Monetary Fund.

The State Department released its first Trafficking in Persons (TIP) Report in July 2001 to great fanfare and controversy. For utter disregard for trafficking within its borders, it relegated twenty-three countries to Tier 3, including Russia, Israel, South Korea, Romania, Albania, and Greece. Even the most cynical observer had to be pleased that the State Department objectively shamed even some of its closest political allies. It was disappointing, on the other hand, to see perched on Tier 1 several European countries, like the Netherlands and Germany, that have significant trafficking problems.

As might be expected, the countries that received abysmal marks cried foul and engaged in serious political lobbying leading up to the 2002 TIP Report. Once that report was released, the United States's closest political allies had miraculously improved their performance. Abolitionist and human-rights groups expressed their displeasure that geopolitical politics had so obviously influenced the report.

The 2006 TIP Report confirms that bias that plays a strong role in the evaluation process. Among only a handful of nations relegated to Tier 3 can be found Cuba, Burma, Venezuela, North Korea, Sudan, Zimbabwe, Syria, and Iran. These nations just happen to be on not-so-friendly terms with the U.S. government. Meanwhile, countries like Albania, Romania, Serbia, Russia, India, Israel, Turkey, and Thailand, all of which have an abysmal record on trafficking, do not receive a Tier 3 ranking.

Several of these countries do appear on a Tier 2 "Watch List," a category established in the 2004 TIP Report. The countries on the Watch List teeter on the cliff above Tier 3. They show increasing numbers of trafficking victims and fail to demonstrate progress in complying with minimum standards of law enforcement. Again, it is not clear what it would take to tip these U.S. allies over the cliff and in to Tier 3.

Despite the uneven application of the TIP Report, it nevertheless has the potential to be a very useful tool. The more evidence that abolitionist groups can collect and publicize on the performance of specific nations, the more difficult it will be for the State Department to sanitize the performance of any given country. The overall goal, of course, is to create tangible incentives for government action on trafficking.

The U.S. Congress took another positive step when it authorized the creation within the State Department of a unit specifically charged to fight trafficking. In 2003 John Miller was appointed the first ambassador of the Office to Monitor and Combat Trafficking in Persons. Miller, who retired from his post in December 2006, turned out to be a tireless and effective advocate in the antislavery campaign.

At his swearing-in ceremony as ambassador, Miller eloquently raised a moral challenge to American abolitionists:

> The people of eastern Europe thank us for freeing them from Soviet tyranny.... In the future, if we are successful, millions of men in forced peonage and millions of women and children forced into prostitution and sex slavery will thank the United States for their freedom.[13]

Nadia—A Surprise Ending

Nadia considered herself very lucky to spend only a month in the brothel in Shkodra. The Albanian pimps kept the girls moving on a treadmill. On one single day, Nadia counted twenty-five individual encounters with men paying to have sex with her.

It was easy to pick out the girls who had "served a sentence" of more than six months in Shkodra. They looked utterly wasted. If a girl complained or demonstrated the least bit of resistance to her handlers, she would be treated harshly. Even if a girl acted 100 percent docile, the pimps would occasionally throw her a punch or put a gun to her head as a reminder. They beat one girl so badly that they had to remove her from the brothel, and Nadia never saw her again.

Nadia's age turned out to be her salvation; at twenty-two, she was considered over the hill. "We have sold you to the Italians," the cruelest of the pimps revealed to her out of the blue one day. "They don't mind old hens in Rome, I guess," he scoffed.

The next night Nadia was sitting in a motorized rubber raft once again. But this boat was at least four times the size of the dinghy that had carried her into Albania. If the dinghy operated like a taxi, this raft was a bus. Nearly forty passengers of all ages—even a mother who cradled a baby in one arm and sat a toddler on her knee—crammed into the boat.

Once they had moved off the shore some distance, the sea turned rough. The boat carried them up and down steep water valleys. Passengers who leaned their heads over the side of the raft to vomit more often than not received a sharp slap of water in the face. The children at first screamed in terror and then whimpered.

Two Albanian goons sat at the front, keeping a watch for any sign of lights from Italian coast guard crafts. The pilot had his hands full keeping the boat heading straight into the waves lest they get sideswiped.

Even though it was pitch-black out, Nadia kept her eyes tightly shut. She tried to focus on Stefan, wondering how her son might be faring back in Chisinau. Tears streamed down her cheeks as she admitted to herself that she would likely never see him again.

She opened her eyes and saw bright lights on the distant shore ahead. "Italy?" she asked one of the goons positioned in front of her.

"Yes, Italy," he said without looking back at her.

Nadia lost her mind for a moment. "Italy? Italy? Italy?" she kept repeating, now practically screaming.

"Damn it! I already told you! It's Italy over there," growled the goon angrily.

That afternoon before she had boarded the raft, the cruelest of the pimps had handed her a plastic baggie. Inside she could see her passport, a bit of Italian money, and a small card with scribbled text.

"When you reach the beach near San Foca, your new owner will be waiting," he said. "If for some reason you get lost, I have given you his phone number and enough money to make a phone call. He will drive you to Rome, where you will work for him."

Nadia nodded. He took the gun from his belt nonetheless and put it to her head. "If you try to escape, we will hunt you down. There would be no place to hide; we have people on both sides of the sea."

Now, perched in the hull of the raft, she had a more pressing concern. The pilot had taken the boat within twenty yards of shore, and the Albanians were yelling for everyone to jump out before the authorities detected them. Those passengers who did not comply got tossed forcibly into the sea.

As she entered the sea, the water reached up to Nadia's nose. As the waves crested, she lost contact with the sandy floor and took in large gulps of salty water. She floated, stumbled, and fought her way to shore. A number of other passengers washed ashore on the beach at about the same moment. After a pause to gain their bearings, they all made a chaotic rush to get off the beach and avoid detection.

Nadia slept until daylight nestled in a crevice in the middle of three large rocks. The sound of a loud horn jarred her awake. Peaking over the top of the rocks, she saw a roadway no more than fifty yards in the distance. She reached inside her pants to see if the plastic baggie had survived her ordeal, and she was pleased to discover that all the documents had remained dry.

Now Nadia had to consider her next move. She knew the fate awaiting her if she called her new owner. She could never willingly go back to that hell. If the mafia wanted to track her down, so be it.

Absent a plan, she started walking in search of food. It did not take her long to reach San Foca. She used her "phone money" to buy a loaf of bread at a small bakery and started eating it greedily as soon as she hit the sidewalk. Propped against the wall of the bakery, she luxuriated as the sun came out brightly to take away the shivers that had troubled her sleep.

During the course of the morning, the owner of the bakery strolled outside her shop and noticed that Nadia had not left. Based on their brief encounter, she realized that Nadia did not understand Italian. Taking a look at her ragged appearance, the woman guessed that Nadia had recently washed ashore from Albania.

"Regina Pacis?" the woman asked.

Nadia shrugged her arms to indicate that she did not understand.

"Regina Pacis?" the woman repeated, saying the words slowly this time. "Padre Cesare?"

Once again, Nadia gave her a puzzled look. The woman smiled and gestured for Nadia to wait on the sidewalk. She went inside and made a call to the shelter.

Nadia did not know it at the time, but her torturous trek had reached its end. Years later—long after she had married a man from the village and Stefan had joined her in San Foca—she would walk by that bakery wall and smile. It was there, at that spot, when the sun had come out brightly to take her shivers away.

Sheltering the Lost Children: Peru

We often look at heroes and think, "I so admire who they are, but I could never do what they do." The truth is that a heroic path usually begins with a humble act that opens a gate into a new universe.

Lucy Borja passed through that portal in 1991. She reached out to help two boys—both around twelve years old—who feared to spend the night on the rugged streets of Peru's capital city, Lima.

She had only recently learned of the existence of a subculture of "street kids." As part of an HIV/AIDS-prevention program she directed called Generación—literally "generation," as in "youth generation"—Lucy started visiting Peru's prisons for juveniles. The children shared with her their personal stories of life on the streets, where they faced the threat of violence daily. Sex traffickers had moved some of them to Lima from Peru's rural provinces, while others had fallen victim to poverty or sexual abuse at home.

The president of Peru at the time, Alberto Fujimori, declared that his government would "cleanse" the city of street kids. The dead bodies of several children showed up in city parks shortly thereafter; many more went missing. The street kids reported to Lucy that police used brute intimidation against them, putting a gun to their heads and pulling the trigger on an empty chamber.

So when Lucy met two young boys who were too frightened to spend another night on the streets, she invited them to sleep in the Generación office. She told them to extend the offer to any other child who shared their fears. Since Lucy already had plans to attend a family party that evening, she informed the custodian to give entry to any child who arrived at the office.

After her party ended, Lucy decided to check in with her young guests. She hoped that the custodian, upon meeting the ragged vagrants, had not balked at her instructions. She half expected to find the boys sitting on the curb in front of her office, locked out.

Street kids around the world suffer from a cascade of curses. A traumatic incident initially tears them away from their families. Once displaced, they become vulnerable to predators of every stripe: traffickers set traps to ensnare them, the police consider them outlaws, and "decent folk" regard them as less than human. The stigma of rejection brands their tiny bodies.

Lucy indeed had a surprise awaiting her that evening when she arrived at the Generación office. Her key unlocked the front door, but try as she might, she could not shove it open. It felt like a rolled-up carpet had been lodged behind the door to block the entry. With the help of her sons, Lucy finally moved the door to create enough space to squeeze through.

As she reached blindly in the dark in search of the light switch, Lucy tripped over the "carpet roll." She deftly caught her balance and leaned her body against the wall. Her fingers searched the wall until she eventually found the light switch.

Once the light came on, Lucy looked down at her feet and discovered several young kids curled up on the floor sleeping, their bodies jammed against the door. She cast her vision around the room, though it was hard to register what she was seeing. Sleeping children covered every nook and cranny of the office. "I even found young kids snuggled tightly inside the cupboards where we stored our office supplies," Lucy recalls.

Lucy counted over six hundred children who slept in the office that night. The word had passed like wildfire on the streets of Lima. Found: a safe shelter from the storm.

Lucy did not know all the details that caused these boys and girls to run scared, but she clearly sensed that her life would never be the same. "Stacked one against the other, asleep on the floor of my office, those children seemed so vulnerable," Lucy says in a slow, soft voice. "They had no one to be their advocate, to defend their rights," she adds. "I knew then what path I had to take."

Making a stand against injustice generally requires us to make some painful personal choices. Lucy soon found herself at one of those crossroads. The kids of Lima kept coming back to the office each night for sanctuary. Her Generación staff got fed up with this ongoing invasion. "It's either us or the kids," they told her.

"OK, then, it's the kids," Lucy calmly answered.

SEX IN THE STREET

Save the Children, the international aid and children's rights group based in Sweden, sponsored a team of investigative journalists to conduct a study of child sex trafficking in Peru in 2004. Their research was designed originally to focus on the johns— "to find out what goes on in the hearts and minds of human beings capable of violating the rights of [children]."[1] But they cast their net wide and delivered one of the best analyses of sex trafficking of minors in a single country.

Due to the difficulty of getting perpetrators to openly admit to their illicit behavior, the journalists established a fictitious child pornography magazine they called *Sex in the Street*. They placed employment ads—open positions for administrators, lawyers, writers, drivers, janitors, and more—in major Peruvian newspapers. Applicants from across the socioeconomic spectrum spoke openly with undercover investigators in "job interviews" about their background in the child sex industry and their understanding of the needs of that market.

The final report—published under the title *The Client Goes Unnoticed*—describes how traffickers run a sex trade in children that stretches across Peru. A substantial number of these kids eventually end up on the streets of Lima. Sadly, Save the Children investigators found "very few organizations currently assisting prostituted children and adolescents, and it is very disturbing that there is no effective support from the state to incorporate these young people into the country's labor."[2] Their research in fact confirms that Generación practically stands alone—with only a handful of courageous allies—in its fight to protect sexually exploited children and bring justice to the streets of Lima.

Sandra—Biography of a Sex Trafficker

Sandra does not match the stereotype of a dangerous pimp. She agreed to be interviewed in exchange for a box of diapers for her newborn child. As the baby fed off her breast, Sandra shared her disturbing passage from street urchin to sex trafficker.

A consistent thread emerges in her story: Sandra is a survivor. She never knew her father. Her grandmother and mother raised her with meager resources. When she turned eight, they kicked her out with explicit orders that she not return until she had some money to contribute to the household income. Sandra slept in the streets of Lima for several nights, and it scared her to death. So she returned home, hoping that her mother and grandmother might have missed her and would reconsider their ultimatum.

"So, did you bring any money back with you?" her grandmother asked as soon as Sandra passed through the door.

"Grandma, no one wants to pay an eight-year-old to work," Sandra replied tearfully. "And it is scary out there alone."

"Don't be such a baby," her grandmother replied unsympathetically. "Your mother and I have a hard enough time feeding ourselves."

"But Grandma, it's dangerous—" Her grandmother's slap across her face cut off Sandra in midsentence.

"Now, get out of here. Come back when you have cash."

Sandra ran out the door, her eyes blurred by a flood of tears.

CHILDREN ARE NOT PROSTITUTES

Young boys and girls in every city on the globe today are forced to serve as sex slaves. Sex traffickers target twelve- to seventeen-year-old children as their choice candidates. The johns who pay regular visits to brothels prefer adolescents above any other age group. Looked at from the cold perspective of a slaveholder, adolescents also have a longer shelf life. Any older and they start to lose their youthful appeal. Any younger and they may draw the attention of law enforcement authorities.

Because sex trafficking masks itself as prostitution, the general public does not feel outraged. The children are perceived to be criminals or sexual deviants or at best victims of their environment: desperate for survival, the kids "choose" to sell their bodies for profit.

The real criminals hide in the shadows. An illicit network of traffickers, pimps, recruiters, brothel owners, and johns preys on vulnerable kids and forces them into a life of sexual commerce. Once the inner workings of that criminal network are exposed, common sense prevails. Of course a child would not volunteer for the repeated trauma of ten (or more) grown men penetrating their bodies every evening. We have a word for exploiting minors that way: rape.

It should be noted that the same mechanisms of financial bondage and violent intimidation that enslave children are practiced on females of all ages. Adult "prostitutes" too can recount shocking testimonies of pimps locking them in closets, flogging them with coat hangers, and forcing them to service a staggering number of clients. The pimps quite explicitly refer to these women as "my property" and will attack anyone who acts to compromise their control.

Donna Hughes, an influential activist in the campaign to stop the flow of sex trafficking, explained to the U.S. House Committee on International Relations that prostitution and sex trafficking are inextricably linked: "To not understand the relationship between prostitution and trafficking is like not understanding the relationship between slavery in the Old South and the kidnapping of victims in Africa and the transatlantic shipment of them to our shores."[3]

Without a doubt, we need a more nuanced understanding of prostitution. Katherine Chon, cofounder of the Polaris Project, points to a conversation she had with a Korean woman in her early twenties whom she suspected was a victim of sex trafficking. When Katherine asked the woman whether she had been coerced into coming to the United States to work in the sex trade, the woman adamantly denied that was the case.

Katherine decided to change her tack: "Well, on a scale of 0 to 100 percent, how much control do you feel you have over your decisions each day to continue selling your body to men?"

Given the flow of the conversation up to that point, Katherine expected the woman to give a response that might fall close to 90 percent. But after considering for a few seconds, the woman gave Katherine a surprising answer: "Oh, I'd say maybe 5 percent."

Confused by her answer, Katherine started digging a bit deeper: "So why do you feel such loyalty for the owner of the brothel where you work?"

"The owner told me that if I got into trouble, she would bail me out of jail and pay for an attorney," the Korean woman replied. "I am not from here [the United States]; the police can do bad things to you, so I need security." The Korean woman went on to explain that the brothel owner also keeps possession of all her "savings." If she were to leave the brothel, the owner would not give her the money back. Her pimp also provides her protection, though he threatens to beat her if she tries to leave him.

Is she a slave? It would not be much of a stretch to identify her as such, even though she technically does not live under lock and key. Tragically, the woman herself rejects the label. She has come to accept her destiny—the coercion weaves so seamlessly into her surroundings that she no longer recognizes it as a chain.

Coercing children into the sex trade entails much less ambiguity. The actual process of enslavement varies from place to place; the most influential independent variable is the strength of law enforcement in a particular region. Research across five continents uncovers a disturbingly common pattern in child sex trafficking, regardless of whether international crime networks are involved or the operation runs on a regional level with ad hoc players. The process of enslavement involves five predictable elements:[4]

Recruitment—Traffickers target children most commonly from communities that lack social power, at times with the consent of the victims' parents.

Extraction—Traffickers remove recruits from their home community and shift them to a destination where they are unlikely to get support from law enforcement bodies or the general citizenry.

Control—Slaveholders seek control over every aspect of the child's life so that escape becomes unthinkable.

Violence—Slaveholders exercise violence as a means to reinforce their control and ensure compliance.

Exploitation—Slaveholders show slight regard for the physical or emotional health of the child in their pursuit of financial gain.

Lucy Borja—Dark Alleys and Bright Office Lights

The street kids kept coming back to Lucy's shelter. After one especially brutal incident in a city square, she had to find medical attention for eighteen kids that the police had shot.

Generación had to evolve into something more than a short-term crisis shelter, of that Lucy had no doubt. She above all wanted to bring some normalcy and structure into the lives of the children.

Lucy has a remarkable gift for connecting with youth in crisis. Despite being in her late fifties, she builds an easy rapport with them and earns their trust. Almost any minute of the day she can be found surrounded by a cadre of kids. Their high-paced energy does not seem to overwhelm her. In fact, Lucy keeps steadfastly calm—she neither demands attention nor deems it necessary to use a loud voice to bring order. Yet she can exercise a steely determination when the occasion warrants it.

Once the first wave of street kids made Generación their home base, Lucy established a rule: to stay at the shelter, the kids had to attend school. While the teens could work in the morning hours, they still had to attend classes in the afternoons.

Soon after "Lucy's rule" took effect, a group of seven Generación boys—from fourteen to sixteen years old—found work at a hair salon. About a month after they were hired, Lucy asked the boys about their jobs. When they told her that they cleaned dishes and washed bedsheets and towels, she became suspicious—the tasks did not seem like the kind that would be required at a hair salon. Lucy checked her sources and discovered that the hair salon was a front for a brothel. She urged the boys to quit their jobs without delay.

The boys went to the salon the next day to collect their earnings and inform the managers that they would be leaving. The women offered to pay them in sex with the young girls whom they controlled. They put a pornographic movie on the television and told the boys to go to the back rooms of the salon and select a girl. When the boys refused and demanded cash for their wages, the managers locked the doors to the salon and said they could not leave until they performed sex with their girls. The boys became quite upset and began ransacking the premises. The managers called the police and reported that street kids were vandalizing their property. All of the boys were arrested except one, who escaped out a back window and ran back to the Generación office to inform Lucy about what had taken place.

When Lucy arrived at the local police station, the officers in charge claimed that they did not know anything about the incident. In actual fact, they were holding the boys in a cell at the station. So Lucy reported the incident to a judge of the court, Regina Chavez, a woman of high integrity. Judge Chavez made a personal visit to the salon and found a library of homemade pornographic movies featuring minors. The judge found additional evidence to convince her that the salon was indeed operating as a brothel.

A few hours after Judge Chavez had completed her investigation, the police showed up at Generación to arrest Lucy on charges of trespassing and impersonating a judge of the court. Judge Chavez promptly exposed the setup and confirmed that she herself had entered the salon.

A subsequent court investigation revealed what motivated the police actions. The salon was located directly across the street from an office building for several important government agencies, including the police headquarters for Lima. Many of the salon's regular clients walked in from their offices across the street.

Bit by bit Lucy began to put together the pieces of the puzzle. "The criminals exploiting children in Peru do not only hang out in dark alleys," she explains. "They also sit comfortably behind desks in the halls of power."

TRAFFICKING CHILDREN: RECRUITMENT AND EXTRACTION

Only on rare occasions will a sex trafficker abduct a child from a neighborhood that enjoys social power. Doing so carries too high a risk. A family from an empowered community is more apt to mobilize legal and political authorities to conduct an extensive search for an abducted child. If caught, recruiters face a higher probability of prosecution and place their entire operation at risk. Why would recruiters take that risk when so many candidates can be found in relatively powerless neighborhoods?

Furthermore, recruiters can deceive destitute families more easily with promises of a better life. The allure of a steady job may cause parents to overlook the risks of sending their child off to a faraway destination. Teenagers might be promised a modeling job in another country or less glamorous, yet high-paying work in a restaurant or a retail store. Parents of young children in the rural areas are told that a wealthy family in the big city needs a domestic servant or a nanny. These offers are crafted to extract children from the reaches of those who might care for them. Recruiters have no intention of fulfilling their promises of course; they intend to sell the children to a brothel owner at their first opportunity. But their game depends on maintaining the illusion of a golden path out of the depressed conditions that the families face.

In that regard, lower-middle-class families with heightened aspirations can be as vulnerable to traffickers as the most impoverished family. A shortcut to upward social mobility holds tremendous appeal.

Consider the case of Lan, a seventeen-year-old Laotian girl living in Bangkok. Her mother migrated to Thailand with Lan and her two siblings when the children were all under ten years old. The mother worked in a local street market, and the children contributed to the family business. Years passed, and the family's hard work lifted them out of dire poverty. Lan works today in a luxury tourist hotel in Bangkok as a waitress. She owns her own car and a modest wardrobe of fashionable western clothes.

Lan has tasted enough of the "good life" to entertain aspirations for an even more glamorous lifestyle. Her best friend met an American visiting Bangkok on a business trip, and he occasionally sends her friend a plane ticket to meet him in some exotic holiday spot. The American recently invited Lan along and sent her a plane ticket, too. Despite the prevalence of sex trafficking in Thailand, this invitation did not raise a red flag for Lan. She in fact aspires to find a "friend" who will offer her nice gifts and travel like her friend receives. It will be only a matter of time before a well-heeled trafficker will ensnare Lan unless her attitude changes.

Parents with material aspirations are at times willing to put their children in dangerous situations. It is not uncommon for parents to deliver a child to a recruiter even when they are fully aware that the child will be exploited sexually. The recruiter might pay the parents a cash advance for their child's future earnings, with the promise of more payments to come. For their part, recruiters make these arrangements so that they can establish a steady trade in a region. Neighbors will witness the recruiter's credibility, as well as the financial rise of the family that has sold their child, and will become more willing to sell their own children.

Abolitionists fighting sex trafficking in both Southeast Asia and Latin America report that parents commonly sell their kids so that they can make an improvement on their home or purchase a vehicle or other consumer item. These stories align with a report in the *New York Times* that parents in Albania sold their children to traffickers so that they could buy a color television.[5]

Nonetheless, the sex trafficker who deals in children usually wants to extract recruits from their home region as expeditiously as possible. When kidnapping is involved, the trafficker has more reason to fear arrest. Even if the parents of the abducted child do not get involved, an adult relative or friend may advocate for the child and press the police to take action.

An anonymous individual who bears the stigma of "child prostitute," on the other hand, is much less likely to have an advocate. Foreign children evoke even less sympathy than those who share the nationality or ethnicity of the mainstream population. For that reason, traffickers typically shift child slaves to the other side of the country or, even more effectively, across an ocean.

In that regard, Save the Children investigators discovered that kids who are trafficked from the rural regions of Peru become invisible to law enforcement officials in the capital: "It is alarming to view the impunity with which networks trafficking in minors operate in [Lima], in full view of authorities who not only do nothing, but who ... also do not consider that children and adolescents are people who need to be defended and protected."[6]

The testimony of nine-year-old Guadalupe in Lima illustrates a more unusual case: how a parent and a trafficker might work together as allies. Guadalupe's mother had made a financial arrangement with a pimp "to employ" her daughter. As a way to introduce very young girls into sex commerce, pimps in Lima commonly place them on the street only to tempt passing clients. Once a john stops and inquires of her availability, the pimp will bring in a slightly older, more experienced girl to turn the trick. This bait-and-switch role does not last long, especially once the pimp has made a tidy sum selling the young girl (usually multiple times) as a virgin.

Guadalupe fortunately met a street counselor from Generación before the pimp had the opportunity to sell her off as a virgin. She moved into one of Generación's high-security shelters where the pimp could not touch her. Guadalupe's mother then visited the shelter and demanded, "I want my daughter back!" At great institutional risk, Generación denied the mother her request; the staff knew what Guadalupe's fate would be if they relented.

Neither Generación nor any other child service agency wants to be in a position where it has to wrestle with parents over the well-being of their child. But abolitionists have to deal with an uncomfortable truth: Not every parent has come to the firm conviction that a child, their child, is not for sale.

Sandra—The Temporary Gardener

Sandra eventually met up with other street kids who shared her lot. They traveled in packs, finding safety in numbers. After police officers threatened one night to make her gang of friends "disappear," she crashed at a shelter called Generación for the first time. It became her home for the next seven years.

Most of Sandra's friends had given up on the option of going back to their families: those bridges had burned down and would never be rebuilt. But Sandra still hoped that she could prove herself worthy to move back in with her mother and grandmother.

Generación began creating jobs for the kids. Noting that the parks in Lima were poorly maintained, Lucy proposed to city officials that they hire the kids of Generación to be Lima's public gardeners. With characteristic panache, Lucy called it an "environmental company" in order to leave the door open for future development. As the kids improved their skills, they could shift up market and offer landscaping services as well.

Sandra, now twelve years old, was one of the first kids to sign up for gardening work. But after only a couple of weeks of labor, she visited the city contractor and demanded her pay. The supervisor told her that she would be paid at the end of the month along with everyone else. Sandra threw down her rake and quit on the spot.

The city supervisor just scratched his head. He had never met a young kid so eager to get her hands on money.

Lucy Borja—The Dangerous Games Adults Play

Lucy Borja easily qualifies as one of the most controversial living figures in all of Peru. At last count, she has twenty-two legal denunciations pending against her in Lima's courts, including charges of kidnapping children, giving false testimony to the police, and "acting against the public interest." On any given day it is not unusual for a political figure to make a disparaging remark about her on the evening news.

To meet Lucy Borja—and track her movements over a substantial period of time—confounds all expectations. She is neither argumentative nor cantankerous; in fact, her gentle spirit and compassion lead some people to call her "the Mother Teresa of the streets of Lima."

How can we square this bipolar public image? It's quite

simple: Lucy speaks the truth about what she sees around her. That habit can create formidable enemies in Peru.

On Mother's Day in 1992, for example, Lucy received an invitation to participate in a press conference at the juvenile prison, along with the wife of President Fujimori and Ana Kanashiro, the national director for children's welfare. Once the press conference began, Kanashiro proudly announced to a television audience that the national government had set aside $5 million to resolve "the problem of street children." The symbolism of making this pronouncement at the juvenile prison was not lost on anyone.

When the camera turned to the founder of Generación, she proposed that rather than use government funds to punish exploited children, the money should be used to open "healthy homes" for them. Lucy referred to the hundreds of street kids who slept in her office each night. "While children in the prisons are ill treated," she said, "the street kids at Generación study in the classroom and develop life skills that will move them in a new direction."

Kanashiro was livid at being upstaged, and from that day forward she made it known that Lucy was to be banned from visiting the juvenile prison and from providing HIV/AIDS courses in the public schools. A friend of Lucy's in the national congress rose to her defense. She distributed for television broadcast a video of interviews with children testifying to their treatment inside juvenile prison and the trumped-up charges that incarcerated them. A major television personality in Peru, Juan Carlos, watched the interviews and became inspired to produce a series of special reports on the struggles of street kids in Lima.[7]

Overjoyed that a news reporter of his stature would be interested in their cause, Lucy arranged for Carlos to portray the stories of three young boys who lived at Generación. Carlos devoted a considerable amount of time to interviewing the boys and filming their daily activities. Using Generación as a base, the journalist then dove deep into the netherworld of street life. He filmed the story of Alicia, a young girl who for many years dressed as a man so that she would not be raped on the streets. His short documentaries ran on national television and won critical acclaim both inside Peru and internationally, even winning a prestigious cultural award from the United Nations Educational, Scientific, and Cultural Organization (UNESCO).

Lucy, however, could not enjoy watching the documentaries. Just as Carlos was wrapping up production, the kids at Generación berated her for bringing him into their lives. The boys divulged how Carlos had supplied them with drugs and then raped them. One of the more memorable scenes in his documentary shows street kids using drugs and alcohol at a popular street hangout. In actual fact, the boys reported, Carlos had bought the substances and distributed them before he started filming. It was the first time that many of the younger kids had ever used drugs. The kids also reported to Lucy that Carlos had exploited his connection to Alicia. He paid her to find young children and bring them to his own house for sex; later he had her pimp children to the homes of his friends as well.

It saddens Lucy today to look back fifteen years and recognize the pivotal role that Juan Carlos played in the buildup of sex trafficking in Lima. Up until that point, the child sex industry was more or less opportunistic—an adult might find a child in desperate circumstances and induce him or her to engage in sex for money. Carlos initiated a more systematic practice of trafficking. Alicia, for example, began recruiting kids into the sex trade at his urging and went on to become one of the country's most notorious pimps.

Yet try as she might, Lucy could not bring Juan Carlos to justice. The courts would never convict a man of his stature based solely on the testimony of street kids, and that was the only hard evidence that she had. Nonetheless, Lucy reported his criminal activities to the police and persistently urged them to investigate.

In a vicious retaliation, Carlos produced a television news report on Generación that he called "The House of Terror: Where Children Go to Contract AIDS." But his assault on the shelter's reputation backfired. When a judge ordered that the kids at Generación undergo HIV testing, not one of the kids tested positive. The kids actually turned the tables and testified to the judge of Carlos's sexual crimes with minors.

Worried about a possible arrest, Carlos fled the country and worked for many years as a journalist in the United States. He recently returned to Peru and resumed his successful television career.

TRAFFICKING CHILDREN: CONTROL AND VIOLENCE

Once traffickers extract victims from their home community, they typically sell the children to slaveholders who deal in commercial sex—for example, pimps or the owners of strip clubs, sex bars, brothels, karaoke clubs, or massage parlors. Most traffickers have a steady relationship in place with the slaveholder; hence, they know who the buyer will be before they recruit the child. Although it is more rare, some traffickers act as both recruiter and operator of their own "retail" sex shop.

The slaveholder acts swiftly to take complete control of the child's life. Passports, birth certificates, national identity cards, and any other documents of citizenship are stripped from the child's possession. The child is kept closely guarded and locked in a room when not accompanied. Even if escape were possible, the child has no money, probably does not speak the local language, and does not know to whom he or she could turn for help. Given their past experience, slave children would not instinctively trust public officials or the police.

The slaveholder also generally manipulates a relationship of financial dependence with the child. Basic life necessities like food, clothing, and shelter are charged to the child's "account." Until that money is repaid, the child is obligated to continue in the slaveholder's service.

Slaveholders will buttress these social controls with the constant threat of violence. Almost all trafficked children will testify that they were victims of an extreme act of violence within the first forty-eight hours of their abduction. Whether through rape or brutal beatings, slaveholders use violence to imprint their dominance. In the logic of the trafficking world, a terrified child is a compliant child. The slaveholder therefore will never let the child slip out of a state of terror.

Ranchers refer to "breaking the spirit of a wild horse"; in a macabre sense, that is how slaveholders approach child sex slaves. The sex slaves will have to learn to comply happily with whatever sexual act a client requests. The liberal application of violence early on will crack the resistance they will inevitably mount. If a client ever complains that the sex slave was less than accommodating, swift and brutal punishment will be meted out.

The threat of violence becomes a ubiquitous force in the life of a sex slave. The child knows that a failed escape attempt would result in a severe beating. Moreover, the slaveholder may threaten to harm the child's family even if the child does manage to get away. To remind the child of that fact, the slaveholder may occasionally drop some piece of current news about family members, whether real or fabricated, as if to say, "Yes, I am watching them, so don't do anything stupid."

Dina, a sixteen-year-old girl who presently finds refuge at Generación's center for rescued sex slaves, relates how she spent four years under the control of a pimp because she feared for her family's welfare. She has three younger sisters and a brother. The pimp threatened to pursue them as replacements if she ever left him. He would taunt Dina with a stream diet of comments: "Hey, I saw your sister on the bus in Lima this afternoon. Geez, chica, she is turning out to be as pretty as you."

Many mornings Dina would wake up and tell herself that she could not spend one more day in her hell. But then she would see a mental image of her sisters, and she steeled herself to endure whatever might come her way.

Sandra—Pimping for a Living

After Juan Carlos initiated Alicia into pimping, she evolved a lucrative trafficking operation. Her strategy to train a network of pimps to serve as her agents on the streets turned into a big success.

Alicia convinced Sandra that she could make a ton of money trafficking young children. As a recruiter, Sandra would earn a piece of the action every time the child engaged a paying client. As the queen pimp, Alicia also would earn a share off of Sandra's recruits. Their third financial partner would be a mami who would give the child a place to live, usually in a hotel though sometimes in a private residence.

Sandra, then fifteen and no longer living at Generación, quickly earned a reputation as one of the toughest pimps on the street. Her style of recruitment was not very sophisticated. She would spot a child walking alone in the streets—whether day or night it made no difference. Acting quickly, she dialed any one of a number of taxi drivers who formed part of the trafficking network. After informing the driver of her location, she would move in on her target and concoct some excuse to start a conversation. Then, once the cab pulled up along the curb, she would force the child inside the car, using violence if necessary. Sometimes the taxi drivers would rape the child; other times they would sell the "virgin rights" to a client.

The taxi driver would return the child to Sandra after the rape. He would be sure to give the child a dollar or two for "the service." As soon as the shell-shocked victim stepped out of the cab, Sandra shifted into psychological coercion. "Now that you have lost your virginity, you might as well keep making money with me," she would say matter-of-factly. "Face it. You're now a tramp."

The victim at this stage is wholly disoriented and traumatized, so Sandra delivers the child to the mami. At the first meeting, the mami shows motherly warmth and sympathy. She offers the child secure accommodations and provides a hot meal and maybe new clothes. Each of these "expressions of sympathy" gets the tab running on the debt that the child will owe the mami.

Though the child does not yet realize it, she (or he) has just become a sex slave.

Lucy Borja—Extending the Family

It does not feel right to call Generación an "agency" or an "orphanage" or even a "shelter." It does fulfill all of these important roles for the children who go there for help. But none of these labels conveys the sense of extended family that permeates the place.

Certainly it starts with Lucy, who makes a personal connection with every child who walks through Generación's doors. Mention a particular resident's name, and she can rattle off the child's history, habits, passions, strengths, and weaknesses. Thousands of youths have run to Generación over the past two decades, and Lucy is mother to them all.

Like a caring mother, Lucy forgives all failures and betrayals, of which there are many. One mention of Sandra and Lucy's face fills with pain. She knows full well what has become of the little girl who first came to Generación when she was eight years old. Ironically, Lucy now strives to rescue the children whom Sandra seeks to enslave. "I really do believe that down deep she wants to change, to be a different person," Lucy says, refusing to give up on her "prodigal daughter." Then, as if speaking to herself, she adds softly, "One day she will find her way."

The family atmosphere at Generación extends to Lucy's husband, Juan Enrique, and their five grown children, who also embrace the street kids as their own.[8] Lucy's children grew up with a constant stream of visitors invading their home, so it would be understandable if they felt some bitterness about having had to share their mother. If they harbor such sentiments, it does not show. Now that they are adults in their twenties and early thirties, the children still chip in passionately to help their mother.

One of Generación's most dynamic programs revolves around surfing. Lucy's own children are avid surfers, and they infused the younger street kids with their love for riding waves. Generación now runs a house in a coastal town about an hour from Lima, and fifteen to eighteen kids live there full-time. It is a remarkable scene to head down to the beach late in the afternoon and watch a pack of ex-street kids mixing in with the local surf bums. Some of Generación's kids are now entering surfing competitions and performing at a high level.

Juan Enrique, Lucy's husband, has partnered with Save the Children's programs in Latin America for almost twenty-five years. An erudite and reflective man, he has helped to establish graduate programs for children's rights advocates at major universities around the world. Juan Enrique and Lucy offer the perfect complement of academic and activist, all in the service of abolition.

Save the Children in turn has been a good friend to Generación. The children's rights agency bought an enormous house in 1994 that Lucy uses rent free to house the street kids. The office was never a suitable place to shelter so many children, but Lucy did not have the finances to fund an alternative. In the ensuing years, Generación has set up more specialized shelters for teen mothers with children and females of all ages recently rescued from sex trafficking.

Generación approaches its mission like a family that has suddenly adopted hundreds of children. First off, it aims to rescue children in crisis and offer them a safe living environment. Next, it aims to equip the children with the education and work skills they will need to be self-sufficient young adults. Lucy aims to get the kids involved in school as soon as they are emotionally able to handle it. She often has to negotiate with public school principals who do not want to accept street kids into their classrooms. Finally, as they move into adolescence, Generación wants to give its youth meaningful jobs that offer a positive work experience.

The "environmental company" has evolved into a true success story. Nearly a decade after it was launched, over a hundred former street kids daily labor for wages in Lima's parks. The managers of the company grew up in Generación and have developed into responsible leaders.

Just about all of Generación's financial help over the past twenty years has come from European foundations. For some reason even Lucy cannot explain, she has never had much luck persuading U.S.-based agencies to support her work. In 2002 a German foundation donated equipment for Generación to launch several new bakery ventures.

The most thriving bakery operates on the ground floor of a new shelter that Generación opened specifically for females that it has rescued out of sex slavery. The women are taught how to bake bread and pastries and learn the rudimentary skills needed to run a retail shop.

All the same, Lucy has a good laugh at her own expense whenever she speaks about Generación's business ventures. She spawns microenterprises not because she has a passion for business; in fact, she considers herself an inept entrepreneur. But when she sees a critical need, she rolls up her sleeves and figures out a solution. She dreams of the day when a skilled business professional will roll into town and offer to build companies that transform the lives of the employees. "Work," Lucy stresses, "is both therapy and empowerment for former sex slaves."

TRAFFICKING CHILDREN: AN INDUSTRY OF EXPLOITATION

The classic concept of prostitution invokes the image of a client who pays a sole individual for sexual activity. Most johns like to maintain this illusion because they do not like to think of their "date" as a sex slave. As Save the Children investigators exposed, "[The clients] say that because they do not use violence to force the child or adolescent to have sex, the situation does not violate the minor's human rights. They do not identify the children and adolescents as victims of sexual exploitation."[9]

Most people are vaguely aware, however, that women and children who sell their bodies for sex rarely operate independently. Even in the movies, pimps control the activities of the prostitutes.

But the tentacles of the "sex industry" go much deeper. An entire underground economy is built around sex slaves. Whether it's Munich or Phnom Penh or Lima, similar economic sectors profit from exploitation.

The conference industry serves as a useful analogy. Major cities hire an entire staff to persuade professional associations and trade groups to host an annual convention or other big event in their city. Not only does the city's convention facility benefit from a successful bid, so do the city's hotels, restaurants, night clubs, taxis, airports, and so on. In other words, a major conference delivers a financial bonanza across the city's commercial sector.

In like manner, the growth of the sex industry in a city like Lima benefits many parties, but much of the money flows through underground channels. Nevertheless, it is safe to say that a substantial number of Lima's hotels could not survive without the sex trade.

The financial interdependence that the sex trade spins can be observed even when scaled down to the microlevel. A single child trafficked into the center of Lima brings a significant bonanza to the owner of the hotel where the victim is lodged. The food vendors and bars in the immediate vicinity will benefit from the daily visits of a dozen johns. They will in fact negotiate deals with sex slaves to bring the johns into their place in exchange for a free meal. Multiply these connections thousands of times over, and a lucrative industry begins to take shape.

The only people who do not reap financial benefits from the sex industry are the ones upon whom the whole network depends: the slaves.

Sandra—The Long Road Back

The last person in the world that the Generación staff expected to find knocking at the door of their shelter for rescued sex workers in fact showed up recently. It was Sandra, and she was holding the hand of a tiny eight-year-old girl. The child had bloodstains on her face and severe scrapes and bruises on her limbs. "Please take this girl in," Sandra told the director of the shelter. "She was badly treated by a john today, and she won't survive another day on the streets." Once the director agreed to help, Sandra turned and walked away.

The news of this good deed certainly brought a smile to Lucy's face. Perhaps Sandra has started to "find her way" as she anticipated. But even Lucy knows the road back is a long one.

Sandra, now twenty-two years old, has given birth to two children. In many respects, she feels trapped in the same dilemma that has long cursed her life: how to make the money she needs to go "back home." The father of her kids has been in and out of jail over the past five years. It pains him to see Sandra work in sex trafficking, so he twice has tried to steal a big chunk of money that would allow her to walk away from that life. On each occasion he landed in jail, and Sandra's cycle of desperation continues.

Lucy paid a visit to Sandra after her good deed with the little girl. She delivered a message that Sandra had heard many times before but that has never lost its power to move her: "I am always here for you, my Sandra, but I cannot walk the path for you."

Lucy Borja—Justice at the Center

Lucy dedicates herself wholly to the children who live on the fringes of her society. She does not view a single relationship as a waste of her time. But no matter how many kids she rescues from the gutter, more arrive to take their place. "Nothing will change for street kids until we put justice at the center of our society," she declares. "At the moment, we are ruled by corruption and greed."

To make her point, she tells the story of a failed mission to rescue an eleven-year-old Generación girl who had fallen into sex slavery. The girl just disappeared one day, and no one knew where she went. A few weeks passed, and then Lucy received a phone call from a former street kid who had sighted the missing girl. She had entered a known brothel in the company of an older man.

Despite the prevalence of the child sex trade in Peru, the law states that sex with a minor is a crime. So Lucy was able to persuade three members of the local police force to go with her to the hotel and intervene on the girl's behalf. While two police officers waited outside with Lucy, one officer went inside and found the john with the little girl. But instead of arresting the john, he led him out a back door and allowed him to escape. One can only guess that he received a bribe for his favor. The little girl, on the other hand, was arrested and taken down to the police station.

Outrageous, certainly, but not out of the ordinary in the streets of the poor. "We need a police force and a judicial system that are incorruptible and will defend the rights of every citizen," Lucy stresses. "To say that the poor have rights means to accept that street children hold the exact same value as our own children. Our society is not yet ready to affirm this truth."

Proving the inestimable value of abandoned kids has been the hallmark of Lucy's work. Be it riding a surfboard across Peru's emerald waves or baking delectable pastries for commercial sale, Generación's kids show their potential: they can flourish in a family environment where they feel loved.

Sex trafficking in children can be a heavy scene and leave the abolitionist in despair. But it's hard not to be inspired after visiting the Generación's home for young musicians. Nearly fifteen boys and girls, once marginalized on the streets of Lima, live together in a dynamic community of music. Most of these teens have learned to play the soulful tones of the Peruvian pan flute, which the kids enhance with the rhythmic beat of hand drums. They perform wherever they can spontaneously create an audience, maybe on a crowded bus or a bustling city square. In the not-so-distant future the tables will turn, and audiences will seek them out and pay to hear them in concert. But these ex-street kids are not waiting around for others to recognize their talent. They know their music is good, and playing it together transports them to a place where they want to stay.

Building a New Underground Railroad: USA

Louis Etongwe, age fifty-two, liberates slaves from the homes of wealthy families in the states of Virginia, Maryland, and New Jersey.

No, that's not a news bulletin from pre–Civil War America. Louis lives in modern-day Williamsburg, Virginia, and in seven separate incidents since 1999 he has rescued teenage African girls from domestic servitude and sexual bondage. Remarkably, Louis has no training in immigration law, he has no social services organization standing behind him, and he funds his activities with the money he earns from a modest salary working for the telephone company. "I act out of principle," Louis says without a trace of hubris. "I can't sit by passively when predators take advantage of the defenseless."

His odyssey toward abolition began over a Thanksgiving meal at his cousin's home in Richmond, Virginia. His cousin was helping out a family friend by giving shelter to a teenager from Cameroon—an African country located just south of Nigeria in West Africa—who was "fleeing captivity." The term *captivity* piqued Louis's curiosity. He thought maybe the girl had run into political problems back in the country where he himself had been born. So after the meal ended, he asked the teenager directly about her troubles.

His jaw dropped as she detailed her enslavement in the home of a wealthy family in the Richmond area. Her "masters" had promised her parents in Cameroon that, in exchange for work in their home, the fourteen-year-old girl would receive an education. Moreover, they offered to send her wages back to Cameroon on a regular basis. The American couple used their own daughter's passport—fabricated with a photo of their new recruit—to bring the girl into the United States.

Once the girl arrived in Virginia, the slaveholders forced her to work at domestic chores from dawn to dusk. She never attended school; for that matter, she could not leave the house unless accompanied by the husband or the wife. The slaveholders prohibited her from having any communication with her family back in Africa, though they assured her that they were sending them regular payments.

While relating her story to Louis, the girl dropped a hint that she was not the only girl from her tribe in Africa who had been trafficked to the United States. Louis seized on that reference. "What do you mean that there are 'others that have fallen into the same trap'?" he asked.

"Several of us from our region were brought here," she replied.

"Do you know their names and where they went?" Louis asked.

"Certainly, I can provide you with names and locations," she said softly. "I cannot feel totally free while they stay in captivity. You must help them."

At that moment, Louis knew he had been called to a noble cause. He had no choice—he had always stood up for the defenseless. As a young boy in grammar school in Cameroon, he never allowed the playground bullies to take advantage of the weakest kids. "Even when the fight was none of my business," Louis recalls, "I would step in and defend a kid before he got pummeled."

Now, hearing the testimony of this frightened adolescent, a familiar wave of responsibility welled up inside of him. When his cousin confessed that he could not offer refuge to the girl for more than a few days, Louis and his wife agreed to take her into their own home. The following day Louis called an FBI hotline to report an incident of international abduction and forced labor. As strange as it felt to say, he told the FBI that he was harboring an escaped slave in his home.

SLAVERY IN MODERN-DAY AMERICA

One shining star of global abolition work is the Washington, DC–based organization Free the Slaves. Kevin Bales established the organization in 2000 to educate the American public about the existence of slavery and to push governments to enact and enforce antislavery laws. The organization reflects the ethos of its founder. Kevin speaks about slavery in a style that is local yet global, strategic yet nonpartisan. Moreover, Free the Slaves consistently produces the most insightful and accurate research on trafficking networks available anywhere.

Between January 1998 and December 2003, Free the Slaves conducted a research project in collaboration with the Human Rights Center at the University of California, Berkeley. The final report, published under the title *Hidden Slaves: Forced Labor in the United States,* thoroughly documents the nature and scope of slavery inside American borders.[1] The investigation exposed a number of noteworthy trends:

- Foreigners are trafficked into the United States from at least thirty-five countries. Most victims originate in China, followed by Mexico and then Vietnam.

- The states with the largest incidence of slavery are California, Florida, Texas, and New York.

- Mexican, eastern European, and Asian crime syndicates run extensive trafficking rings inside the United States. They particularly target migrant groups.

- U.S. citizens and permanent residents import thousands of domestic servants into this country as slaves.

- Seventy-five percent of all New York apparel manufacturing firms are sweatshops, using forced labor or paying workers below minimum wage.

- Forced labor is most prevalent in five sectors of the U.S. economy: prostitution and sex services (46 percent); domestic service (27 percent); agriculture (10 percent); sweatshop/factory work (5 percent); and restaurant and hotel work (4 percent).

It is hard for many Americans to believe that slavery still exists on a grand scale in the world, let alone that it may have a foothold in their community. Yet there is no denying the fact that tens of thousands of people labor each day in the United States without pay and under the threat of violence. Because forced labor is often hidden in unregulated work environments or where cheap labor is the norm, most Americans will walk by an incidence of slavery and pay it no notice.

Given a widely held misconception, it must be emphasized that not all incidences of slavery involve undocumented immigrants. For instance, the *Detroit Free Press* reported in January 2003 that Michigan police had uncovered a multistate sex-trafficking ring involving the abduction of midwestern females, some as young as thirteen years old. The criminal network was exposed when a seventeen-year-old girl fled into a store in a Detroit, Michigan, strip mall and pleaded with a security guard for assistance. Soon thereafter, her traffickers burst into the store in pursuit. The security guard noted that the girl was battered and terrified, so he thwarted the predators and called in the local police.

The girl informed the police that she had been kidnapped while waiting at a bus stop in downtown Cleveland, Ohio. Her captors drove her to Detroit, where she was forced to engage in commercial sex.

The girl subsequently led the police to the house in Detroit where she had been held, and they arrested the leader of the trafficking ring. Upon further investigation, the police learned that the perpetrators had been kidnapping teenage girls for eight years and trafficking them to cities around the Midwest.

The mother of the girl whose escape triggered the bust declared, "The whole thing is unreal—it's like slavery. They lure and coerce these girls into doing whatever they want. It's a sick game they are playing with our children."[2]

The Polaris Project—A Star Shall Guide Them

After two commercial airliners crashed into the World Trade Center in New York City on September 11, 2001, Katherine Chon was not the only university student who grew concerned about the world's future. In the days that followed the attack, the dinner conversations she shared with her Brown University friends regularly turned to global social issues.

"So, what do you think: is religion a tool that people use to justify acts of terror and human oppression?" asked Brown senior Derek Ellerman. "Look at U.S. history," he continued. "Christians used the Bible to sanctify the practice of slavery."

"True," Katherine acknowledged, "but that same Bible inspired other Christians to become the prime movers in the abolitionist movement."

The conversation took off from there as the handful of students around the table argued over what social forces "really" ended the African slave trade in the nineteenth century. Then Derek suddenly shifted the topic: "Well, what do you think it will take to end slavery today?"

Katherine gave him a confused look. "What are you talking about?"

"Women and children all over the world are being abducted or sold and forced into the sex industry," Derek informed his stunned peers. "And millions of people of all ages have fallen into forced labor in India, Nepal, and Pakistan."

Surely Derek must be exaggerating, Katherine thought to herself, otherwise she would have heard about it in her classes at Brown. Still, she could not get the idea out of her head when she sat down to study that evening. So she put aside her books and searched the Internet for information about human trafficking. Up popped a human-rights report that detailed the millions of people caught in modern slavery. Another respected Web site claimed that human trafficking was the third most lucrative criminal activity in the world today.

Katherine looks back now and recalls her reaction: "Here I was in my senior year at an Ivy League university, and I didn't even know that this huge problem exists!" The following day she sought out the most politically aware students and professors she knew and pumped them for information about the global slave trade. They, too, confessed their ignorance.

Katherine decided to pursue her own line of research. She stumbled across a newspaper article recounting a police raid on an Asian massage parlor located only a few miles from her campus. Someone had tipped off the police that the establishment operated as a brothel, and their raid recovered six South Korean women. Traffickers had brought the women to the United States under false pretenses, took away their passports once they arrived inside its borders, and forced them to sell their bodies for sex. Despite the corroborating testimonies of the women and obvious signs of torture, the police arrested all six women on charges of prostitution.

Katherine was shocked that this could be happening in her own backyard. But it got even more personal: she herself had been born in South Korea and was about the same age as these trafficked women. Under different circumstances, she might have fallen prey to the traffickers herself.

As she learned more about the modern slave trade, a fire grew inside her. When she told Derek of her desire to become an active abolitionist, he did not skip a beat: "I'm in—we can't let this go on without a fight."

The passion to help individuals trapped in exploitation ran deep for Derek. Some of his closest friends growing up in Welles-ley, Massachusetts, had fallen victim to sexual assault and incest. At the time, he felt powerless to do anything but be a supportive listener when his friends shared their trauma. Now he felt as if he could do something more.

Katherine knew that Derek did not make commitments lightly. He had already proved himself to be a dedicated activist. During his sophomore year, the local police had used excessive force against several Brown students at a campus protest. Derek created a student task force to carry out an independent investi-gation of the incident. His dedication to public justice led him to take a two-year sabbatical from his university studies so that he could head up a nonprofit agency to monitor policy brutality and establish a civilian review board for the city of Providence.

Now he and Katherine had bumped into a colossal law en-forcement challenge. They searched for opportunities to be useful. To their consternation, they struggled to find any mean-ingful volunteer opportunities. The few abolitionist groups that did exist were looking for highly qualified professionals. The only viable options for students came down to organizing a fund-raiser or showing a film on campus.

The duo desired a deeper engagement, but they realized that they first had to better understand the mechanisms of the modern slave trade. So they persuaded two of their Brown professors to alter their standard curriculum in the coming semester and re-quire students to carry out original research on human traffick-ing. The yield of that semester's research at Brown set the early foundation for a Web site that Derek and Katherine launched and still run today, HumanTrafficking.com.

Brown offers an annual event for entrepreneurs to develop a business plan for a start-up company. Though the competition is geared toward applicants starting a for-profit enterprise, Derek and Katherine saw themselves as entrepreneurs as well, even if their bottom line was social justice. So they wrote up a business plan to launch an agency that would utilize communi-cation technologies and organizational ingenuity to resist the slave trade. Despite their unorthodox approach, they won second place and received a cash prize of $12,500, enough to launch a new antislavery agency. They named it the Polaris Project, referring to the North Star that guided slaves toward freedom along the Underground Railroad.

The Zambian A Cappella Choir—Slavery in the Church

Sandy Shepherd presumed she was doing God's work. The mother of three daughters in Colleyville, Texas—a suburb of Dallas—had taken an active role in bringing the Zambian A Cap-pella Choir to her Baptist church. The choir's members came from impoverished families in Zambia, a country that borders Angola and Zimbabwe in the center of Africa.

A pastor from Texas, Keith Grimes, had formed his TTT (Teaching Teachers to Teach) ministry to bless constituencies on both sides of the Atlantic. Church audiences in the United States would be moved to hear young African boys sing songs of Christian praise—so deeply touched, in fact, that they would open up their wallets to fund education projects back in Zambia.

When he was recruiting boys for the choir, Pastor Grimes told parents that American donations would fund the construction of local schools. Moreover, their boys would receive cash stipends that they could send back home. While on tour, his staff would provide tutoring for the boys, and upon their return to Zambia they would be the first students in a newly built schoolhouse.

Pastor Grimes brought his first boys' choir to the United States in 2003 and scheduled a tour that would last three months. Over that period, revenue from donations and CD sales of the boys' performances totaled nearly $250,000. The cash receipts exceeded the pastor's wildest dreams, and so he unilaterally extended the tour for an additional half year without the consent of the boys or their parents. The financial success of the tour continued to soar.

After the first tour group returned to Zambia, Pastor Grimes set out to recruit another choir. Between 1993 and 2000, the pastor formed five boys' choirs from Zambia and one from Liberia. The Liberian choir featured blind children.

During a tour, families from the churches where the choir performed provided the boys with hospitality. Between tour dates, the boys stayed at the TTT headquarters, located on a property in rural Texas.

Sandy signed up to host some of the boys when the choir gave its first performance at the Colleyville Baptist Church. The total experience—the beautiful a cappella songs, Pastor Grimes's graphic description of their impoverished lives back in Zambia, and a shared meal with the boys in her home—made Sandy ache for Africa. She enthusiastically joined a church delegation to visit Zambia and see firsthand the region where the boys came from and the site planned for the new school.

On that trip, Sandy witnessed Pastor Grimes in action. Being a white preacher with a freshly pressed shirt and tie gave him credibility, while his kind, charismatic personality won over the hearts of Zambian villagers. Sandy noted how proud the parents were that Pastor Grimes had selected one of their sons to join the boys' choir. They signed contracts written in English that they could not read, but they trusted that the pastor would take good care of their sons. "I sympathize with the Zambian families," Sandy says. "I could not imagine that a pastor, in the guise of Christian ministry, could enslave young kids just so that he could put money into his own donation plate."

On the choir's first visit to Colleyville, the boys who stayed at Sandy's home kept very quiet. Their behavior did not seem especially unusual for young kids who had landed in a wholly foreign culture.

Behind the scenes, the TTT staff had threatened the boys to keep quiet about their life in the choir. If a host family gave them a gift, the boys were required to hand it over to the leaders. Even phone numbers and addresses of host families were treated like contraband. The leaders directed them to "be polite yet stay silent whenever possible."

After Sandy returned from Zambia, the boys' choir made a number of return engagements to her church. The boys opened up slowly and began sharing tidbits of information that alarmed their hosts. The TTT staff screened their letters to and from Zambia, the boys claimed, and forbade phone calls home. The choir averaged four concerts a day performing in shopping malls, churches, and schools. On heavily scheduled days they might put on as many as eight separate performances. If any boy fell ill or became exhausted, Pastor Grimes threatened to send him back to Zambia, subjecting him to utter shame in the eyes of his parents. Finally, the boys revealed to their hosts that they lived in squalor here in America because TTT did not pay them stipends as they had been promised.

When Sandy called Keith Grimes and voiced her concerns, he lashed back with red-hot fury. She never saw this side of his personality on the mission field in Zambia. His heated denial only fanned her suspicions, so she called federal law enforcement agencies to request an investigation. "At that time I did not know much about human trafficking," she admits, "so I spoke to the federal agents about a cut-and-dry case of child exploitation."

FBI agents did investigate TTT, but they dismissed accusations of forced labor and bondage because they did not uncover any signs of shackles or bruises on the boys' bodies. Pastor Grimes explained to agents the mission of the boys' choir, and they accepted his motives at face value. The pastor even produced contracts that the Zambian families had signed that proved his rightful guardianship over the choir members within the United States.

Despite this setback, Sandy persisted. She contacted state law enforcement officials in Texas, the Immigration and Naturalization Service (INS), and the office of Attorney General Janet Reno. Unfortunately, her efforts yielded very few tangible results.

In 1998, the boys' choir to which Sandy had grown close returned to Africa. She heard reports that Pastor Grimes had recruited a new choir of sixty-seven Zambian kids. But she could no longer bear fretting daily about TTT's control over the boys, and her campaign to pursue legal justice waned.

For its part, TTT sought to avoid the Colleyville Baptist Church. Pastor Grimes warned his new crop of boys that an "evil church" existed in Texas and that they should reject any invitation to visit families there. "If you go to that church," the pastor warned, "they will deceive you, and you will end up in terrible conditions of abuse." It was the voice of a wolf warning the sheep to watch out for the hens.

CAST—Bringing Slavery out of the Closet

In August 1995, federal agents swooped in on an eight-unit apartment complex hidden behind a barbed-wire fence in El Monte, California, a municipality of metropolitan Los Angeles. Seventy-two garment workers had been kept captive inside the compound for as long as seven years. The slaveholders recruited females from poor, rural communities in Thailand and promised to give them high-paying sewing jobs in the United States. Once the workers arrived in Los Angeles, the slaveholders took away their passports and informed them that they had to pay back the expenses of their trip.

The garage of the apartment complex served as the sewing factory. Industrial machines stood side by side in a space so cramped that the workers could barely walk between stations. The garage offered no ventilation, and the windows were covered wholly with posters.

The roach-infested bedrooms in the apartment complex held no furniture—just mattresses lying on the floor. No light could get through the covered windows. A typical American family would find the bedroom space tight for two people, yet ten Thai women shared a single bedroom in El Monte.

The slaveholders operated two additional sewing factories in the bustling garment district of Los Angeles. While some of the Thai women sewed in the El Monte garage, others were shuttled back and forth each day to the other factories. The women labored sixteen-hour shifts while armed guards monitored their movements around the clock.

The slaveholders paid the workers about 70 cents an hour and then recouped that money immediately as a debt repayment. Because they did not allow the workers to leave the compound unguarded, the slaveholders established a commissary for toiletries and essential food. A bar of soap sold for $20; a bag of rice went for $10.

After the intervention at El Monte, Secretary of Labor Robert Reich called it "the worst case of slavery in America's recent history."[3] Nevertheless, the multiagency strike force that raided the compound treated the victims like illegal aliens. Having survived seven years of enslavement, the women now had to endure another form of captivity—behind bars and forced to wear prison uniforms. Their treatment sent a horrible message to slaves held anywhere in the United States, supporting the slaveholders' warning: "Report us to the authorities, and you will be the ones thrown in jail."

A loose network of human-rights and Asian community groups based in Los Angeles fought the detention of the ex-slaves and raised funds to post their bail. Once the women were released, the groups quickly realized that no single organization could handle medical care, legal representation, immigration issues, and the daily livelihood needs of the trafficked women. In the months to follow, the Thai Community Development Center and Little Tokyo Service Center, academics, and legal aid groups marshaled their resources to form CAST—the Coalition to Abolish Slavery and Trafficking. The group functioned informally in the aftermath of the El Monte case and then became an independent organization in 1998.

The shocking revelation of the El Monte case—that more than seventy women could be held in slavery in a Los Angeles

residential neighborhood for seven years and not be detected—
and the high-profile trial that followed raised the alarm in political and legal circles that the United States lacked effective
legislation to combat human trafficking. Foreign nationals who
were trafficked into the country were typically classified as violators of immigration law. As "illegal immigrants," they were detained and deported back to potentially dangerous situations.

CAST and other nationally active nongovernmental organizations (NGOs) pressed federal lawmakers to engineer comprehensive legislation that would protect the rights of trafficking victims
and shift the focus of law enforcement onto the real criminals.
They also encouraged the U.S. government to provide measures
for the physical, psychological, and social recovery of victims of
trafficking.

THE U.S. CONGRESS GETS IN ON THE ACT

A major piece of legislation, the Trafficking Victims Protection
Act (TVPA), passed the U.S. Congress in late 2000 with the express purpose "to ensure just and effective punishment of traffickers, and to protect their victims." Most important, the law
recognized that human trafficking is simultaneously a domestic
U.S. problem and an international crisis.

The TVPA gave law enforcement better tools to prosecute
criminals who engage in involuntary servitude, sex trafficking,
and forced labor. Under the new law, trafficking in human beings
for any of these reasons became a felony with penalties of up to
twenty years in prison, and sentencing could be increased to life
imprisonment in cases involving severe sexual abuse, kidnapping,
or murder.

The TVPA also created a new category of visa, the T visa, especially important for trafficking victims who were brought
across the border illegally or were forced to overstay their visa

admission. The statute allows them to remain in the United States if it is determined that they could suffer "extreme hardship involving unusual and severe harm" if returned to their home countries. Another requirement for eligibility: victims must be willing to cooperate with law enforcement against those responsible for their enslavement. After three years in "T status," qualified candidates may apply for permanent residency. The regulation allows them to apply for nonimmigrant status for their spouses and children. Victims under the age of twenty-one may apply for nonimmigrant status for their parents as well.

Under the auspices of the TVPA, the Congress further mandated specific government departments to launch new mechanisms to combat trafficking. The U.S. State Department, for instance, was ordered to establish an office to monitor international trafficking activity and to submit an annual report to Congress detailing how effectively individual governments had performed in confronting trafficking within their own borders. The Department of Health and Human Services (HHS) was charged with increasing the American public's awareness of trafficking and extending the range of services available to trafficking victims.

The TVPA went a long way toward creating a new legal environment so that trafficking victims would feel safer identifying themselves to law enforcement authorities, would be confident that they would not be criminalized, and would benefit from social programs specifically designed to help them. Despite this strong legal framework, antitrafficking enforcement since the TVPA's passage in 2000 has been tepid. Only about six hundred victims of trafficking have either received a T visa or been granted "continued presence" in the United States. Those figures are anemic when put next to the tens of thousands of people who have been trafficked into the United States since 2000.

The data on successful prosecution against traffickers also pale in comparison with the level of criminal activity. In 2005, the

U.S. Attorneys' offices nationwide initiated prosecutions against ninety-five defendants, 87 percent of whom were charged with violations under the TVPA. The good news: that's more than twice the number of defendants who were prosecuted in 2004.[4]

In the last couple of years, agencies at the federal and local levels have reached the right conclusion, that they cannot fight the slave trade alone. A plethora of community partnerships (or "task forces") are springing up around the country to link NGOs that specialize in trafficking, social service and health care providers, and local police departments.

Anna Rodriguez—Breaking a Curse

When U.S. Attorney General John Ashcroft signed the TVPA legislation at a major press conference in Washington, DC, Anna Rodriguez and Chica Garcia stood behind him in prominent positions. Ironically, less than two years earlier neither Anna nor Chica were even remotely aware that a modern slave trade existed. Now they had front-row seats for arguably the most important piece of antislavery legislation in over a century.

A twist of fate drew the two Hispanic women close together in 1999. Anna was working with the sheriff's office of Collier County, Florida—which includes the fertile agricultural region of Immokalee—as an advocate for victims of crime. She was frequently called in to help with cases of domestic violence.

The sheriff's office alerted Anna one morning to an assault in a neighborhood heavily populated with migrant workers. Its officers had responded to a 911 call the previous day. At the premises a battered Guatemalan woman told of how she had come home and found her husband in bed with their "domestic helper." When the wife protested bitterly, he violently assaulted her. No one from the sheriff's office bothered to interview the "domestic helper," and rather than try to untangle a complex marital spat, the sheriff's office passed the case along to Anna for evaluation.

When Anna visited the home, she interviewed the couple separately and then asked to speak to the "domestic helper." The husband became very nervous, but he could not refuse her request. Her suspicion raised, Anna made sure to find a private space to talk to the young girl. The girl introduced herself as Chica and said she was fifteen years old. Six months earlier, the master of the house had kidnapped her from a rural village in Guatemala, where her abductor's brother was mayor. The man brought her through the U.S.-Mexico border on a bus, and then across the southern United States to Florida. She now lived with her slaveholder, his wife, and their children.

Over a six-month span, she was a field slave during the day and a sex slave at night. The slaveholder forced Chica to work in the tomato fields, always hovering close by to ensure that she did not talk to other field laborers. He claimed that it cost him $2,000 to bring her to the United States, and so he would keep her wages until he had recouped his expenses. The man's wife worked in the evening, and that is when the master violated her sexually.

Anna was stunned. She had dealt with many cases of sexual abuse and domestic violence, but this was blatant slavery. She nevertheless kept her composure and gave comfort to Chica, telling her that she could find immediate shelter for her. To Anna's surprise, the girl strenuously resisted the option of leaving the home.

Anna alerted the sheriff's office to the man's crime, and that afternoon he was arrested and put in jail. Over the next week, Anna returned several times to the home and tried to convince Chica to move out and get into a shelter. Each time the girl refused.

As the trust in their relationship grew, Anna began to unravel the mystery. First off, she learned that Chica was really nineteen years old. The man had instructed her to say that she was fifteen so that other people might think she was his niece. Then she learned why the man had such a hold over her. Witchcraft carries tremendous sway in many parts of rural Latin America. The slaveholder had taken a lock of the girl's hair and had told her that he had gone to a witch doctor to bind her to him. If she tried to escape, she and her family would face a calamity. As long as the slaveholder held the lock of hair, Chica was terrified to leave the property and unleash the curse.

When the police checked the man's wallet, they found the lock of hair exactly where Chica had said it would be. On Anna's next visit, she used her own deception to get the girl help. Anna told Chica that she had just come back from visiting the slaveholder at the county jail and that he had forfeited the lock of hair and had forgiven the money she owed him.

Freed from her psychological chains, Chica happily left the property and within a year became the first recipient of a T visa in the United States. Chica has since married and with her husband is raising three children, among whom is a daughter named Anna.

The Polaris Project—
Building an Underground Railroad

The day after college graduation, Katherine and Derek loaded up a U-Haul and moved the Polaris office to Washington, DC. Itching to move from study to action, the duo had determined that major policy changes in the government and the public justice system would be needed to make a dent in the global slave trade. If they were going to concentrate first and foremost on the United States—and subsequently develop an international strategy—they needed to be in the nation's capital.

All the same, Katherine and Derek did not want to address policy issues in a vacuum, so they immersed themselves in the metropolitan DC trafficking scene. Days after setting up their new office, they read in the *Washington Post* a news item about two Chinese women whom police had arrested in a local massage parlor. The women were being detained and were awaiting deportation back to China. The case had all the signs that pointed to slavery: the women had been arrested after a raid at an Asian massage parlor, they were not in possession of a passport or other official documentation, and they did not speak a word of English. Katherine and Derek contacted the defense attorneys handling the case and asked to speak to their clients. The attorneys welcomed any kind of help that they could get on a case that remained a mystery even to them.

The Polaris founders arranged two sessions, and each time the Chinese women blatantly lied about the circumstances of their presence in the United States. As usual, their traffickers had threatened to kill the women if they told the truth. Finally, on the third visit, the women revealed to Katherine and Derek their abduction in China and coercion into the DC commercial sex industry. Polaris subsequently secured legal aid to stop their deportation and win their release from prison. Both women were eventually granted a T visa that enabled them to stay and work freely in the United States.

Katherine and Derek cut their teeth on dozens of similar domestic trafficking cases. Human slavery, they came to realize, is not only a serious crisis in China, Thailand, Nepal, Ukraine, and other poor nations. Strong trafficking networks operate covertly within U.S. borders as well and even reach to massage parlors within a few blocks of the White House. The Polaris team therefore shaped a plan to deliver a U.S.-based outreach program that would follow the entire course of the human trafficking process, starting with direct services for victims, prosecution of criminals, and structural policy changes at all levels of government.

It was an ambitious agenda, but one should not underestimate these young activists. The Polaris Project has accomplished much since its move to DC in mid-2002. It has provided a full range of social services—shelter, medical and legal aid, language classes, and job placement—for 130 individuals trafficked within the metro-DC area. The agency employs nine full-time staff workers in its Washington office and has opened satellite offices with full-time directors in Denver, Newark, and Tokyo. It manages three Web sites—HumanTrafficking.com, SlaveryStillExists.com, and PolarisProject.org—that offer substantial, fresh data. It runs four multilingual, twenty-four-hour telephone hotlines that reach across the United States and into Japan. Polaris staff members have testified before congressional committees on a range of human-trafficking policy issues and have assisted legislators in over a dozen states to draft antitrafficking laws.

As its name suggests, Polaris aims to build a modern Underground Railroad. Katherine points out that the original nineteenth-century version did not rely solely, or even primarily, on elite sectors of American society. Grassroots activists, many of whom had no formal education, built the movement. "At that time it didn't matter who you were, or what kind of education or experience you had," she says, "only that you were willing to join in the fight to stop slavery."

To that end, Katherine and Derek are training a shock troop of young abolitionists, and they are the secret behind the agency's impressive record of achievements. Nearly 175 "leadership fellows" from around the United States have come to DC for a four-month internship. Polaris runs three sessions each year, and hundreds apply for only twelve available slots in each session. Candidates, mostly university students in their twenties, go through a competitive application process that includes a written submission and several personal interviews. The fellows are responsible for finding their own housing in the DC area, while

Polaris provides hands-on experience in antislavery work. "Lots of young people want to do something meaningful about slavery, but there's so few options available," notes Katherine, who only a few years ago found herself in the same boat. "I don't want Polaris to be the only group doing this," she adds. "I just wonder why other agencies aren't tapping into their volunteer potential."

The word *intern* is practically banned from the Polaris lexicon because it is typically code for "menial jobs." At Polaris, after a two-week immersion education in antislavery activism, the fellows are placed in responsible positions that demand the exercise of leadership skills and decision making. The enthusiasm and dedication of young activists grows when they realize they are doing tasks that make a difference

Bradley Myles, an alum of the Polaris fellow program, today serves as Polaris's national program director. Other fellows have returned to their home communities and created Polaris chapters in the cities of Seattle, Los Angeles, Columbus/Toledo, Providence, and Boston. The DC office does not set the agenda for its chapters. The chapters are encouraged to tap into local expertise and existing networks and to design a strategy that makes sense for their locale. To that end, the Los Angeles chapter organizes itself around forced labor slavery, while the Seattle chapter aims to raise legal pressure on the demand side (the johns) of the commercial sex trade.

Bradley suggests that the reason 90 percent of the fellows continue on as active abolitionists is their sense of joining a movement that is bigger than themselves, yet at the same time one that craves their contribution. He points to a graduate student from Ohio, Kathleen Davis, who returned to Wright State University after her four-month stint as a fellow and initiated an Ohio chapter of Polaris. She then single-handedly wrote an eighty-page document detailing the incidence of human trafficking in the state of Ohio—its different forms, hot spots in the state, and the demographic of its victims. Davis sent the unsolicited report to law enforcement agencies, state legislators, and social service organizations across the state. It created such a stir that two Ohio legislators were inspired to propose an antitrafficking bill to the state senate.

To Bradley and his colleagues at DC headquarters, this success in Ohio meets the agency's objective to build a movement. He points to a number of former fellows who work in government antitrafficking posts or staff positions at abolitionist NGOs other than Polaris. "We shine brighter as an organization when we put the spotlight on emerging leaders and give them the tools they need to shine wherever they go."

To arrest the global slave trade, abolitionists will have to build social movements that do not wilt before the threat of powerful trafficking syndicates. Nothing builds toughness like the hard knocks of experience, and, frankly, very few abolitionist groups have a deep well of experience from which they can draw. At this early stage of movement building, inspired individuals have to be willing to make mistakes and make brave forays into uncharted territories.

"People assume that I have had this heart for social justice my entire life," Katherine remarks. But she admits that up until 2001 she rarely picked up a newspaper. "If you had told me five years ago that this is what I would be doing, I would not have thought it was possible," she says.

When she was growing up in a small New Hampshire town, her family did not discuss politics. In 1980 her parents had emigrated to the United States from the region of Kwangju in South Korea. A massacre had occurred there just months before their departure—government troops sent to squash a civic demonstration killed two thousand defenseless Koreans. Katherine knew nothing about this family history until 2004, when she was twenty-four years old. A documentary about the Kwangju massacre came on the television, and her father remarked nonchalantly, "Oh, yes, that happened around the time you were born; in fact, it's the reason you weren't born in the United States, because martial law was in place."

Her parents had passed along to Katherine their inclination to steer clear of politics to avoid trouble. So when she was first asked to speak about human trafficking at workshops in DC forums, she admits to feeling insecure: "Who am I? I'm a recent college graduate with a degree in psychology, and I just started learning about human trafficking a few years ago."

But once she and Derek attended a few congressional hearings and agency briefings, they found that their on-the-ground experience in the streets of DC was so much more real than what passed for reality in the Beltway. "I discovered that people who are in a position to make decisions are not always equipped with the best knowledge," Katherine remarks. "Developing an expertise that is rooted in real-life experience can make a big impact."

For his part, Derek gravitates toward policy work as his primary vocation. Based on the research and field work that Polaris has accumulated, he points to five strategic initiatives that he feels will make a real dent in the slave trade inside the United States.

First, abolitionists have to focus on the suppression of regional markets. In most U.S. cities at the moment, traffickers enjoy the luxury of high business profits with a low risk of arrest. Once law enforcement starts closing down operations that use forced labor, however, that equation starts to shift. Even if the traffickers decide to relocate to a new city, the cost of doing so cuts into their profit margins. The antislavery movement will know it is making progress, says Derek, when it can point to the suppression of slave markets in major metropolitan areas like Los Angeles, New York, Miami, Washington, DC, San Francisco, and Chicago.

A second key initiative involves changing the common perception of the trafficking victim. Twenty-five years ago, society treated domestic violence as a private family matter. But a new paradigm swept across the country that changed our understanding. Today we consider all men who attack women—be they husbands or boyfriends, it does not matter—guilty of a crime, and we treat the abused women as victims. Derek believes the trend is moving in the same direction with the victim of trafficking. The TVPA was a critical piece of legislation pushing the American legal system in that direction.

The next initiative also deals with the proper identification of a criminal. Derek argues that it will be critical to decriminalize the children involved in the sex industry. No child under seventeen years old who operates in the commercial sex industry should be treated as a criminal. "In every major city across America today, we arrest and punish eleven-year-old girls for the fact that they are sexually abused! How crazy is that?" Derek declares.

Fourth, Derek recognizes that the state courts are the workhorse of the judicial system. Federal law enforcement alone can never handle the load of cases involving human trafficking. Therefore, priority should be given to passing antislavery laws in state legislatures. Once again, momentum is moving in this direction. As of September 2006, twenty-two states have passed antitrafficking legislation, and seven more states are considering such legislation.[5]

Derek acknowledges that his final priority is much more ambitious. He would like to see grassroots activists track the supply chain of every consumer product we buy to determine how it is produced. Armed with that data, we could shape a policy to hold companies accountable that use slave labor in any way to produce products that they offer to consumers in the United States. Derek admits that this strategy has the least amount of momentum, but it will be a necessary step to undercut the economics that make slavery so favorable.

Despite hopeful signs, Derek stresses that the abolitionist movement has a long way to go. In his testimony before the House Subcommittee on Human Rights and Wellness, Derek gave a report card: "The standard I use to evaluate how well the U.S. is doing against trafficking is, 'Have the traffickers noticed yet?' and particularly, 'Have the majority of victims noticed yet?' The answer overwhelmingly, even almost half a decade after the passage of TVPA, is no."

Louis Etongwe—Never Waste a Perfect Opportunity

The FBI was slow responding to the report Louis had made about finding slavery in Richmond, he felt, so he tried engaging the INS and the local police. They showed polite interest, too, but no one made his houseguest's case a priority, nor would they pursue his leads on other girls from Cameroon who might be enslaved.

"I realized that if I didn't take action, no one else would," Louis says. So he dialed the home phone number of a New Jersey family on the list of names that his houseguest had provided. In hopes that the enslaved girl might be in the house alone, he called in the middle of the day. The scheme worked—a seventeen-year-old Cameroon girl picked up the phone and confirmed that she had spent three years in captivity subject to the same abuses as the first victim that Louis had met. The girl on the phone confessed that she had resigned herself to a lifetime of slavery, and so this call out of the blue felt like a miracle.

When Louis asked the whereabouts of her home village in Cameroon, he was mildly surprised that she named a place only two miles from his own childhood home. The real shocker came when he inquired about her family background. She blurted out the name of his first cousin—he had known this girl's mother for most of his life. The daughter had been a toddler when Louis had emigrated to the United States. And here they were, making a first contact in a foreign land at the worst of times.

Then again, perhaps their paths had crossed at the best of times. The girl now had no doubts that a miracle was unfolding. Before she had left Cameroon, her mother had urged her to contact Mr. Louis Etongwe if she ran into trouble in America. She had lost his phone number, but here was Louis on the phone offering to rescue her. "Please, Mr. Etongwe," she pleaded, "free me from this prison! I fear for my life!"

Louis subscribes to the theory that a perfect opportunity should never be wasted; the window may never open again. "The masters of the house have left you at home alone," he noted, "so we must seize this chance to get you out."

They hatched an impromptu escape plan. The girl explained that she was tending three young children and did not feel right simply abandoning them without a caretaker. The mother arrived home promptly at 4:00 each afternoon, and the girl could see her car approaching up a long driveway. As soon as her car entered the driveway, the girl could sneak out the back door and run to a side street. Louis has a brother-in-law who lives in New Jersey, and he would call in a favor—the brother-in-law would be waiting in the side street with the car running. He would take the girl back to his home, and there they would wait for Louis, who would be driving up to New Jersey that evening after he got off work in Virginia.

The plan came off without a hitch, and the girl was rescued. On the long trip back to Virginia, she filled Louis in on the details of her captivity. She had not had contact with her family for three years. On one occasion, she had caught a glimpse of a letter from Cameroon with her mother's handwriting on the envelope, but the letter had disappeared. She assumed that other letters had been confiscated as well.

By 2002, Louis had rescued two additional girls from domestic slavery. So now four young girls lived with him and his exceedingly generous wife. But try as he might, Louis had trouble lighting a fire under the justice system to offer the girls protection. Investigation into a trafficking crime generally moves at a snail's pace, even in cases like these where the testimonies of the victims are solid. As commonly happens, the slaveholders claimed that the girls' parents back in Cameroon had consented to an employment contract, and they had signed documents to prove it. Neither local nor federal law enforcement agents were likely to send an investigator over to Africa to unravel the truth.

Louis therefore bought a plane ticket and a video camera and headed over to Cameroon on his own. He visited the families of each girl now living in his home and filmed their testimonies detailing how the traffickers had promised an education and a well-paying job for their daughters. None of the families had heard directly from their daughters from the moment they arrived in the United States, and their "employers" had not sent any money.

Louis particularly relished a visit to his home village. When he arrived, his cousin was in mourning, dressed completely in black. "Dear cousin," she spoke tearfully to him upon his arrival, "I wish it were with joy that I could mark your visit from America. But I have received sad news that my daughter went missing in your new homeland and is presumed dead."

His news that her daughter was alive and safely sharing his own home became a cause for great celebration. He then played for them a video message from the girl to her family and friends. There was not a dry eye in the village.

CAST—Shifting Paradigms

Kay Buck became executive director of the Coalition to Abolish Slavery and Trafficking in 2003. The Canadian-born visionary has an extensive international background in antislavery work. From 1990 to 1996, Kay lived in Asia and supported the efforts of abolitionists in Thailand and Japan to design strategies that would reduce the incidence of trafficking in rural communities. While creative economic and social interventions helped build stronger communities, Kay could not help ignoring the fact that a destructive cultural pattern persisted: society tolerates violence against women.

An objective analysis of the global slave trade supports her conclusion. Select a random sample of five individuals who have fallen victim to trafficking, and four will be females. The statistics would not change radically even if sex slavery were separated from forced labor. Though females certainly are the prime targets for sex traffickers, they also dominate the ranks of coerced factory workers, rug and loom weavers, and domestic servants, just to name a few major categories of forced labor. Research further shows that regardless of their form of slavery, a female in most cases will be subject to sexual violence as part of her domination.

When Kay left Asia, she returned to North America and joined a Canadian NGO that focused on societal violence against women. Though the semantics changed—from human trafficking to gender violence—she felt as if she continued to address many of the same issues that she confronted in Asia. When the top post at CAST opened up, she jumped back over the fence into the dynamics of human trafficking.

The first private foundation to support CAST's work was the Women's Foundation of California. They appreciated what Kay and a growing number of abolitionists have seen. The tidal wave that could sweep over trafficking networks worldwide will begin to crest when women organize internationally to empower other women.

It would not do CAST justice, however, to categorize it as a "women's organization." The agency has pioneered community-based models that bring help to trafficking victims and grief to traffickers. CAST has distinguished itself in the area of police training: how to identify and rescue potential victims and how to usher them into victim aftercare. Since 1999 the CAST staff has trained more than five thousand officers and has a project in place with the Los Angeles Police Department (LAPD) to train all ten thousand of its officers by the end of 2007.

Imelda Buncab heads up the training and outreach programs at CAST. She trains police units in regions far beyond Los Angeles. In 2006 she led workshops in the Virgin Islands, Arizona, Texas, Washington, Kansas, Alaska, and Hawaii. Imelda admits that she can never quite predict what response she might get from police officers.

When she led a training workshop for the police in Tucson, Arizona, in 2005, the controversy over border patrols was at its height. A self-styled vigilante group called the Minutemen had taken it upon themselves to stop immigrants from crossing into the United States. So when Imelda began talking about trafficking, the Tucson police were adamant that they were not responsible for enforcing immigration laws. Smuggling, which is what they interpreted trafficking to be, was a federal issue. Eventually Imelda enabled them to see the distinction between smuggling (a crime in which individuals help migrants cross borders without proper documents or official approval) and human trafficking (a crime in which individuals are coerced or deceived into entering the United States and then forced to work against their will).

Captain Kyle Jackson, the commanding officer at the LAPD who oversees human trafficking cases, heralds the CAST training as invaluable for his officers. "Trafficking usually is so underground, we had to shift our mindset to notice the signs," he says. "In the past we would focus solely on the crime at hand. In a domestic violence case, for instance, we did not ask a victim what country she was from or how she might have fallen under the control of the owner of the house."

Captain Jackson also underscores the importance of partnering with an NGO like CAST to obtain the trust of victims and potential witnesses in a trafficking case. Foreign nationals particularly may fear to speak to a police officer. A community NGO can help assure victims that the police are on their side to stop their predator. At the same time, the NGO can help the police understand the unspoken cultural assumptions that the victim or witness is bringing to the case. Captain Jackson notes that law enforcement has to approach human trafficking with a fresh pair of eyes: "Local police work changes dramatically in a global village."

The Zambian A Cappella Choir—Smile and Sing

When Pastor Grimes recruited him to join his choir in 1998, Given Kachepa was an eleven-year-old orphan. His mother had died when he was in the second grade, and his father passed away two years later. Given and his five siblings moved in with their Aunt Margret, who already had six children of her own.

The promises that Pastor Grimes made to Given and Aunt Margret seemed like a dream come true. The boy could earn some money for his destitute family and gain a top-drawer education in the United States. Pastor Grimes also pledged that the boys would be baptized once they reached the United States, which to a Christian convert in Zambia means a great deal. "When you are from a poor country, and you have someone from a rich country tell you that they can provide all the things that you are missing in your life, you treat it like a gift from God," Given explains.

It is almost impossible for a poor Zambian to obtain a visa to visit the United States. But a senior officer in the Zambian national police collaborated with Pastor Grimes to facilitate the visa process for hundreds of choir boys. Other government officials must have been on TTT's payroll as well, for the American pastor had the birth dates on the boys' passports altered. Once he learned that U.S. audiences would donate more generously to help small children, Pastor Grimes fabricated the image of a choir of extraordinarily young boys.

Not one of the pastor's promises to Given came to fruition in the United States. Each day at TTT headquarters in Texas, the staff woke up the boys at the crack of dawn and forced them to dig by hand a deep hole to build a swimming pool. After hours of hard physical labor in the blazing summer sun, they would rehearse songs in the afternoon and into the evening.

Despite the exhaustion they felt at the end of a day at TTT headquarters, it was nothing compared to the pace they kept on tour: eighteen-hour days, seven days a week, for perhaps a month at a time. The boys would travel from one location to the next crammed into an overcrowded van. Once they arrived at a venue, they set up the stage for the performance, and then dismantled it after the concert was finished. They repeated this drill multiple times each day. "I felt like a puppet on a string being moved around," Given says. "I was told to smile and sing with an expression of joy for my God, but eventually singing to the Lord lost its meaning for me."

Given had his heart set on an education, and so three months into his U.S. stay he asked Pastor Grimes and his daughter, Barbara Grimes Martens, when the boys' tutoring might begin. They passed into an angry frenzy, screaming at Given, even swearing at him, for being so ungrateful for the opportunity to live in America. It was the last time he inquired about study. Their baptism in a church also turned out to be an empty promise. Given concluded that the TTT leadership spoke only in lies.

Pastor Grimes died in 1999, and his daughter and her husband, Gary Martens, picked up where he had left off. The couple had been involved in "the ministry" from the start. Barbara kept track of the finances, and Gary handled the tour schedule. Not much changed in the daily lives of the boys after the pastor's death. Given and his peers kept on their grueling pace.

Barbara and Gary Martens lacked the pastor's smooth diplomacy and shrewdness. At one point, they determined that two of the boys had become a negative influence on the choir, and so they called the INS to pick the boys up and deport them back to Zambia. On the way to the airport, the boys divulged to the INS agent the truth of what went on behind closed doors in the Zambian A Cappella Choir. The agent found their stories credible and took the boys to a safe house instead of to the airport.

The agent then launched an in-depth investigation into TTT. Given recounts the day that INS agents came to TTT headquarters to conduct interviews. Barbara and Gary Martens had scripted how the boys should answer questions and had warned the boys that the agents would throw them into jail and torture them if they felt that something was amiss. "We believed that no one would help us," Given explains. "In our country, government officials take bribes every day. We do not trust men in uniforms."

Because the boys refused to come forward, the INS investigation did not yield immediate results; in fact, it lasted another seven months. Finally, in January 2000, the INS rescued the boys from the grasp of TTT. Given was thirteen years old, an orphan cut off from his siblings, left in limbo in a foreign land.

That's about the time Sandy Shepherd received an unexpected call from the pastor of her church. The INS had just contacted him with a report that a group of boys from the Zambian A Cappella Choir had been rescued from TTT, and they needed safe houses. If the church could not accommodate the boys, the agent would have to detain them in an INS holding cell.

Sandy was not about to let that happen. She jumped on the phone and found some good Samaritans in her community who were willing to help out on short notice. Given stayed with Sandy, and she walked him through the endless hoops of health screenings, depositions, work permits, and visa applications.

In 2001, Sandy and her husband, Deetz, gained legal custody of Given and enrolled him in the seventh grade. He excelled in high school and is now a second-year university student in Texas. He worked part-time jobs in high school at a grocery store and a landscaping business and sent most of the money back to his siblings in Zambia. He even helped three of his brothers start a small business. Given has worked with Texas state representative Lon Burnam to pass a statute on human trafficking. He is also doing something that TTT promised but never delivered: he is raising funds to build schools in his native Zambia.

Given and Sandy remain devoted to putting an end to human trafficking. Given speaks nationally to groups about his experience and what it feels like to be a victim. "Look beneath the surface," he tells audiences. "People who are trafficked usually are hidden, so pay attention to signs that seem out of the ordinary."

The Polaris Project—
Americans Trafficking Other Americans

About half of the sex slaves that Polaris assists in the metro-DC region are foreign nationals, and the other half are internally trafficked U.S. citizens. At some point, they all end up in deep gratitude to Tina Frundt, the woman who pulls them through their darkest night.

Tina has been rescuing sex slaves from the streets of DC for the past six years, three in her capacity as the Polaris outreach coordinator. It troubles her that Americans still think sex trafficking only happens to women and children overseas. "We run into a foreign victim of sex trafficking, and we instantaneously sympathize with her coerced passage into the sex industry," Tina says. "But when we encounter an American girl on the street, we think, 'Why did she make this choice? Surely she can walk away any time she wants.'"

Tina explains that most domestic trafficking victims are between twelve and fourteen years old. "How many girls at that age do you know who would choose to be sexually assaulted a dozen times a night?" she asks poignantly.

A domestic trafficking episode can begin with any number of scenarios. Traffickers sometimes kidnap children and transport them to another region of the United States, or they might buy a child from parents addicted to drugs. Pimps may court young teens as if they were looking for girlfriends and then coerce them into sex slavery. The pimps also troll strip clubs and juvenile jails, which they consider target-rich environments.

Tina recounts a "typical case" that took place in early 2006. Two young women—one eighteen years old and the other nineteen—called her hotline number from the bathroom of a DC hotel. They had turned on the shower so that the pimp and his "bottom" who shared their hotel room could not hear them make the phone call.

Pimps often select one of the women whom they control to be their "bottom," or go-to girl, for recruiting new sex slaves. The bottom may be the woman who has been with him the longest, or his favorite, or the most trusted. Regardless, the bottom will carry out much of the dirty work that the pimp could probably not do as effectively alone.

Tina instructed the frightened girls to stay in the bathroom while she made an emergency call to the local police. By the time the police arrived at the hotel, Tina was there waiting for them. She called the girls back on their cell phone and told them to ask the pimp if they could buy a soda from the vending machines outside the hotel room. Once the girls emerged, the police rushed inside and arrested their abductors.

Once they were free, Tina learned more about their story. The two girls live in the Midwest. The bottom had been a longtime acquaintance of theirs, and she asked them for a favor. She and her boyfriend needed to get to Washington, DC, where they had landed new jobs, but their car had broken down. She offered to pay the girls to drive them out East.

The girls considered it a great deal to be paid to take a road trip and visit DC. But once they arrived in the nation's capital, the man bluntly informed them that they were his property. He invited several friends over to the hotel their first night in town, and the men took turns raping the women. "You might as well get used to it because this is what you will be doing from now on," he said matter-of-factly.

Luckily, he never thought to search the girls to see if they possessed a cell phone. The night before, during their orientation to street life in DC, a community advocate was handing out Polaris hotline cards. The girls grabbed one and kept it hidden, waiting for the right moment. Their hotline call passed directly to Tina's cell phone.

Tina knows intimately about the trauma of being trafficked. When she was fourteen years old, growing up in Chicago, a man coerced her into sexual commerce. Ten years her senior, he pretended that he had fallen in love with her—a classic recruitment technique called "the lover boy." After several months of courtship, he suggested that they run away from her "meddling parents."

They ended up in Cleveland, Ohio, where he said they were going to visit his relatives. That evening, several of his friends came by the hotel where they were staying, and her "boyfriend" told her to have sex with them. She refused, and the men raped her. After they left, her boyfriend simply said, "That wouldn't have happened to you if you had just listened to me in the first place."

Tina today tells clients, "You don't have to explain to me everything that happened to you because I have been in your situation." At that point the client typically breaks down in tears, the dam released simply because someone else knows the deep pain she has endured. "What happened to me twenty years ago is still going on today," Tina notes sadly.

Tina realizes that slaveholders will not surrender their trade easily because they make so much money off of it. She reports crossing paths with a DC-based trafficker who held three young girls in his "stable," each of whom was bringing in about $1,500 a day. Multiply those figures out and this one slaveholder was making about $45,000 a month, or $540,000 a year, tax-free selling these girls every night.

"The pimps are cocky now, not afraid of the police, not afraid of the judicial system, because they feel like they are untouchable," Tina informed a House committee that was seeking to understand the criminal syndicates behind the sex trade. "We, as Americans, have made them untouchable by not recognizing the problem and solving it."[6]

Louis Etongwe—Passing a Test

After gathering crime evidence in Cameroon, Louis faced tribulations of his own back in the United States. The slaveholders had discovered who had facilitated the escape of "their property," and they began making threatening phone calls to his home. Louis received angry phone calls as well from other Cameroon foreign nationals living in the United States who believed that his activities had tainted the reputation of their entire community. "Why don't you just leave good enough alone," they told him bitterly. "You know as well as I do that these girls were as poor as dirt back home; they are much better off here."

Meanwhile, Louis's wife had tired of the constant drama that the rescued slaves had brought to their lives, not to mention the mounting costs of meals, medical care, and legal aid. On one of the many long trips that Louis made to the INS district office, his car broke down and he did not have the money to fix it. Louis's wife wanted it all to end—and soon.

His troubles reached an apex in mid-2002 when he came home from work and saw several police cars parked in his driveway. The police had been tipped off that Louis was harboring illegal aliens and running a brothel out of his home. The "tips" had come from the slaveholders, who wrote slanderous letters to local social service agencies and the police. The police now threatened to throw Louis and the girls into jail.

Fortunately, Louis had kept meticulous documentation of his work on behalf of the girls. He also had kept the business cards of those immigration attorneys and law enforcement agents who had invited him to call any time he might need help. That moment had arrived, and he passed the cards on to the police. Once the police called his references, they received confirmation that Louis was "one of the good guys."

Following the raid on his home, the local newspaper published a feature story on Louis's activities and lauded his sacrifice to liberate enslaved teens. Neighbors stopped by to congratulate him and sheepishly acknowledge that they had been asked to monitor his activities. "Now we understand why so many investigators were coming to our homes and asking about you," they told him.

Almost as if he had passed his test, everything started to fall into place following the police raid on his home. The attorney general's office arrested the slaveholders and brought them to trial. Once juries had watched Louis's videotape of the parents and heard the testimonies of the girls, they convicted the perpetrators of abduction and sexual assault. The girls obtained residency in the United States, found boyfriends and jobs, and maintain regular contact with their families in Cameroon.

For his part, Louis has rescued three additional girls enslaved in domestic labor and is working covertly on a few other unresolved cases. He is reticent to talk about his work, mostly because he wants to deflect attention from himself. He desires no greater reward than what he has already gained. "I've never felt so much strength and passion in my life as I have liberating these girls," he explains. "I feel like I tapped into a gold mine of meaning for my own life."

Asked from where he draws his strength, Louis points to his grandparents. When he was a young boy, his village had the good fortune to land one of the first schoolhouses in all of Cameroon. Families from distant regions hoped against hope that their children might attend the school, but they did not know how they could manage the logistics. Louis's grandparents offered to take in as many as a dozen kids at a time so that they could attend school. Walking into his grandparent's home felt like entering a dormitory.

"But they did not treat it like a sacrifice," Louis recalls. "To help someone in need felt like a gift." Louis ponders that comment for a moment, then adds, "I think my grandparents would be very proud of what I am doing today."

Indeed, the Etongwe legacy has crossed an ocean but has lost none of its power to move mountains.

Anna Rodriguez—
Community Action Against Trafficking

Anna began helping victims of violent crimes as a second career. Born in San Juan, Puerto Rico, she came to Florida at the age of eighteen when her father's company transferred him to "the citrus state." She married young and together with her husband raised a family. After her children had grown up, Anna explored how she might help her local community. The director of a domestic violence program invited her to volunteer a few days each week at its shelter.

Anna loved working at the shelter and discovered that she had a knack for treating crises with a cool head. People quickly come to believe that she could help them resolve their problems. That's due in part to the fact that she is blessed with a unique mix of personal qualities. On the one hand, she radiates compassion in such an affable way that crime victims do not feel pitied. Yet she conducts herself with a hard-nosed, let's-do-whatever-it-takes-to-get-this-job-done demeanor. In sum, she's someone you definitely want on your side, not battling against you.

At the shelter, Anna teamed up with the public justice system to bring domestic violence cases to trial. Previously, county crime investigators and prosecutors could not coax abused women to talk about what their boyfriends or husbands had done to them. Furthermore, most migrant workers in her county do not trust the police. They fear being deported if they so much as report a crime. As a result, the justice system in her county had lots of open cases that never came to trial.

In 1995 Anna joined the county sheriff's office to act as a bridge to the community. She aimed to be available. Because most farm laborers start their day at four in the morning and finish at dusk, she worked evening shifts several times a week. Once the migrant community viewed her as a trusted advocate, the sheriff's office filled up like a doctor's waiting room. The county saw a sharp increase in the number of cases flowing through the court system.

After her first slavery case with Chica, Anna detected an increasing number of human trafficking incidents. But the scarcity of services geared to trafficked victims exasperated her. In one single incident, the sheriff's office rescued seven children who had been trafficked to the county as sex slaves. Anna could not find a single place that could give them shelter; the justice system was set up to send runaways and minority offenders to juvenile prisons. But jail was no place to send victims of a crime.

Anna also became frustrated that so many trafficking cases would languish and never come to trial. Prosecuting a trafficking case demands extraordinary dedication because it is so costly and time-consuming. Many times an investigator needs to travel to a foreign country to check out the original scene of the abduction. Moreover, victims are often slow to cooperate because they have been psychologically terrorized or told not to testify under threat of death. Sex traffickers might videotape a victim being violated and threaten to show the tape to the victim's family and neighbors in the home village if she testifies.

Observing firsthand all the reasons why a slavery case might fall through the cracks, Anna resigned from the sheriff's office to establish the Florida Coalition Against Human Trafficking. Her primary goal as executive director was to create a liaison linking law enforcement bodies, social service agencies, and trafficking victims. She secured funding from several government agencies—above all, the federal Department of Health and Human Services—and a few individual donors.

She set up the coalition's headquarters in Bonita Springs, an agricultural community between Naples and Fort Meyers in southwestern Florida. A large concentration of migrant workers and construction workers can be found in Bonita Springs, which—added to the fact that it is located off a major transportation artery (Interstate 75)—makes it a trafficking hot spot.

Anna is convinced that it will take community-wide action to shut down the slave trade. So she runs workshops for any group that is likely to have contact with people in their homes or at their places of work. For example, she teams up with the power company to train the workers who read the meters in residential neighborhoods. She also delivers workshops for home-care nurses and social workers who are likely to make home visits. "The more people who know about the indicators to look for, the more trafficking victims we can save," she notes.

In her workshops, Anna identifies hot spots where slaves turn up time and time again:

> Housecleaning services
> Landscape and gardening businesses
> Domestic (home) workers
> Large-scale agricultural labor
> Construction sites
> Casinos
> Garment factories
> Hotels (housekeeping)
> Nail salons
> Migrant or transitional communities
> Zones known for prostitution
> Strip clubs/massage parlors
> Domestic violence cases

After reviewing common destination sites, Anna suggests a series of questions to evaluate a potential case of slavery:

- Does the individual have freedom of movement?

- Is the individual allowed to socialize with other people or attend community events and religious services without accompaniment?

- Does a minor appear to be under the control of an adult who is not his or her parent?

- Does the residence have doors with locks on the outside, or is it surrounded with a barbed wire fence directed internally to keep people inside the property from getting out?

- Are the windows at the residence boarded up?

- Is there a steady flow of males in and out of the residence?

- Do male guardians appear to be constantly monitoring women who come in and out of the residence?

- Has the individual been threatened with deportation or law enforcement action?

- Has the individual, or a relative, been threatened with harm if he or she attempts to leave?

- Is the individual in possession of identification documents (like a passport); if not, who has control of the documents?

- Does it seem as if the individual was coached on what to say when questioned by law enforcement officers?

- Is the individual coerced to engage in some kind of work?

- Is the individual forced to perform sexual acts?

- Has the individual been deprived of food, water, sleep, medical care, or life necessities?

Anna's experience proves time and time again that good things happen once people learn the warning signs of slavery and feel confident to take action. For example, in April 2005, a social worker approached Anna after a training workshop and told her that she had a client in the fast-growing resort town of Cape Coral who fit her profile of a trafficking victim.

A few days later, Anna accompanied local police on a raid of the property. They rescued a fourteen-year-old Guatemalan girl who had been enslaved for almost three years. The slaveholder owned a landscaping business and forced the girl to make meals for his workers. When the landscaping team went out to work, he locked her inside the house. The slaveholder also sexually abused her and pimped her out to workers and suppliers to whom he owed money.

"Finally, someone believes my story." That's the first thing the girl said to Anna after the raid. A year earlier, when she was six months pregnant, her slaveholder had beaten her badly. A neighbor rushed her to the hospital, and she gave birth to a one-pound baby who survived. The neighbor reported the crime, but the police never responded. They treated it like a family dispute.

Anna tells this story to highlight the difference that a community coalition makes. The police did intervene and arrest her trafficker, who pleaded guilty to child sex trafficking. The girl was not treated like a criminal, and she received her T visa. Not only did the trafficker go to jail, but his sister, who lived in the house, was convicted for aiding and abetting a crime. One of the associates who accepted sex as payment for a debt was also convicted for rape of a minor.

Anna stresses how much has changed in the last five years, and much of it has to do with creating a united community front that can deal a blow to trafficking networks. She is busy extending Florida Coalition offices to the cities of Jacksonville, Pensacola, and Miami. Each office will be staffed with full-time case managers who can offer help to rescued victims and develop strong alliances with the local public justice system.

Anna is quick to point out that the smallest action can make a difference. "Human trafficking can only work if the victims remain invisible to the public eye," Anna says. "We have to remove the veil of ignorance."

Conclusion
Ending the Slave Trade in Our Time

I believe in the power of individuals to change the world. Social movements take root and blossom when enough individuals take personal action. When you tell yourself that there is nothing that you can do to arrest the global slave trade, you underestimate your own potential and abandon hope for those trapped in captivity.

I speak from experience. In the early 1980s I went to the country of El Salvador to visit grassroots organizations that provided food and medical aid to impoverished communities. I had no grand plan in mind beyond seeing if there was anything I could do to support their work.

At the time, a military government terrorized the civilian El Salvadoran population. The generals especially did not like groups that preached democracy and social development for the poor. Two years before I arrived, the archbishop of the Roman Catholic Church, Oscar Romero, was shot in the heart in the middle of mass as he stood behind the altar. During his sermons, Romero had boldly addressed military atrocities against civilians.

A year later, military death squads savagely raped and murdered four U.S. religious women who worked in El Salvadoran refugee camps. In response to these murders, President Jimmy Carter induced Congress to cut off tens of millions of dollars of economic aid to the government of El Salvador. That act certainly got the attention of the generals.

Up until that moment, military death squads had acted with near impunity. They would conduct intelligence on individuals working for social change and then at night take off their uniforms and visit their homes. In the morning, neighbors would find their mangled bodies with a note attached: "This is what happens to subversives."

During my first visit, my new El Salvadoran friends implored me to start a human-rights program that would protect them from the death squads. I had no background in this type of work. In fact, I had never been involved previously in any kind of political work or international diplomacy. A couple of years earlier, I had earned a degree in psychology from Westmont College, a small liberal arts college in Santa Barbara, California.

After about nine months, the U.S. Congress restored economic and military aid to El Salvador, but the generals in El Salvador had learned a lesson: it was fine to kill El Salvadorans, but not U.S. citizens. I, too, took note of the skewed rules of international politics, and so I leveraged the value of a U.S. citizen to save an El Salvadoran life. I recruited friends and acquaintances to go to El Salvador as unarmed bodyguards, and their only shield would be a U.S. passport.

The initial plan was simple. A team of six U.S. citizens would pass a month in El Salvador on twenty-four-hour alert. One member of the team would accompany any El Salvadoran health care worker or pastor or literacy worker who received a threat from a death squad. Two more of my "bodyguards" would stay at the family home of the individual at risk. I assigned an additional two bodyguards to stay full-time at the threatened individual's agency office: the death squads would at times bomb the offices of grassroots organizations that they sought to destroy. The final member of the six-person team would visit the chief of the military police of El Salvador, as well as a senior El Salvadoran government official and the U.S. ambassador. These authorities would be informed that U.S. citizens had aligned their fate with the targeted community leader.

I participated in the first team of six that went to El Salvador in 1984. We had been in the country for only a few days when the executive director for all the Baptist churches in El Salvador, Rev. Carlos Sanchez, contacted us. He held in his hand a note from one of the more notorious death squads. The message was clear: "Unless you leave the country within forty-eight hours, you and your family will be killed."

On two previous occasions, Rev. Sanchez had received similar death threats and had taken his family out of the country for a year at a time. But now that he was responsible for over fifty Baptist churches in his country, he did not want to leave. If a high-profile church leader fled when he received a death threat, how would the parish pastor in a rural village feel? What motivation would that give a health care educator teaching peasants community medical models? So Rev. Sanchez asked if we could help him and his family stay in the country and continue their work.

We swiftly put our plan into action. A young U.S. seminary student from Las Vegas, Nevada, accompanied Rev. Sanchez around the clock. Two members of the team went to his house to stay with his wife and four children, and two others camped out at the national headquarters for the Baptist church. I took on the role of visiting the authorities, essentially warning them of a major international incident if they did not take quick action to stop the death squad. Each authority I visited denied knowing the identity of these "shadowy groups," the death squads. I politely responded that it was in their power to stop this assassination. I relayed our commitment to stay by the side of our El Salvadoran friends.

Fortunately, the gambit paid off. Rev. Sanchez and his family survived and continued their valuable work in local communities.

Over the months to follow, our project sent a new team of six U.S. citizens to El Salvador every month to play a similar role. On each occasion, the life of an El Salvadoran was protected by the presence of U.S. citizens.

The El Salvadoran authorities eventually discovered the leadership behind our human-rights work. I was banned from entering the country, and many of our team members had trouble securing visas. Quickly shifting to Plan B, we decided to launch a fake economic development agency as a front for our human-rights group.

I still get a chuckle when I recall the phone call I made to one of my Westmont College friends, Jim Morgan, asking him to go to El Salvador and become our first agronomist. Jim had graduated with a degree in religious studies, and at the time of my call, was driving a forklift at a yogurt factory. His initial response was reasonable: "But I hardly know anything about agriculture." I explained that it did not matter, since his primary role was to serve as a human-rights presence and he only had to pretend to be an agronomist. I made similar calls to other friends asking them to take on other roles—a nutritionist, a health care worker, and so on—in our new "economic development agency." Every one of us was around twenty-five years old and lacked experience for the job we set out to do.

A long story could follow—we stayed in El Salvador for more than a decade, until a peace treaty ended the violent civil war—but I will cut to the chase. Not only did we continue to carry out human-rights work and rescue the lives of many El Salvadorans, we also evolved into a proficient economic development agency. Jim Morgan became one of the most highly respected agronomists in El Salvador. He initiated an experimental farm where he introduced peasants to new ways of farming on steep, poor land. Our other staff also developed excellent skills in areas for which they had no formal training. What we did have going for us was an education, a compassion for the defenseless, and the courage to stand up for what is right. We did not listen to family, friends, and politicians who told us that this international problem was too big for us, that it was beyond our means to make a difference.

So today I am convinced that every single individual can make a valuable contribution to arrest the global slave trade. If you doubt that fact, it is probably because you underestimate the power of your personal resources. Twenty years ago, all it took for a U.S. citizen to save the life of an El Salvadoran was to hold up a passport. Sometimes it is simply who you are, and not only what you can do, that can make a difference. Truly, the hardest step to take is the first one: the commitment to take action. The ensuing steps have a way of revealing themselves.

THE ABOLITIONIST'S VOCATION

As a university professor, I frequently challenge my students about their obsession with a career beyond college. I tell them that they will be far more fulfilled if they seek a vocation instead. To build a career, they will stitch together jobs into a valuable résumé; to build a vocation, they will design and pursue meaningful endeavors. Those two paths often take an individual in different directions.

How do you find your vocation? You locate where your passion meets the needs of the world. The first part of that equation is to engage yourself in those activities that you feel you were put on this earth to do. The second part of the equation is to carry out those activities so as to benefit others. The world is filled with unhappy people who are doing work that they do not care about, all for the sake of making more money or because they are trying to fulfill someone else's dreams.

A new underground railroad is emerging that aims to put an end to human slavery once and for all. It desperately needs reinforcements, a new wave of abolitionists, to join in the struggle. Lawyers are needed to protect the rights of victims and prosecute their predators. Business entrepreneurs are needed to launch enterprises for freshly liberated slaves. Students are needed to carry out research and influence policy. Health care workers and mental health professionals are needed to pick up the pieces of broken lives. Construction workers are needed to build shelters. Employers are needed to offer jobs. Owners of two blankets are needed to donate one. On the list goes—mention a resource and the abolitionist movement needs it. The movement needs your time, money, and talent.

Join an existing group, or create a project of your own. Volunteer on a part-time basis, or make it your full-time work. Whatever your inclination, do something that will help this abolitionist movement blossom. To stir your imagination, here are several examples of creative abolitionist work.

Shoot a Home Movie and Project It Around the Country

Lots of university students know about the night commuters in Uganda, thanks in large part to the efforts of three college students from Southern California. Immediately after graduating from college, these three friends made a trip to Sudan. They brought along a video camera to document their adventures. It was serendipity that took them to northern Uganda, where they stumbled across a sea of children migrating to safety.

The boys filmed as much footage as they could, then returned to California and edited it into a documentary that they called *Invisible Children*. They then traveled tirelessly to campuses across the country, showing the movie and hosting follow-up discussions.

The film has done wonders to raise awareness on American campuses about "the forgotten war" in Uganda. Every time I speak about modern slavery at a university, I am asked if I have seen the film.

Whenever young people tell me that they feel powerless to make a difference on big issues like global slavery, I think of those three friends from Southern California.

Launch a Second Career Where Your Skills Are Needed

Pierre Tami, the founder of Hagar in Cambodia, would be the first to admit that he does not have the necessary expertise to launch some of his business enterprises. But in his shelter live an army of women freshly liberated from sex slavery who need jobs. So Pierre moves forward in faith that the right people will show up in due course to help him figure out how to make the company work.

Hagar Catering is a prime example. Pierre knew very little about how to operate a company that prepares and delivers food. Once he got the enterprise up on its feet, Pierre tried handing over responsibility for the day-to-day operations to a series of general managers who knew as little about the catering business as he did. The business floundered, and Pierre feared that it might not survive.

The future of the company was weighing heavily on his mind when he toured Australia to speak about Hagar's work. Over lunch with supporters in the city of Perth, he shared his burden. Once he had finished, one of his companions suddenly blurted out, "Hey, Pierre, look. Up at the front of the restaurant I can see Frank Woods eating lunch with a friend. Frank is one of the most successful caterers in all of Perth. On our way out I'll introduce him, and you can ask his advice."

Pierre felt somewhat sheepish interrupting a stranger's lunch to tell him about his struggling catering business in Phnom Penh. But he figured that he did not have anything to lose. So he met Frank and explained what Hagar was trying to accomplish with its entrepreneurial ventures and the roadblocks it had met along the way. After a friendly fifteen-minute chat, Pierre apologized for the interruption and walked to the front of the restaurant, where he waited for his friends to pay the bill.

After a minute or two, Frank rose from his seat and approached Pierre with a proposal. "I have done quite well with my business career here in Perth," he said to Pierre. "What do you think about my coming over to Phnom Penh and lending a hand?"

Pierre could only think to ask, "How soon can you come?"

Frank moved to Cambodia and soon turned the business around. He set up new business practices that might be common sense to a seasoned veteran of the catering industry but would never have occurred to a novice. The company has thrived since 2004. It now employs seventy-three ex-slaves and turns a profit that helps support Hagar's philanthropic programs.

Abolitionists all over the world are launching microenterprises in an effort to create sustainable jobs for ex-slaves. Frankly, most of these erstwhile entrepreneurs are out of their depth: they have backgrounds in social work or religious ministry, not business management. They badly need a Frank Woods to step in and apply expertise honed from years of experience.

Shape a Government Policy That Could Impact Millions of Lives

For the past twelve years Joe Mettimano has worked in Washington, DC, to advocate on behalf of children in crisis. He began with a seven-year stretch at the United Nations Children's Fund (UNICEF) and has led World Vision's advocacy efforts since 2001.

The forced recruitment of child soldiers looms high on Joe's current list of priorities, and the war in northern Uganda puts that crisis into sharp focus. "As long as this war continues, children will suffer," Joe declares. "That's why we are encouraging the United States government and the international community to intervene."

Joe does not believe that the United States should police the world wherever a political conflict arises. But leadership from the United States—through its own diplomatic efforts and its leverage at the United Nations—would be a crucial factor in brokering peace in northern Uganda. At the moment, however, the U.S. government does not value the conflict enough to expend its political capital.

Joe's team at World Vision has designed a public advocacy campaign to change that perception. First, Joe hopes to secure a million signatures on a "Children Should Never Be Soldiers" petition.

The gist of the petition declares, "Innocent children [in Uganda] are brutalized and mutilated, forced to commit atrocities, and given as sex slaves to military commanders. This targeted abuse of children is unacceptable.... All children deserve to have a childhood free from torture and a future free from cruelty." It can be signed in hard copy or over the Internet (www .worldvision.org/nochildsoldiers). Once he gathers the signatures, Joe will take the declaration to the U.S. president, the Congress, and the United Nations and press them to take meaningful political action.

On a second level of advocacy, Joe and his team promote "Gulu Walks" that give concerned citizens the chance to publicly show their support for the night commuters. Any group can sponsor a walk in its own city, and World Vision will provide an organizing kit that contains everything that the group might need to pull off a successful event.

Heightening concern for Uganda in the Congress and in the White House enables Joe to translate advocacy into effective public policy. Though NGOs like World Vision obviously cannot enter a piece of legislation directly in the Congress, they can help elected officials craft better policy. When I met with Joe at his office in Washington, DC, he had just finished assisting congressional aides in drafting a bill called the Child Soldier Prevention Act. A group of powerful members of the House had already agreed to champion the bill.

Every year the U.S. government gives foreign governments a range of military assistance, including training, weapons, and "nonlethal" funding. The Child Soldier Prevention Act would prohibit the delivery of such aid to any government that deploys children in armed conflict within its own ranks and to any government that gives support to a paramilitary group violating that ban.

Taken in isolation, no one of these political acts delivers the total solution to child slavery in northern Uganda. But each advance in policy and public awareness builds an environment wherein kidnapping children from their homes and forcing them to perform heinous acts will not be tolerated. "One policy change," Joe says, "can affect millions of lives permanently."

Create an International Network of University Research Centers That Focus on the Practice of Slavery in Local Communities

The slave trade operates most efficiently when it is hidden from sight. Once a trafficking ring is exposed to the public eye, the slaveholders become more vulnerable to arrest, and slaves are more likely to be rescued. Moreover, clients who engage in commercial transactions with slaveholders—for example, a john who visits a massage parlor or a retailer who sells dresses made in a slave-labor factory—find comfort in covert conditions. They are less likely to engage in business once the slave operation comes under public scrutiny.

Imagine the impact if research centers could spring up all over the world to identify and monitor trafficking activity in their own region. And what better site for this kind of study than colleges and universities? A growing number of schools in the United States already require their students to participate in "service learning" as part of their degree program. Some of these students, working in collaboration with their professors, could use their service hours to conduct community-based research on human trafficking. It would not be that difficult to conduct interviews with community residents, local police, social workers, probation officers, migrant workers, and a host of others to aggregate local intelligence on trafficking. An annual report of updated data could then be supplied to local service agencies, government officials, and law enforcement agencies for appropriate action. The research center would also want to partner with the local media to feature the latest trends and expose trafficking sites.

An investigative report on human trafficking featured on the front pages of the *San Francisco Chronicle* for four separate days in October 2006 suggests the impact that public monitoring and exposure can have.[1] A *Chronicle* reporter, Meredith May, related the story of a teenage girl whom a sophisticated international sex-trafficking ring had moved from South Korea to San Francisco. May revealed that San Francisco had become a key commercial center in the global sex trade: "There are at least 90 massage parlors in San Francisco where sex is for sale ... [and] on average there are about eight women working in a massage parlor, police say. That would mean more than 700 Asian masseuses are working in San Francisco."[2]

May's report created quite a stir. In the days to follow, Mayor Gavin Newsom expressed his dismay that San Francisco could be an international destination and transit point for the global slave trade and announced that he was working with law enforcement agencies to come up with more effective strategies to close down sex-trafficking establishments.[3] "It's time to let these traffickers know San Francisco is not the city to be operating in," Newsom said.

To be completely fair to the mayor, he had previously directed his office to address the illicit activities of massage parlors. But the high-profile coverage that the *Chronicle* gave to the crisis of human trafficking in San Francisco led him to admit that those efforts had fallen short, and he dedicated his office to more aggressive antitrafficking efforts.

Ironically, journalist May gathered much of her research on San Francisco massage parlors from a Web site that sex predators had created to review their experiences for the benefit of other johns. Less than half of the establishments listed on the Web site have city-issued permits, and ten parlors are evidently up and running again after being closed in a July 2005 federal raid that led to the arrest of forty-five traffickers in a California-wide sex-trafficking ring. The Web site unintentionally provides abolitionists with a useful tool; as Newsom suggests, "What they've done is provide us a virtual road map for enforcement."[4]

The dynamics of the San Francisco case could be replicated in university research centers all over the United States. Following May's model, researchers could gather data from a broad range of sources and highlight the hot spots and trends for specific regions.

Hire One Ex-Slave and Make Your Purchase Count

About 80 percent of the individuals who are trafficked for the purposes of slave labor each year are females. If women's groups in every professional association, religious community, and funding network would get behind abolition, they would fuel an international movement that could eradicate slavery. That's a strategic proposal, not a normative one: women obviously have no more ethical burden to end slavery than men do. But it's an educated guess that women will carry the abolitionist movement forward.

Ambassador John Miller passes along an idea that he received from a government minister in South Korea. The minister has initiated a national campaign in her country asking every women-run business to hire at least one freed slave for a legitimate job. Ambassador Miller was inspired to consider how that kind of campaign might take root in the United States and Europe. The aggregate impact of such an employment scheme would be far-reaching.

In like manner, with their consumer dollars women could give a tremendous lift to microenterprises around the globe. Annie Dieselberg's enterprise for women in Bangkok, NightLight Design, relies heavily on women in the United States who organize jewelry-buying parties in their homes or in church communities. Hagar Design in Cambodia produces a wide product line of handbags, purses, and clothing. A shift of just a few consumer dollars could make an enormous difference for these early-stage companies.

Take Advantage of Your Access to Power for the Sake of the Powerless

David Arkless is the senior vice-president of corporate affairs for Manpower, the world's largest private employer. An associate asked him in January 2006 what he and his company were doing about human slavery. David admitted that he had no idea what the woman was talking about. Once he started investigating the prevalence of human trafficking, he was appalled.

He decided to do a test case on the screening that a Manpower office in southern Europe might use to ensure that a slave would not be utilized for a work assignment. To his surprise, the office did not even check into an individual's background or otherwise check out whether they might be forced to perform the job.

David was a human cyclone in 2006, using his networks to bring about changes inside Manpower and in other international companies. He persuaded his own company to take the lead in the private sector, and Manpower became the first global corporation to sign the Athens Declaration covering human trafficking. The seven-point compact commits a business to

Pledge zero tolerance for trafficking in human beings

Provide awareness training and education for its workforce

Develop a corporate strategy for antislavery that will permeate all its activities

Ensure that its personnel comply with its antislavery policy

Encourage its business partners, including suppliers, to apply antislavery protocols

Call on governments to revise laws and regulations to enhance antislavery enforcement

Report and share its best practices

Manpower has declared a zero tolerance to slavery worldwide and is urging that its principles be adopted among its three hundred thousand customer and supplier companies. The company's worldwide offices are now required to screen for forced labor and possible cases of human trafficking. David is leading the charge to sign up the top one thousand corporations in the world to the Athens Declaration by 2008.

Though some social activists may be cynical about the tangible benefits of a company's signing a policy declaration, the act has a key strategic purpose. Subsequent third-party monitoring by nongovernmental organizations (NGOs) and research centers can help identify the practice of slavery in any corporation's supply chain. When the company has already made a public commitment to a standard of behavior, the obligation to address the violation becomes all the stronger.

THE TEARS OF THE OPPRESSED

The book of Ecclesiastes is one of the extraordinary pieces of ancient wisdom literature. The author beautifully expressed the desperation of the powerless: "I saw all the oppressions that are practiced under the sun. Look, the tears of the oppressed—with no one to comfort them! On the side of their oppressors there was power" (Eccles. 4:1).

In our world today, 27 million individuals live as slaves. Frankly, power is on the side of the oppressors at the moment, but a wave of abolitionists is on the rise. They will wipe away the tears of the oppressed and deliver justice to the oppressors.

The movement gains momentum each time a new individual joins. If you are unsure what you can do, offer your time, talent, and money to one of the following groups.

ANTI-SLAVERY INTERNATIONAL

www.antislavery.org

Founded in 1839, Anti-Slavery International is the world's oldest international human-rights organization. It has consultative status with the United Nations Economic and Social Council and engages in extensive research and advocacy for antislavery work.

BAL VIKAS ASHRAM

**www.freetheslaves.net/about/partners/
bal-vikas-ashram**

Bal Vikas Ashram is a rehabilitation center for children age eight to fourteen who have been rescued from slavery in Uttar Pradesh in northern India. The ashram organizes raids to free children who have been taken hundreds of miles from their home villages and sold to carpet loom owners. In 2006 alone, the ashram carried out at least nineteen raids and released more than one hundred children.

CAMPUS COALITION AGAINST TRAFFICKING (CCAT)

www.ccatcoalition.org

The Campus Coalition Against Trafficking is a university campus movement cosponsored by the FAIR Fund and the Polaris Project. The main goal of CCAT is to build the antitrafficking movement by training emerging leaders, fostering youth empowerment, raising awareness about human trafficking, and encouraging linkages among social justice issues.

CHILDREN OF THE NIGHT

www.childrenofthenight.org

Children of the Night has rescued more than ten thousand American children from prostitution since it was founded in 1979. It is dedicated to helping children between the ages of eleven and seventeen who are forced into the commercial sex trade.

CHURCHES ALERT TO SEX TRAFFICKING ACROSS EUROPE (CHASTE)

www.chaste.org.uk

Churches Alert to Sex Trafficking Across Europe has been developing a network of European churches to respond to the increasing trade in trafficking for sexual exploitation. It works within a network coordinated through the Churches Commission on Migration in Europe, an EU-funded project connecting churches and church agencies involved in antitrafficking initiatives and survivor support.

CHURCH MISSION SOCIETY (CMS)

www.cms-uk.org/united/index.htm

The Church Mission Society stands in solidarity with the abducted child soldiers in northern Uganda and with ordinary citizens who are victims of terror and war. CMS engages in education and advocacy in churches primarily in the United Kingdom.

COALITION AGAINST TRAFFICKING IN WOMEN (CATW)

www.catwinternational.org

The Coalition Against Trafficking in Women promotes women's human rights by working internationally to combat sexual exploitation in all its forms. Founded in 1988, CATW was the first international nongovernmental organization to focus on human trafficking, especially sex trafficking of women and girls. CATW has regional networks in Asia, Latin America, Europe, Africa, and Australia.

COALITION OF IMMOKALEE WORKERS (CIW)

www.ciw-online.org

The Coalition of Immokalee Workers is a community-based worker organization. Its members are largely Latino, Haitian, and Mayan Indian immigrants working in low-wage jobs throughout the state of Florida. Over the past several years, through campaigns like the Taco Bell boycott and antislavery work, Immokalee has evolved from one of the poorest, most politically powerless communities in the country to become a new and important public presence.

COALITION TO ABOLISH SLAVERY AND TRAFFICKING (CAST)

www.castla.org

The Coalition to Abolish Salvery and Traficking opened the first shelter for trafficked women in the United States, offering a model for the development of services to victims of trafficking. CAST's programs include social services, legal services, and training and advocacy, which have assisted over two hundred victims of trafficking in some of the most well known cases in the United States.

DEVELOPMENT AND EDUCATION PROGRAM FOR DAUGHTERS AND COMMUNITIES (DEPDC)

www.depdc.org

The Development and Education Program for Daughters and Communities is a nonprofit community-based NGO working in Thailand to prevent trafficking of women and children into the sex industry or other exploitative child labor situations. It offers free education, vocational training, and full-time accommodation for young girls and boys in an effort to achieve these goals.

FLORIDA COALITION AGAINST
HUMAN TRAFFICKING (FCAHT)

www.stophumantrafficking.org

The Florida Coalition Against Human Trafficking aims to identify victims, provide advocacy, and understand how to pursue justice for victims. It actively participates in human trafficking cases and provides outreach and advocacy services to at-risk people who live and work in target areas, especially in southwestern Florida.

FREE THE SLAVES

www.freetheslaves.net

Free the Slaves fights slavery all over the world by helping people to freedom and to stable lives after liberation, by removing slave labor from the products we buy, and by helping governments enforce their own antislavery laws.

GENERACIÓN INSTITUTE

www.notforsalefund.org/projects.html

Generación is a human-rights organization committed to the promotion and protection of street children's rights in Peru. Generación provides a shelter that offers educational, artistic, recreational, and employment opportunities. Its goal is to rescue vulnerable children and teenagers, especially young women who have been exploited sexually, and offer them reintegration programs.

HAGAR

www.hagarproject.org

Hagar is a Christian-based development organization in Cambodia that provides a number of projects and for-profit enterprises that focus on prevention, rehabilitation, and reintegration of women and children who have been abused, abandoned, trafficked, and impoverished.

INTERNATIONAL JUSTICE MISSION (IJM)

www.ijm.org

The International Justice Mission is a human-rights organization that rescues victims of violence, sexual exploitation, slavery, and oppression. IJM documents and monitors conditions of abuse, educates the public about the abuses, and mobilizes intervention on behalf of victims.

LA STRADA INTERNATIONAL

www.lastradainternational.org

La Strada International works on the prevention of trafficking in women from central and eastern Europe. It seeks to make the issue of trafficking in women visible; to influence authorities, the media, and public opinion about the possible dangers of trafficking, and to refer victims to support networks. It has offices in nine European countries: the Netherlands, Poland, the Czech Republic, Ukraine, Bulgaria, Belarus, Bosnia and Herzegovina, Macedonia, and Moldova.

NIGHTLIGHT DESIGN

www.nightlightbangkok.com

NightLight Design is a Christian ministry in urban Bangkok that reaches out to women and children exploited in the city's sex bars. It aims to intervene when children are solicited for sex trafficking and to provide women with job training and employment through a self-sustaining business.

NOT FOR SALE FUND

www.notforsalefund.org

The Not for Sale Fund, the charitable arm of Right Reality, aims to create and support projects that equip former slaves to have a hand in their future destiny. The organization collaborates with economic, political, religious, and other social groups to leverage their assets on behalf of individuals in crisis, above all those who have fallen victim to the slave trade. The organization also educates world citizens on the existence and plight of slaves around the world, and shows them how to be part of building an abolitionist movement to arrest slavery.

POLARIS PROJECT

www.polarisproject.org

Based in the United States and Japan, the Polaris Project brings together community members, survivors, and professionals to fight trafficking and slavery in the spirit of a modern-day Underground Railroad. It runs a shelter for trafficking victims and, in addition to its organizational Web site, runs HumanTrafficking.com and SlaveryStillExists.com.

PROTECTION PROJECT

www.protectionproject.org

The Protection Project is a human-rights research institute based at the Johns Hopkins School of Advanced International Studies in Washington, DC. The project documents information about the scope of the problem of trafficking, with a focus on U.S. and international laws, case law, and implications for foreign policy.

REGINA PACIS FUND

www.reginapacis.org/en

The Regina Pacis Fund is carrying out protection programs for victims of sexual trafficking through projects in Italy and Moldova. It offers material and psychological assistance, employment, and reintegration facilities for girls who decide to return home.

RUGMARK

www.rugmark.org

Rugmark works to end child labor and offers educational opportunities for children in Nepal, India, and Pakistan. The Rugmark label assures consumers that no illegal child labor was employed in the manufacture of a carpet or rug.

SALVATION ARMY

www.salvationarmy.org

The Salvation Army is an international agency that is committed to policy, resources, and public action against sex trafficking. It assists trafficking victims and has launched an international awareness campaign. A free download of the Salvation Army's "Anti-Trafficking Training Manual" is available on the organization's Web site.

SANKALP

www.sankalpindia.net/drupal

Sankalp assists the indigenous Kol people who live in the northern Indian state of Uttar Pradesh and have subsisted for generations as bonded laborers with an illegal debt that they can never pay off. Sankalp helps them organize into micro-credit unions and collaborate with volunteer lawyers to acquire small-scale quarrying leases from the state and to win their freedom.

SOJOURNERS

www.sojo.net

Sojourners is a Christian ministry to organize for social justice, inspire hope, and build a global movement to transform individuals, communities, the church, and the world. It links with U.S. and international faith-based groups to combat poverty and the global slave trade.

STANDING AGAINST GLOBAL EXPLOITATION (SAGE) PROJECT

www.sagesf.org

The Standing Against Global Exploitation Project is a unique collaboration between law enforcement, public health, social services, and private agencies. SAGE partners work for restorative justice that benefits individual communities and the whole of society.

STOP THE TRAFFIK

www.stopthetraffik.org

Stop the Traffik is a global coalition of organizations working together to fight human trafficking, with a focus on advocacy and education. Currently over three hundred member organizations, including businesses, faith groups, community groups, and charities, have joined the coalition.

TINY STARS

www.tinystars.org

Tiny Stars is committed to exposing the growing multibillion dollar industry of the child sex trade and is working behind the scenes alongside law enforcement to capture international child predators. It also aims to educate the public to the magnitude of the commercial child sex trade industry and give a voice to vulnerable victims.

WORLD VISION

**www.worldvision.org/worldvision/wvususfo.nsf/
stable/globalissues_childprotection_sexexploit**

**www.worldvision.org/worldvision/wvususfo.nsf/
stable/globalissues_uganda**

World Vision is a Christian humanitarian organization dedicated to working with children, families, and their communities worldwide to reach their full potential by tackling the causes of poverty and injustice. It has dedicated projects and Web sites for child sex trafficking and child soldiers.

Notes

INTRODUCTION: FINDING SLAVERY IN MY OWN BACKYARD

1. The 27 million figure is widely cited and traces back to research done by Kevin Bales and his Free the Slaves organization. Precise numbers for slaves are hard to come by because the slave trade operates in the shadows. Though statistics in this book are documented, the author holds no illusion of their 100 percent accuracy.

2. U.S. Department of Justice, *Report on Activities to Combat Human Trafficking: Fiscal Years 2001–2005* (Washington, DC), p. 31.

3. George W. Bush, speech to the United Nations General Assembly, New York City, September 23, 2003.

4. U.S. Department of State, *2004 Trafficking in Persons Report* (Washington, DC).

5. International Labour Office, *A Global Alliance against Forced Labour* (May 2005).

6. Barry Tang quoted in Meredith May, "Sex Trafficking," *San Francisco Chronicle,* October 6, 2006, p. A21.

7. U.S. Department of State, *2006 Trafficking in Persons Report* (Washington, DC).

8. Derek Ellerman, "The John Miller Interview," Polaris Project, February 13, 2003, http://www.humantrafficking.com/humantrafficking/Interviews/Miller_Page/Interview_Miller.htm

9. Miron Varouhakis,"Trafficked Women Are Victims," *Global Outlook* (Centre for Research on Globalization, July 26, 2002).

10. Varouhakis, "Trafficked Women Are Victims."

11. Benita Ferrero-Waldner, speech at conference on Combatting Trafficking in Human Beings, Vienna, Austria, March 17, 2006.

12. United Nations, *Ten Million Children Exploited for Domestic Labor* (June 14, 2004).

13. Kim Meston gave her testimony to Risa Medrick. I met with Meston and Medrick in Newton Center, Massachusetts, in September 2006.

14. U.S. Department of State, *2005 Trafficking in Persons Report* (Washington, DC).

15. Kevin Bales, *Disposable People: New Slavery in the Global Economy* (Berkeley: University of California Press, 2004), pp. 3–4.

16. Senator Sam Brownback, press conference at U.S. Capitol, Washington, DC, September 23, 2003.
17. Bales, *Disposable People.*
18. Bales, *Disposable People,* p. 9.

CHAPTER 1: SHINING LIGHT INTO THE SEXUAL DARKNESS:
CAMBODIA AND THAILAND
1. U.S. Department of State, *2006 Trafficking in Persons Report* (Washington, DC).
2. Save the Children USA, *2005 State of the World's Mothers Report* (Washington, DC).
3. Interview with Janejinda Pawadee, a staff worker for International Justice Mission, Chiang Mai, Thailand (June 17, 2006).
4. Bales, *Disposable People,* p. 45.
5. Andrew Perrin, "Special Report: Child Slavery," *Time Asia* (August 26, 2002), p. 25.
6. J. K. Reimer, "At What Price Honour?: Research into Domestic Trafficking of Vietnamese (Girl) Children for Sexual Exploitation" (Phnom Penh: Chab Dai Coalition, 2006), p. 4.
7. Center for the Protection of Children's Rights, "Case Study Report on Commercial Exploitation of Children in Thailand" (Bangkok, November 2003), p. 37.
8. World Vision, "Report on Sex Tourist" (May 2002).
9. Perrin, *Child Slavery,* p. 25.
10. Bales, *Disposable People,* p. 45.

CHAPTER 3: RESCUING THE CHILD SOLDIERS: UGANDA
1. Jan Egeland, interview on the BBC, November 10, 2003.
2. Grace Grall Akallo, "The Endangered Children of Northern Uganda," testimony before the House International Relations Subcommittee on Human Rights and International Operations, April 26, 2006.
3. Library of Congress Country Studies: Uganda, http://hdl.loc.gov/loc.gdc/cntrystd.ug.
4. World Vision, *Pawn of Politics: Children, Conflict and Peace in Northern Uganda* (2005), p. 18.
5. World Vision, *Pawn of Politics,* p. 26.
6. Jeffrey Gettleman, "Uganda Peace Hinges on Amnesty for Brutality," *New York Times,* September 15, 2006, p. A6.
7. Akallo, "The Endangered Children."

CHAPTER 4: UNDERMINING THE SEX SYNDICATE: EUROPE
1. Donna M. Hughes, "The 'Natasha' Trade: The Transnational Shadow Trade of Trafficking in Women," *Journal of International Affairs,* 53:2 (Spring 2000), pp. 8–15

2. Mira Med Institute, *Preliminary Survey Report on Sexual Trafficking from the CIS Countries,* 1999 (http://www.miramedinstitute.org/trafficking.eng.html).

3. Moldovan Intelligence and Security Agency, cited in United States Aid and International Development Agency, *USAID Anti-Trafficking Assessment: Critical Gaps in and Recommendations for Anti-Trafficking Activities* (Washington, DC, 2002).

4. U.S. Department of State, *2003 Trafficking in Persons Report* (Washington, DC).

5. International Organization for Migration (IOM) Counter-Trafficking Center, *Changing Patterns and Trends of Trafficking in Persons, the Balkan Region* (July 2004). See also Martti Lehti, *Trafficking in Women and Children in Europe,* European Institute for Crime Prevention and Control, paper no. 18, Helsinki, Finland, 2003.

6. Anna Diamantopoulou, "Trafficking in Women: Prevention and Protection," speech at the Second Conference on Women in Democracy, Vilnius, Lithuania, June 16, 2001.

7. C. J. Gomez, *Sex Trafficking of Women in the United States: International and Domestic Trends* (Coalition Against Trafficking in Women, March 2001).

8. Lehti, "Trafficking in Women and Children in Europe."

9. Karin Alfredsson, *No to Prostitution and Trafficking* (Stockholm, Swedish Institute, 2005).

10. Alfredsson. *No to Prostitution and Trafficking.*

11. U.S. Department of State, Bureau of Democracy, Human Rights, and Labor, *Country Report on Human Rights Practices* (2004 and 2005).

12. Regina Pacis, *Focus Moldova* (San Foca, Italy, 2005).

13. U.S. Department of State, "Swearing-in of John R. Miller as Senior Advisor to the Secretary of State and Director of the Office to Monitor and Combat Trafficking in Persons," March 4, 2003, http://www.state.gov/g/tip/rls/rm/ 18200.htm.

CHAPTER 5: SHELTERING THE LOST CHILDREN: PERU

1. Verushka Villavicencio, et al., *The Client Goes Unnoticed,* Save the Children (Stockholm, 2004), p. 7.

2. Villavicencio, *The Client Goes Unnoticed,* p. 40

3. Statement of Donna Hughes, professor of women's studies at the University of Rhode Island, hearing before the Committee on International Relations, U.S. House of Representatives, 107th Congress, June 19, 2002.

4. I note my debt to Kevin Bales, *Understanding Global Slavery: A Reader* (Berkeley: University of California Press, 2005).

5. Nicholas Wood, "For Albanians, It's Come to This: A Son for a TV," *New York Times,* November 13, 2003.

6. Villavicencio, *The Client Goes Unnoticed,* p. 40.

7. "Juan Carlos" is a pseudonym for an actual televison personality in Peru who acted in the way described in this chapter.

8. Luis Enrique Bazan, Lucy's oldest son, is a partner in my social-venture firm, Right Reality, and serves as executive director of our Not for Sale Fund.

9. Villavicencio, *The Client Goes Unnoticed,* p. 47.

CHAPTER 6: BUILDING A NEW UNDERGROUND RAILROAD: USA

1. Free the Slaves and Human Rights Center, *Hidden Slaves: Forced Labor in the United States* (Berkeley, September 2004).
2. Suzette Hackney and Ben Schmitt, *Detroit Free Press,* January 15, January 16, February 15, September 16, 2003. Cf. *Hidden Slaves,* p. 12.
3. Robert Reich, press release, U.S. Department of Labor, Office of Public Affairs, September 15, 1995.
4. Department of Justice, *Assessment of U.S. Government Efforts to Combat Trafficking in Persons in Fiscal Year 2005* (Washington, DC, 2006).
5. Department of Justice, *Asessment of U.S. Government Efforts to Combat Trafficking,* p. 3.
6. Statement of Tina Frundt, hearing before the Subcommittee on Domestic and International Monetary Policy, Trade, and Technology, Committee on Financial Services, U.S. House of Representatives, April 29, 2005.

CONCLUSION: ENDING THE SLAVE TRADE IN OUR TIME

1. Meredith May, "Diary of a Sex Slave," *San Francisco Chronicle,* October 6, October 8, October 9, October 10, 2006.
2. May, "Diary of a Sex Slave." October 6, p. A21.
3. Meredith May, "Mayor's Plan to Curb Sex Trafficking: SF Could Fine, Jail Landlords Renting to Illicit Massage Parlors," *San Francisco Chronicle,* October 11, 2006, p. A1.
4. May, "Mayor's Plan to Curb Sex Trafficking."

Acknowledgments

This book project began over a casual lunch with Mark Tauber, a longtime friend and deputy publisher at Harper San Francisco. I owe Mark a tremendous debt for recognizing how my background uniquely qualified me to investigate the global slave trade and the emerging movement to resist it. The entire Harper San Francisco team was spectacular. It's uncanny how my editor, Mickey Maudlin, can go straight to the heart of the matter, and I came to treasure his friendship during this project. My appreciation extends as well to Julie, Jan, Claudia, and Laina for going the extra mile to get the word out about the book.

My admiration goes out to Steve Privett, S.J., Jennifer Turpin, and Dean Rader for their unyielding support and inspiring leadership at the University of San Francisco. My university life changed radically the day I teamed up with Mike Duffy at USF. Teaching the Erasmus Program with Mike has helped me find my vocation as a professor. My heartfelt thanks goes out to all of the Erasmus students with whom I have shared wonderful classroom dramas and global immersion trips.

A number of people played significant roles in helping me find my way through the invisible world of trafficking. I am deeply grateful to Pamela Livingston, Mark Rhode, Joe Mettimano, Margaret Larson, Ambassador John Miller, Pierre Tami, Lucy Borja, Annie Dieselberg, Sean Litton, Blair Burns, Gary Haugen, Kevin Bales, Michael Kane, Imelda Buncab, and Kay Buck. My partners at Right Reality, Kique Bazan and Mark Wexler, are unfailing friends and talented cohorts. Kique accompanied me to

Peru and made a valuable contribution to the chapter on his home country. Many thanks to Jim Wallis, Jeff Carr, Jim Rice, and the entire Sojourners staff for giving the world a compassionate religious story. Robert Marcarelli and Steve Crisman helped me to "visualize" the antislavery movement and gave of themselves freely to produce the *Not for Sale* film documentary. Michael and Frannie Kieschnick and Anne Howard of the Beatitudes Society remind me that the true measure of a movement is twenty years out. Thanks to Michael for cold-hard realism and warm friendship.

Other good friends have helped to build a Not for Sale campaign. T-Bone Burnett, Callie Khouri, and Ed Solomon opened their hearts to do whatever they could to raise up a strong abolitionist movement. Randy Newcomb and I turned a coffee chat in a San Francisco cafe into an impromptu planning session for a media communications network. Randy's entrepreneurial spirit is a real gift. A special thanks go out as well to Bono, Ricky Ross, Lorraine McIntosh, Martin and Meg Wroe, Simon and Hilary Mayo, Peter Stanley, Heather Somaini, Brent Gudgel, David Mahanes, Laryn Bakker, and the Walden Media crew of Micheal Flaherty, Erik Lokkesmoe, and Penny Hunter. Todd Sheffield continues to come through at unpredictable moments to provide help at the right time.

Above all, words alone cannot convey my love and appreciation for Wendy, Jade, Zachary, Jesse, and Caelin. Each family member made real sacrifices to bring this book to fruition. Wendy showed a remarkable ability to hold our chaotic family life together while I sank deep into the book. Beyond that, her photographic contribution to the Peru trip was stunning. You are a jewel, Wendy. I thank Caelin for being an amazing travel companion to Uganda and South Africa. His journal entries truly inspired me. Each member of the family was extraordinarily patient with my trafficking investigations during our long trip to Europe. I reckon that we all became committed abolitionists during the process of putting this book together.

I am not for sale.
You are not for sale.
No one should be for sale.

JOIN THE
NOT FOR SALE CAMPAIGN

www.NotforSaleFund.org

✠ ✠ ✠

- Get free videos and songs sent to your cell phone or email

- Support the abolitionist groups that you read about in *Not for Sale*

- Get updated research and breaking news on fighting slavery around the globe.

- Read timely commentary from David Batstone, Kevin Bales, Kay Buck, Gary Haugen, and other leading abolitionists

- Find out where you can volunteer

- Meet other people who share your passion

- Make a difference

I am not for sale.
You are not for sale.
No one should be for sale.

www.NotforSaleFund.org

About the Author

PHOTO: TIM PEARSON

DAVID BATSTONE is professor of ethics at the University of San Francisco and is the author of *Saving the Corporate Soul & (Who Knows?) Maybe Your Own,* which won the Nautilus Award for "2004 Best Business Book." For the last six years, Batstone was executive editor of *Sojourners* magazine and the creator of the SojoMail e-zine. He also serves as senior editor of the business magazine *Motto* and was a founding editorial team member of *Business 2.0* magazine. Batstone appears regularly in *USA Today's Weekend Edition* as "America's ethics guru."

Visit www.notforsalecampaign.org to join the cause.

Child Victims in Gulu © 2006, Childvoice International

THE AMAZING CHANGE

**27 million people in slavery. Children held in captivity.
People crying for freedom. Be their answer.**

You can make a difference in the world today by continuing the work begun 200 years ago by William Wilberforce and his friends who worked to end the slave trade. Today victims are still waiting for help. Much is left to be done.

**It's time for action. Time to end slavery in our lifetime.
It's time for The Amazing Change.**

The Amazing Change Campaign is a campaign of justice and mercy inspired by the work of William Wilberforce and the new feature film Amazing Grace. For more information about the film go to www.AmazingGraceMovie.com.

Become an abolitionist!
1. **SIGN** – Give your name to the Petition to Abolish Slavery at www.TheAmazingChange.com
2. **SPEAK** – Get informed and share what you learn with others.
3. **ACT** – Take the knowledge that you have and get involved. You can raise funds to free slaves, organize events to raise awareness and mobilize your community to make a difference. Take a group of friends to see Amazing Grace and discuss how to carry on the legacy of Wilberforce.

WWW.THEAMAZINGCHANGE.COM